Readings in the economics of contract law

Readings in the economics of contract law

Edited by

Victor P. Goldberg

THOMAS MACIOCE PROFESSOR OF LAW

COLUMBIA UNIVERSITY

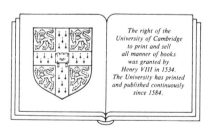

The right of the
University of Cambridge
to print and sell
all manner of books
was granted by
Henry VIII in 1534.
The University has printed
and published continuously
since 1584.

Cambridge University Press

Cambridge
New York   New Rochelle   Melbourne   Sydney

Published by the Press Syndicate of the University of Cambridge
The Pitt Building, Trumpington Street, Cambridge CB2 1RP
32 East 57th Street, New York, NY 10022, USA
10 Stamford Road, Oakleigh, Melbourne 3166, Australia

© Cambridge University Press 1989

First published 1989

Printed in the United States of America

Library of Congress Cataloging-in-Publication Data
Readings in the economics of contract law.
Bibliography: p.
Includes index.
1. Contracts. 2. Contracts—Economic aspects.
I. Goldberg, Victor P.
K840.R43   1989   346'.02   88–20383
                              342.62

British Library Cataloguing in Publication Data
Readings in the economics of contract law.
1. Business firms. Contracts. Law
I. Goldberg, Victor P.
342.6'2

ISBN 0 521 34120 5 hard covers
ISBN 0 521 34920 6 paperback

Contents

Preface   ix

Part I. Some preliminaries

1.1. Non-contractual relations in business: a preliminary study   4
STEWART MACAULAY

1.2. Relational exchange: economics and complex contracts   16
VICTOR P. GOLDBERG

1.3. Production functions, transactions costs, and the new institutionalism   21
VICTOR P. GOLDBERG

1.4. The market for "lemons": quality uncertainty and the market mechanism   24
GEORGE A. AKERLOF

1.5. A treatise on the law of marine insurance and general average, volume I   29
THEOPHILUS PARSONS

1.6. The economics of moral hazard: comment   31
MARK V. PAULY

1.7. The economics of moral hazard: further comment   33
KENNETH J. ARROW

1.8. Efficient rent seeking   35
GORDON TULLOCK

Questions and notes on rent seeking   43

Part II. Contract law and the least cost avoider

2.1. Unity in tort, contract, and property: the model of precaution   53
ROBERT COOTER

CONTENTS

2.2. The mitigation principle: toward a general theory of contractual obligation (1)   61
CHARLES J. GOETZ AND ROBERT E. SCOTT

2.3. Relational exchange, contract law, and the *Boomer* problem (1)   69
VICTOR P. GOLDBERG

Questions and notes on the least cost avoider   72

Part III. The expectation interest, the reliance interest, and consequential damages

A. Property in price

3.1. The reliance interest in contract damages   77
LON FULLER AND WILLIAM PERDUE

3.2. Note on price information and enforcement of the expectation interest   80
VICTOR P. GOLDBERG

Questions and notes on protecting the property interest in the price   84

B. Reliance and consequential damages

3.3. The contract–tort boundary and the economics of insurance   86
WILLIAM BISHOP

3.4. Notes on the reliance interest   92
ROBERT BIRMINGHAM

Questions and notes on fault, consequential damages, and reliance   99

Part IV. The lost-volume seller puzzle

4.1. An economic analysis of the lost-volume retail seller   106
VICTOR P. GOLDBERG

Questions and notes on the seller's lost profits   114

Part V. Specific performance and the cost of completion

5.1. The choice of remedy for breach of contract   122
WILLIAM BISHOP

5.2. Relational exchange, contract law, and the *Boomer* problem (2)   126
VICTOR P. GOLDBERG

Contents

5.3. Cost of completion or diminution in market value: the relevance of subjective value   128
TIMOTHY J. MURIS

Questions and notes on specific performance and cost of completion   133

Part VI. Power, governance, and the penalty clause puzzle

6.1. Transaction cost determinants of "unfair" contractual arrangements   139
BENJAMIN KLEIN

6.2. A relational exchange perspective on the employment relationship   147
VICTOR P. GOLDBERG

6.3. Liquidated damages versus penalties: sense or nonsense?   152
KENNETH W. CLARKSON, ROGER LEROY MILLER, AND TIMOTHY J. MURIS

6.4. Further thoughts on penalty clauses   161
VICTOR P. GOLDBERG

Questions and notes on power and penalty clauses   164

Part VII. Standard forms and warranties

7.1. Institutional change and the quasi-invisible hand   169
VICTOR P. GOLDBERG

7.2. A theory of the consumer product warranty   174
GEORGE L. PRIEST

Questions and notes on warranties   185

Part VIII. Duress, preexisting duty, and good faith modification

8.1. Duress by economic pressure, I   188
JOHN DALZELL

8.2. Gratuitous promises in economics and law   194
RICHARD A. POSNER

8.3. The mitigation principle: toward a general theory of contractual obligation (2)   199
CHARLES J. GOETZ AND ROBERT E. SCOTT

8.4. The law of contract modifications: the uncertain quest for a benchmark of enforceability   201
VAROUJ A. AIVAZIAN, MICHAEL J. TREBILCOCK, AND MICHAEL PENNY

Questions and notes on duress   208

vii

CONTENTS

Part IX. Impossibility, related doctrines, and price adjustment

9.1. Impossibility and related doctrines in contract law: an economic analysis   212
  RICHARD A. POSNER AND ANDREW M. ROSENFIELD

9.2. Impossibility and related excuses   221
  VICTOR P. GOLDBERG

9.3. Price adjustment in long-term contracts   225
  VICTOR P. GOLDBERG

  Questions and notes on impossibility and price adjustment   236

References   241
Index of cases   247
Author index   249
Subject index   251

Preface

The Law and Economics revolution is proceeding in these days apace.*
Economic analysis is being applied by scholars to a wide range of legal
problems. Scholars identified with the use of economic analysis – Richard
Posner, Frank Easterbrook, Robert Bork, Douglas Ginsburg and Ste-
phen Williams – have been named to the federal bench (although not
all have remained on the bench). First-year law students in most law
schools are confronted with the intricacies and paradoxes of the Coase
Theorem in at least one of their classes.

Economic analysis has probably had its greatest impact in its traditional stronghold of antitrust and in the tort/nuisance area. There has
been a reasonable amount of work on the economics of contracts and
contract law, and this too is beginning to have an impact.† This book
represents a sampling of that literature, supplemented by a few pieces
from the more distant past. I do not want to oversell the virtues of the
economic approach – overselling is one of the vices economists have
been accused of in their forays into legal issues. Economics does not
provide all the answers. And some that it does provide are wrong, as
we shall see. Nonetheless, it does provide a powerful analytical framework that can both enhance our understanding of how parties structure
their contractual relationships and illuminate many areas of contract
law.

The scope of these readings is deliberately circumscribed. My primary
interest is in commercial transactions between modern, Western busi-

---

* The phrasing is a play on Cardozo's famous language in *Ultramares Corporation v.
Touche, Niven & Co.*
† Recent scholarship is revolutionizing the study of the law of corporations as well.
The central theme of that literature is that the corporation should be analyzed as if it
were a complex set of contract-like relationships.

ness firms. The emphasis is on legal questions arising under the common law or the Uniform Commercial Code, but the analysis should be applicable with little modification to the civil code countries of Western Europe as well. Consumer transactions will only be touched upon. I do not want to get involved with such questions as whether contract principles that work in the modern American context might work equally well in a socialist system, an underdeveloped country, or New Jersey in 1750. My reason for avoiding these questions is not that they are uninteresting. Quite the opposite – they are too interesting. My concern is that, aside from adding considerable length to the book, pursuing such questions would deflect attention from my basic theme, namely that economic analysis can be extremely useful in illuminating nitty-gritty problems in contract law.

A number of economists have argued that the common law evolves toward becoming efficient even if judges do not consciously take efficiency into account.* The evolutionary process "does" the economics; judges and lawyers needn't bother. I have never been very comfortable with that approach. The statement of a rule to decide a specific case can easily result in a formulation that leads to the improper disposition of other cases. Legal doctrine will evolve reformulating rules to fit new fact situations as they arise. It is quite possible that the categories will take on a life of their own, resulting in pockets of law that make little sense. It is necessary from time to time to step outside the process and assess the meaningfulness of the rules, distinctions, and categories recognized by the current law. To me, that is the most interesting aspect of the application of economic analysis to contract law. It provides a viewpoint that transcends the traditional legal boundaries and gives a fresh perspective on the law, providing additional support for some doctrines and undermining others.

The question of what contract law ought to be can be approached from two different angles. The first is facilitative. If contracting parties would want to do X, how can contract law be designed to enable them to do so? Contract law should strive for efficiency in this sense. The second is regulatory. If contracting parties would want to do X, how can they be prevented from doing so? If, for example, a policymaker wants to provide "job security" to franchised dealers, it will be useful to know why the lack of security is valuable to franchisors and how costly it would be to prevent franchisors from contracting around legally imposed job security. My bias, and that of most of the authors in this

---

* Judge Posner has been a major proponent of this viewpoint; see Posner (1986, pp. 229–33).

volume, is toward the facilitative approach. But much of the analysis would be equally useful for a policymaker who subscribes to the latter position. In this limited sense, much of the analysis is value free.

The book can be used as supplementary material in a number of courses. The target audience is first-year contracts courses. To be sure, some of the material will be too hard for students struggling with contracts concepts for the first time and who have no economics background. Even so, those students will find that economic reasoning can impose considerable order on some of the most confusing areas of contract law. The book can also be used in advanced contracts courses (sales, commercial transactions) and in law and economics courses.

The book is organized as follows. Parts I and II provide general background. Part I is primarily concerned with presenting a number of concepts that economists have found useful in analyzing legal issues in general and contracts in particular: relational exchange, transactions costs, adverse selection, moral hazard, and rent seeking. In Part II we begin the analysis of contract law, emphasizing both the similarity between contract and tort problems and the significance of the fact that contracting parties are often isolated to some degree from market alternatives. It includes a discussion of a well-known, noncontract case, *Boomer v. Atlantic Cement Co.*, to highlight the similarity between contract and tort issues.

Part III concerns some issues regarding damage remedies. The first half develops the notion of a property right in the price as a rationale for enforcing executory agreements. The second focuses on the implications of granting compensation for consequential damages and on the relationship between consequential damages and reliance damages.

Part IV attempts to resolve a difficult problem in contract law: the appropriate treatment of the "lost-volume seller." Part V concerns the specific performance remedy and its close cousin, the cost-of-completion damage remedy.

Part VI is concerned with the exercise of "power" within a contractual relationship and the use of penalties (broadly defined) to influence behavior. Special emphasis is put on the common law's reluctance to enforce penalty clauses. Part VII considers another area in which courts and legislatures have been reluctant to enforce the terms of contracts: express warranties and disclaimers in standard form contracts.

If conditions change after a contract is entered into, one party might request that the contract be modified or that it be excused from performance. Part VIII concerns the possibility that a modification might be accomplished under duress: One party might be taking advantage of the other's vulnerability to a threat of termination. Part IX concerns grounds for excusing performance: acts of God, impossibility, impracticability, frustration of purpose, and the like. It also considers one significant way in which parties can arrange their affairs to anticipate certain changed circumstances: inclusion of a price adjustment mechanism in their contract.

Readings in the economics of contract law

PART I

Some preliminaries

The first paper in this book appeared over two decades ago in a sociology journal. Nevertheless, Stewart Macaulay's paper on the use (and nonuse) of contracts by businessmen has had a considerable influence on economic scholarship. The paper provides a good picture of how businessmen view contracts and why contract language is often of little relevance in describing the behavior of contracting parties and influencing the resolution of disputes. It provides a commonsense backdrop for much of what comes later.

A distinguishing feature of this collection of readings is the focus on "relational exchange" as opposed to "discrete transactions." These are analytical constructs, not categories for classifying existing contractual arrangements. The former concerns arrangements in which contracting parties are isolated, to some degree, from alternative trading partners and the outcomes depend in part upon the behavior of the parties during the life of the contract. The latter concerns exchange of commodities in thick markets (a lot of buyers and sellers); the fact that a buyer enters into a contract with a particular seller today does not give that seller any advantage or disadvantage vis à vis other sellers in subsequent dealings with that buyer. As we shall see, most of the interesting, and difficult, questions of contract law disappear in a world of discrete transactions. In Selection [1.2], I provide a brief introduction to the concept of relational exchange. This is followed by a discussion of "transactions costs," a term I am somewhat uncomfortable with. The reasons for that discomfort are spelled out in [1.3].

The remaining papers in Part I concern some important analytical concepts in the economics of contracts and of law in general. One concept on which many scholars place great emphasis – risk aversion – is not discussed. A brief word on this omission is in order. Risk aversion concerns people's choices between risky alternatives. A risk averse person would prefer receiving $10 with certainty to a 50:50 chance of receiving either $20 or nothing. A risk neutral person would be indifferent between the $10 and the gamble. Contracts allocate risks, and it

1

seems natural to analyze them in terms of the different attitudes toward risk of the contracting parties. If, for example, Smith were more risk averse than Jones, the contract would be arranged so that Jones would bear the risks. However, my experience has been that incorporating risk aversion into the analysis of contracts is seldom useful. It ups the level of mathematical sophistication considerably with little or no payoff in terms of insights into contracting behavior. I prefer to assume that people would be risk neutral and focus instead on their efforts to change the odds (risk management). That is, how can parties design their contracts to increase the probability of good payoffs or decrease the likelihood of bad payoffs? For readers who want to know more about the concept of risk aversion, there is a brief presentation in Selection [9.1].

The first two concepts – adverse selection and moral hazard – arose initially in the insurance context. If a life insurance company sells a policy to a terminally ill person, that is a problem of adverse selection – including the bad risks in the pool. If that same company sells a policy to someone whose beneficiary would prefer to see him dead, there is a problem of "moral hazard."

George Akerlof [1.4] generalizes the adverse selection concept. The insurer's inability to distinguish good risks from bad is analytically similar to a customer's inability to distinguish high-quality goods from others and an employer's inability to distinguish good workers from bad. In all these cases, there are incentives for the above-average to drop out, leaving only the "lemons." Adverse selection now refers to any situation in which an individual has knowledge about his own quality (the goods he sells, his ability to perform, his health status) while whomever he is dealing with knows only about the characteristics of the average member of the group.

Akerlof's paper is followed by a brief excerpt from a treatise written a century earlier by Theophilus Parsons [1.5]. I have included this piece to show how the basic concept of adverse selection has long been recognized by legal scholars, although they have been unencumbered by the economist's terminology.

The "moral" in moral hazard stems from the immoral behavior that might be induced by insurance – murder, arson, and so on. As Mark Pauly [1.6] indicates, the concept need not have any moral content. If insurance reduces the price of medical care, the insured is likely to buy more: Insurance changes the incentives of the insured. Pure insurance covers losses owing to random events beyond the control of the insured. Moral hazard concerns the risks that arise because of the behavior of the insured, that is, endogenous risks. As Kenneth Arrow [1.7] suggests in his response to Pauly, insurance is not the only instance in which endogenous risks are important. The moral hazard concept has been expanded to include this broader class of cases. Interestingly, the concept has been transformed in this manner twice. In his classic *Risk, Uncertainty, and Profit*, which first appeared in 1921, Frank Knight used the moral hazard concept in its modern sense, implying that his readers would be familiar with the term and the usage. However, it disappeared from usage shortly afterward. It was resurrected in the narrow insurance context in the early 1960s and in the past decade has again achieved generality.

We conclude Part I with a discussion of rent seeking by Gordon Tullock [1.8]. This is the most technical paper in the collection; it is followed with some exercises that are intended to make his analysis easier to understand. The rent-seeking concept developed in the context of individuals using the political process and Tullock's examples are all concerned with the political arena. We shall see, however, that the concept has much wider applicability.

CHAPTER 1.1

Non-contractual relations in business:
a preliminary study

STEWART MACAULAY (1963)

Most larger companies, and many smaller ones, attempt to plan carefully and completely. Important transactions not in the ordinary course of business are handled by a detailed contract. For example, recently the Empire State Building was sold for $65 million. More than 100 attorneys, representing thirty-four parties, produced a 400-page contract. Another example is found in the agreement of a major rubber company in the United States to give technical assistance to a Japanese firm. Several million dollars were involved and the contract consisted of eighty-eight provisions on seventeen pages. The twelve house counsel – lawyers who work for one corporation rather than many clients – interviewed said that all but the smallest businesses carefully planned most transactions of any significance. Corporations have procedures so that particular types of exchanges will be reviewed by their legal and financial departments.

More routine transactions commonly are handled by what can be called standardized planning. A firm will have a set of terms and conditions for purchases, sales, or both printed on the business documents used in these exchanges. Thus the things to be sold and the price may be planned particularly for each transaction, but standard provisions will further elaborate the performances and cover the other subjects of planning. Typically, these terms and conditions are lengthy and printed in small type on the back of the forms. For example, twenty-four paragraphs in eight-point type are printed on the back of the purchase order form used by the Allis Chalmers Manufacturing Company. The provi-

Reprinted from Stewart Macaulay, "Non-Contractual Relations in Business: A Preliminary Study," *American Sociological Review* 28 (1963): 55 – 67, with the permission of the American Sociological Association and the author.

sions (1) describe, in part, the performance required, e.g., "DO NOT WELD CASTINGS WITHOUT OUR CONSENT"; (2) plan for the effect of contingencies, e.g., " . . . in the event the Seller suffers delay in performance due to an act of God, war, act of the Government, priorities or allocations, act of the Buyer, fire, flood, strike, sabotage, or other causes beyond the Seller's control, the time of completion shall be extended a period of time equal to the period of such delay if the Seller gives the buyer notice in writing of the cause of such delay within a reasonable time after the beginning thereof"; (3) plan for the effect of defective performances, e.g., "The buyer, without waiving any other legal rights, reserves the right to cancel without charge or to postpone deliveries of any of the articles covered by this order which are not shipped in time reasonably to meet said agreed dates"; (4) plan for a legal sanction, e.g., the clause "without waiving any other legal rights," in the example just given.

In larger firms such "boiler plate" provisions are drafted by the house counsel or the firm's outside lawyer. In smaller firms such provisions may be drafted by the industry trade association, may be copied from a competitor, or may be found on forms purchased from a printer. In any event, salesmen and purchasing agents, the operating personnel, typically are unaware of what is said in the fine print on the back of the forms they use. Yet often the normal business patterns will give effect to this standardized planning. For example, purchasing agents may have to use a purchase order form so that all transactions receive a number under the firm's accounting system. Thus, the required accounting record will carry the necessary planning of the exchange relationship printed on its reverse side. If the seller does not object to this planning and accepts the order, the buyer's "fine print" will control. If the seller does object, differences can be settled by negotiation.

* * *

While businessmen can and often do carefully and completely plan, it is clear that not all exchanges are neatly rationalized. Although most businessmen think that a clear description of both the seller's and buyer's performances is obvious common sense, they do not always live up to this ideal. The house counsel and the purchasing agent of a medium-size manufacturer of automobile parts reported that several times their engineers had committed the company to buy expensive machines without adequate specifications. The engineers had drawn careful specifications as to the type of machine and how it was to be made but had neglected to require that the machine produce specified results. An attorney and an auditor both stated that most contract disputes arise because of ambiguity in the specifications.

Businessmen often prefer to rely on "a man's word" in a brief letter, a handshake, or "common honesty and decency" – even when the transaction involves exposure to serious risks. Seven lawyers from law firms with business practices were interviewed. Five thought that businessmen often entered contracts with only a minimal degree of advance planning. They complained that businessmen desire to "keep it simple and avoid red tape" even where large amounts of money and significant risks are involved. One stated that he was "sick of being told, 'We can trust old Max,' when the problem was not one of honesty but one of reaching an agreement that both sides understand." Another said that businessmen when bargaining often talk only in pleasant generalities, think they have a contract, but fail to reach agreement on any of the hard, unpleasant questions until forced to do so by a lawyer. Two outside lawyers had different views. One thought that large firms usually planned important exchanges, although he conceded that occasionally matters might be left in a fairly vague state. The other dissenter represents a large utility that commonly buys heavy equipment and buildings. The supplier's employees come on the utility's property to install the equipment or construct the buildings, and they may be injured while there. The utility has been sued by such employees so often that it carefully plans purchases with the assistance of a lawyer so that suppliers take this burden.

Moreover, standardized planning can break down. In the example of such planning previously given, it was assumed that the purchasing agent would use his company's form with its twenty-four paragraphs printed on the back and that the seller would accept this or object to any provisions he did not like. However, the seller may fail to read the buyer's twenty-four paragraphs of fine print and may accept the buyer's order on the seller's own acknowledgment-of-order form. Typically this form will have ten to fifty paragraphs favoring the seller, and these provisions are likely to be different from or inconsistent with the buyer's provisions. The seller's acknowledgment form may be received by the buyer and checked by a clerk. She will read the *face* of the acknowledgment but not the fine print on the back of it because she has neither the time nor the ability to analyze the small print on the 100 to 500 forms she must review each day. The face of the acknowledgment – where the goods and the price are specified – is likely to correspond with the face of the purchase order. If it does, the two forms are filed away. At this point, both buyer and seller are likely to assume they have planned an exchange and made a contract. Yet they have done neither, as they are in disagreement about all that appears on the back of their forms. This practice is common enough to have a name. Law teachers call it "the battle of the forms."

Ten of the twelve purchasing agents interviewed said that frequently the provisions on the back of their purchase order and those on the back of a supplier's acknowledgment would differ or be inconsistent. Yet they would assume that the purchase was complete without further action unless one of the supplier's provisions was really objectionable. Moreover, only occasionally would they bother to read the fine print on the back of the suppliers' forms. On the other hand, one purchasing agent insists that agreement be reached on the fine-print provisions, but he represents the utility whose lawyer reported that it exercises great care in planning. The other purchasing agent who said that his company did not face a battle-of-the-forms problem, works for a division of one of the largest manufacturing corporations in the United States. Yet the company may have such a problem without recognizing it. The purchasing agent regularly sends a supplier both a purchase order form and another form which the supplier is asked to sign and return. The second form states that the supplier accepts the buyer's terms and conditions. The company has sufficient bargaining power to force suppliers to sign and return the form, and the purchasing agent must show one of his firm's auditors such a signed form for every purchase order issued. Yet suppliers frequently return this buyer's form *plus* their own acknowledgment form, which has conflicting provisions. The purchasing agent throws away the supplier's form and files his own. Of course, in such a case the supplier has not acquiesced to the buyer's provisions. There is no agreement and no contract.

Sixteen sales managers were asked about the battle of the forms. Nine said that frequently no agreement was reached on which set of fine print was to govern, while seven said that there was no problem. Four of the seven worked for companies whose major customers are the large automobile companies or the large manufacturers of paper products. These customers demand that their terms and conditions govern any purchase, are careful generally to see that suppliers acquiesce, and have the bargaining power to have their way. . . .

A large manufacturer of packaging materials audited its records to determine how often it had failed to agree on terms and conditions with its customers or had failed to create legally binding contracts. Such failures cause a risk of loss to this firm since the packaging is printed with the customer's design and cannot be salvaged once this is done. The orders for five days in four different years were reviewed. The percentages of orders where no agreement on terms and conditions was reached or no contract was formed were as follows:

1953 .... 75.0%
1954 .... 69.4%
1955 .... 71.5%
1956 .... 59.5%

... [I]n Wisconsin, requirements contracts – contracts to supply a firm's requirements of an item rather than a definite quantity – probably are not legally enforceable. Seven people interviewed reported that their firms regularly used requirements contracts in dealings in Wisconsin. None thought that the lack of legal sanction made any difference. Three of these people were house counsel who knew the Wisconsin law before being interviewed. . . . The standard contract used by manufacturers of paper to sell to magazine publishers has a pricing clause which is probably sufficiently vague to make the contract legally unenforceable. The house counsel of one of the largest paper producers said that everyone in the industry is aware of this because of a leading New York case concerning the contract, but that no one cares. . . .

Thus one can conclude that (1) many business exchanges reflect a high degree of planning about the four categories – description, contingencies, defective performances, and legal sanctions – but (2) many, if not most, exchanges reflect no planning, or only a minimal amount of it, especially concerning legal sanctions and the effect of defective performances. As a result, the opportunity for good faith disputes during the life of the exchange relationship often is present.

* * *

Business exchanges in non-speculative areas are usually adjusted without dispute. Under the law of contracts, if B orders 1,000 widgets from S at $1.00 each, B must take all 1,000 widgets or be in breach of contract and liable to pay S his expenses up to the time of the breach plus his lost anticipated profit. Yet all ten of the purchasing agents asked about cancellation of orders once placed indicated that they expected to be able to cancel orders freely subject to only an obligation to pay for the seller's major expenses, such as scrapped steel. All seventeen sales personnel asked reported that they often had to accept cancellation. One said, "You can't ask a man to eat paper (the firm's product) when he has no use for it." A lawyer with many large industrial clients said:

Often businessmen do not feel they have "a contract" – rather they have "an order." They speak of "cancelling the order" rather than "breaching our contract." When I began practice I referred to order cancellations as breaches of contract, but my clients objected since they do not think of cancellation as wrong. Most clients, in heavy industry at least, believe that there is a right to cancel as part of the buyer–seller relationship. There is a widespread attitude that one can back out of any deal within some very vague limits. Lawyers are often surprised by this attitude.

Disputes are frequently settled without reference to the contract or potential or actual legal sanctions. There is a hesitancy to speak of legal rights or to threaten to sue in these negotiations. . . . One purchasing agent expressed a common business attitude when he said:

> . . . if something comes up, you get the other man on the telephone and deal with the problem. You don't read legalistic contract clauses at each other if you ever want to do business again. One doesn't run to lawyers if he wants to stay in business because one must behave decently.

Or as one businessman put it, "You can settle any dispute if you keep the lawyers and accountants out of it. They just do not understand the give-and-take needed in business." . . .

Law suits for breach of contract appear to be rare. Only five of the twelve purchasing agents had ever been involved in even a negotiation concerning a contract dispute where both sides were represented by lawyers; only two of ten sales managers had ever gone this far. None had been involved in a case that went through trial. A law firm with more than forty lawyers and a large commercial practice handles in a year only about six trials concerned with contract problems. Less than 10 percent of the time of this office is devoted to any type of work related to contract disputes. Corporations big enough to do business in more than one state tend to sue and be sued in the federal courts. Yet only 2,779 out of 58,293 civil actions filed in the United States District Courts in fiscal year 1961 involved private contracts. During the same period only 3,447 of the 61,138 civil cases filed in the principal trial courts of New York State involved private contracts. The same picture emerges from a review of appellate cases. Mentschikoff (1954) has suggested that commercial cases are not brought to the courts either in periods of business prosperity (because buyers unjustifiably reject goods only when prices drop and they can get similar goods elsewhere at less than the contract price) or in periods of deep depression (because people are unable to come to court or have insufficient assets to satisfy any judgment that might be obtained). Apparently, she adds, it is necessary to have "a kind of middle-sized depression" to bring large numbers of commercial cases to the courts. However, there is little evidence that in even "a kind of middle-sized depression" today's businessmen would uses the courts to settle disputes.

At times relatively contractual methods are used to make adjustments in ongoing transactions and to settle disputes. Demands of one side which are deemed unreasonable by the other occasionally are blocked by reference to the terms of the agreement between the parties. The legal position of the parties can influence negotiations even though legal rights or litigation are never mentioned in their discussions; it makes a difference if one is demanding what both concede to be right or begging for a favor. Now and then a firm may threaten to turn matters over to its attorneys, threaten to sue, commence a suit, or even litigate and carry an appeal to the highest court which will hear the matter. Thus, legal sanctions, while not an everyday affair, are not unknown in business.

* * *

Tentative explanations

Two questions need to be answered: (A) How can business successfully operate exchange relationships with relatively so little attention to detailed planning or to legal sanctions, and (B) Why does business ever use contract in light of its success without it?

Why are relatively noncontractual practices so common? In most situations contract is not needed.* Often its functions are served by other devices. Most problems are avoided without resort to detailed planning or legal sanctions because usually there is little room for honest misunderstandings or good faith differences of opinion about the nature and quality of a seller's performance. Although the parties fail to cover all foreseeable contingencies, they will exercise care to see that both understand the primary obligation on each side. Either products are standardized with an accepted description, or specifications are written calling for production to certain tolerances or results. Those who write and read specifications are experienced professionals who will know the customs of their industry and those of the industries with which they deal. Consequently, these customs can fill gaps in the express agreements of the parties. Finally, most products can be tested to see if they are what was ordered; typically in manufacturing industry we are not dealing with questions of taste or judgment where people can differ in good faith.

When defaults occur they are not likely to be disastrous because of techniques of risk avoidance or risk spreading. One can deal with firms of good reputation or he may be able to get some form of security to

---

* The explanation that follows emphasizes a *considered* choice not to plan in detail for all contingencies. However, at times it is clear that businessmen fail to plan because of a lack of sophistication; they simply do not appreciate the risk they are running or they merely follow patterns established in their firms years ago without reexamining these practices in light of current conditions.

guarantee performance. One can insure against many breaches of contract where the risks justify the costs. Sellers set up reserves for bad debts on their books and can sell some of their accounts receivable. Buyers can place orders with two or more suppliers of the same item so that a default by one will not stop the buyer's assembly lines.

Moreover, contract and contract law are often thought unnecessary because there are many effective non-legal sanctions. Two norms are widely accepted. (1) Commitments are to be honored in almost all situations; one does not welsh on a deal. (2) One ought to produce a good product and stand behind it. Then, too, business units are organized to perform commitments, and internal sanctions will induce performance. For example, sales personnel must face angry customers when there has been a late or defective performance. The salesmen do not enjoy this and will put pressure on the production personnel responsible for the default. If the production personnel default too often, they will be fired. At all levels of the two business units personal relationships across the boundaries of the two organizations exert pressures for conformity to expectations. Salesmen often know purchasing agents well. The same two individuals occupying these roles may have dealt with each other from five to twenty-five years. Each has something to give the other. Salesmen have gossip about competitors, shortages, and price increases to give purchasing agents who treat them well. Salesmen take purchasing agents to dinner, and they give purchasing agents Christmas gifts hoping to improve the chances of making sale. The buyer's engineering staff may work with the seller's engineering staff to solve problems jointly. . . .

The final type of non-legal sanction is the most obvious. Both business units involved in the exchange desire to continue successfully in business and will avoid conduct which might interfere with attaining this goal. One is concerned with both the reaction of the other party in the particular exchange and with his own general business reputation. Obviously, the buyer gains sanctions insofar as the seller wants the particular exchange to be completed. Buyers can withhold part or all of their payments until sellers have performed to their satisfaction. If a seller has a great deal of money tied up in his performance which he must recover quickly, he will go a long way to please the buyer in order to be paid. Moreover, buyers who are dissatisfied may cancel and cause sellers to lose the cost of what they have done up to cancellation. Furthermore, sellers hope for repeat orders, and one gets few of these from unhappy customers. Some industrial buyers go so far as to formalize this sanction by issuing "report cards" rating the performance of each supplier. The supplier rating goes to the top management of the seller organization, and these men can apply internal sanctions to salesmen, production supervisors, or product designers if there are too many "D's" or "F's" on the report card. . . .

* * *

Not only do the particular business units in a given exchange want to deal with each other again, they also want to deal with other business units in the future. And the way one behaves in a particular transaction, or a series of transactions, will color his general business reputation. Blacklisting can be formal or informal. Buyers who fail to pay their bills on time risk a bad report in credit-rating services such as Dun and Bradstreet. Sellers who do not satisfy their customers become the subject of discussion in the gossip exchanged by purchasing agents and salesmen, at meetings of purchasing agents' associations and trade associations, or even at country clubs or social gatherings where members of top management meet. . . .

Not only are contract and contract law not needed in many situations, their use may have, or may be thought to have, undesirable consequences. Detailed negotiated contracts can get in the way of creating good exchange relationships between business units. If one side insists on a detailed plan, there will be delay while letters are exchanged as the parties try to agree on what should happen if a remote and unlikely contingency occurs. In some cases they may not be able to agree at all on such matters and as a result a sale may be lost to the seller and the buyer may have to search elsewhere for an acceptable supplier. Many businessmen would react by thinking that had no one raised the series of remote and unlikely contingencies all this wasted effort could have been avoided.

Even where agreement can be reached at the negotiation stage, carefully planned arrangements may create undesirable exchange relationships between business units. Some businessmen object that in such a carefully worked-out relationship one gets performance only to the letter of the contract. Such planning indicates a lack of trust and blunts the demands of friendship, turning a cooperative venture into an antagonistic horse trade. Yet the greater danger perceived by some businessmen is that one would have to perform his side of the bargain to the letter and thus lose what is called "flexibility." Businessmen may welcome a measure of vagueness in the obligations they assume so that they may negotiate matters in light of the actual circumstances.

Adjustment of exchange relationships and dispute settlement by litigation or the threat of it also has many costs. The gain anticipated from using this form of coercion often fails to outweigh these costs, which are both monetary and non-monetary. Threatening to turn matters over to an attorney may cost no more money than postage or a telephone call, yet few are so skilled in making such a threat that it will not cost some deterioration of the relationship between the firms. One businessman said that customers had better not rely on legal rights or threaten to bring a breach of contract law suit against him since he "would not be treated like a criminal" and would fight back with every means available. Clearly actual litigation is even more costly than making threats. Lawyers demand substantial fees from larger business units. A firm's executives often will have to be transported and maintained in another city during the proceedings if, as often is the case, the trial must be held away from the home office. Top management does not travel by Greyhound and stay at the YMCA. Moreover, there will be the cost of diverting top management, engineers, and others in the organization from their normal activities. The firm may lose many days work from several key people. The non-monetary costs may be large too. A breach of contract law suit may settle a particular dispute, but such an action often results in "divorce" ending the "marriage" between the two businesses, since a contract action is likely to carry charges with at least overtones of bad faith. Many executives, moreover, dislike the prospect of being cross-examined in public. Some executives may dislike losing control of a situation by turning the decision-making power over to lawyers. Finally, the law of contract damages may not provide an adequate remedy even if the firm wins the suit; one may get vindication but not much money.

Why do relatively contractual practices ever exist? Although contract is not needed and actually may have negative consequences, businessmen do make some carefully planned contracts, negotiate settlements influenced by their legal rights, and commence and defend some breach of contract law suits or arbitration proceedings. In view of the findings and explanation presented to this point, one may ask why. Exchanges are carefully planned when it is thought that planning and a potential legal sanction will have more advantages than disadvantages. Such a judgment may be reached when contract planning serves the internal needs of an organization involved in a business exchange. For example, a fairly detailed contract can serve as a communication device within a large corporation. While the corporation's sales manager and house counsel may work out all the provisions with the customer, its production manager will have to make the product. He must be told what to do and how to handle at least the most obvious contingencies. Moreover, the sales manager may want to remove certain issues from future negotiation by his subordinates. If he puts the matter in the written contract, he may be able to keep his salesmen from making concessions to the customer without first consulting the sales manager. Then the sales manager may be aided in his battles with his firm's financial or engineering departments if the contract calls for certain practices which the sales manager advocates but which the other departments resist. Now the corporation is obligated to a customer to do what the sales manager wants to do; how can the financial or engineering departments insist on anything else?

Also one tends to find a judgment that the gains of contract outweigh the costs where there is a likelihood that significant problems will arise.* One factor leading to this conclusion is complexity of the agreed-upon performance over a long period. Another factor is whether or not the degree of injury in case of default is thought to be potentially great. This factor cuts two ways. First, a buyer may want to commit a seller to a detailed and legally binding contract, where the consequences of a default by the seller would seriously injure the buyer. For example, the airlines are subject to law suits from the survivors of passengers and to great adverse publicity as a result of crashes. One would expect the airlines to bargain for carefully defined and legally enforceable obligations on the part of the airframe manufacturers when they purchase aircraft. Second, a seller may want to limit his liability for a buyer's damages by a provision in their contract. For example, a manufacturer of air-conditioning may deal with motels in the South and Southwest. If this equipment fails in the hot summer months, a motel may lose a great deal of business. The manufacturer may wish to avoid any liability for this type of injury to his customers and may want a contract with a clear disclaimer clause.

Similarly, one uses or threatens to use legal sanctions to settle disputes when other devices will not work and when the gains are thought to outweigh the costs. For example, perhaps the most common type of business contracts case fought all the way through to the appellate courts today is an action for an alleged wrongful termination of a dealer's franchise by a manufacturer. Since the franchise has been terminated, factors such as personal relationships and the desire for future business will have little effect; the cancellation of the franchise indicates they have already failed to maintain the relationship. Nor will a complaining dealer worry about creating a hostile relationship between himself and the manufacturer. Often the dealer has suffered a great financial loss both as to his investment in building and equipment and as to his an-

* Even when there is little chance that problems will arise, some businessmen insist that their lawyer review or draft an agreement as a delaying tactic. This gives the businessmen time to think about making a commitment if he has doubts about the matter or to look elsewhere for a better deal while still keeping the particular negotiations alive.

ticipated future profits. A cancelled automobile dealer's lease on his showroom and shop will continue to run, and his tools for servicing, say, Plymouths cannot be used to service other makes of cars. Moreover, he will have no more new Plymouths to sell. Today there is some chance of winning a law suit for terminating a franchise in bad faith in many states and in the federal courts. Thus, often the dealer chooses to risk the cost of a lawyer's fee because of the chance that he may recover some compensation for his losses.

* * *

CHAPTER 1.2

Relational exchange:
ecomonics and complex contracts

VICTOR P. GOLDBERG (1980)

We begin with an obvious empirical fact. Much economic activity takes place within long-term, complex, perhaps multiparty contractual (or contract-like) relationships; behavior is, in varying degrees, sheltered from market forces. The implicit contract of utility regulation, the contractual network that constitutes a firm, franchise agreements, pensions, and collective bargaining agreements are examples. Granted this, we can then proceed along two different lines. First, we can attempt to explain why relationships take the form that they do; why does a particular firm own its retail outlets rather than selling through franchised outlets or discount stores? Second, what impact does the relationship's structure have beyond the relationship? Do the price adjustment rules used in employment contracts or in regulated industries give the wrong short-run signals, thereby exacerbating unemployment? Since economists attempt both to explain and prescribe, these questions can also be recast in normative terms: How should parties structure their relationships (from the point of view of the parties or other groups – perhaps society as a whole)?

To make headway in understanding the essential features of relational exchange it is convenient to set up a stylized problem. Consider two parties contemplating entering into a contract who must establish rules to structure their future relationship. The parties can have competing alternatives both at the formation stage and within the relationship. The choice of rules will depend upon the anticipated outcomes. The choice will also reflect three significant facts about the world that are so obvious

Reprinted from Victor P. Goldberg, "Relational Exchange: Economics and Complex Contracts," *American Behavioral Scientist* 23 (1980): 337–52, with the permission of Sage Publications, Inc.

that only an economist would feel compelled to recognize them explicitly. First, people are not omniscient; their information is imperfect and improvable only at a cost. Second, not all people are saints all of the time; as the relationship unfolds there will be opportunities for one party to take advantage of the other's vulnerability, to engage in strategic behavior, or to follow his own interests at the expense of the other party. The actors will, on occasion, behave opportunistically. Third, the parties cannot necessarily rely on outsiders to enforce the agreement cheaply and accurately.

If we assume that the agreement reflects the balancing of the parties' interests given the tools available, the efficacy of those tools in different contexts, and the constraints facing the decision makers, then we have the framework for a predictive model. Under conditions M we should expect to observe structure N; or if we observe structure N, then we should expect to find conditions M. This is, of course, an overly mechanical representation. A more modest formulation is that it is a reasonable research strategy to assume that the agreements reflect the purposive behavior of the parties.

The relational exchange framework directs attention to a number of concerns often overlooked in standard microeconomics. It also suggests that in many contexts the significance of the static optimality sort of questions, with which economists typically deal, has been overrated. The parties will be willing to absorb a lot of apparent static inefficiency in pursuit of their relational goals.

Within the contract each party makes expenditures, receives benefits, and confers benefits on the other party at various times. The timing of the streams of benefits and costs need not coincide. For example, X might have planted crops and contracted with Y for harvesting them. Or X might agree to paint Y's house with Y paying upon completion. If X had cheap, effective legal remedies available (or if he could rely on Y's need to maintain his reputation) then the noncoincidence of the streams of costs and benefits to the parties would be immaterial. But if external enforcement is imperfect, X is vulnerable to being held up by Y.

If as the relationship unfolds the costs incurred by X are much greater than the benefits he has received (as in the harvesting example), Y can convincingly threaten to breach the contract even though at this point Y has incurred no costs and received no benefits. Y could conceivably force X to revise the contract price down (or wage up) to the point at which X is indifferent between completing the agreement or terminating it. In the other case, X's vulnerability is even greater. Not only does he incur a cost before receiving payment, but Y also receives benefits before paying.

17

The vulnerability can, of course, be reduced by deliberately structuring the relationship to make the stream of benefits and costs for each party more nearly coincident. Progress payments (for custom-made capital goods or defense contracts) and installment sales contracts are examples of such phased performance in which one party's performance consists of making payment. The parties' options are not restricted to adjusting the payment stream to a fixed production schedule. The timing of production as well as the techniques used in production (e.g., less fixed, specialized capital), and the characteristics of the output (e.g., greater standardization) can all be altered to enhance the contract's enforceability.

Suppose that one party has to make a considerable initial investment and that the value of the investment depends on continuation of the relationship. An employee investing in firm-specific capital is one example; a second would be an electric utility building a plant to serve a particular area. Both will be reluctant to incur the high initial costs without some assurance of subsequent rewards. Other things equal, the firmer that assurance, the more attractive the investment. So, for example, if the utility customers agree to give it the exclusive right to serve them for twenty years, then the utility would find construction of a long-lived plant more attractive than if it did not have such assurance. Of course, if a new, superior technology were likely to appear within three years, the customers would not want the long-lived plant built. Nevertheless, there will be lots of instances in which the parties will find it efficacious to protect one party's reliance on the continuation of the relationship.

Since circumstances will change in many ways not anticipated at the formation stage, the parties will desire some means for adjusting the relationship to take those new circumstances into account. As an example, consider a contract in which X agrees to build a custom-made machine for Y, who will use it to produce a new product. Before the machine's construction is completed, Y decides that marketing the new product will be unprofitable and wants to cancel the order. Ideally, X would want some mechanism in the contract which would require that Y take his reliance into account when weighing the merits of continuation versus breach. (Likewise, Y would want X to take into account his costs of continuing if X had the legal right to enforce the initial agreement.) If the parties acted totally in good faith – if we assume no opportunistic behavior – then this does not present a problem. They can simply inform each other of the costs of continuation versus breach (accurately, by assumption), choose the optimal strategy, and divide in some manner the benefits or costs arising from this optimal solution.

But, of course, both X and Y will have incentives to be less than completely honest. The specter of opportunistic behavior hangs over the relationship. If the parties cannot draw upon a reservoir of trust or rely on the discipline of future dealings, they will require some mechanisms for balancing the reliance and flexibility interests.

The parties must establish some sort of governance mechanism for the relationship. The initial agreement will, in general, be neither self-enforcing nor self-adjusting. Prices (deductibles and copayments in insurance contracts for example) and simple adjustment rules (like indexing) can, of course, be used to influence the parties' behavior. These passive devices can be supplemented by – or supplanted by – more activist forms of governance. These activist forms include extensive monitoring or policing of behavior to detect and punish violations of the agreement. In addition, it will often be advantageous to postpone decisions until more facts are known and to assign to someone the task of making that future decision. If that someone is one of the parties, this arrangement can be characterized as establishing an authority relationship: The decider has authority over the future behavior of the other party (see Simon [1951]). X agrees that Y can tell him what to do. The question of the scope of Y's authority can be a source of great friction, as those familiar with labor history can attest.

Because standard microeconomics emphasizes market exchange and suppresses consideration of behavior that occurs within relationships sheltered from market forces, economists have tended to view elements that facilitate such sheltering with hostility and suspicion. The spirit of the relational exchange approach is quite different. It recognizes that the sheltering is inevitable and, moreover, that it can be functional. Contracting parties will often find it in their mutual interest to increase the isolation of at least one of them from alternatives – to make it more difficult (costly) to leave this particular relationship. To protect X's reliance, for example, the parties would want to make exit expensive for Y. Or, as a second example, A's ability to exercise authority over B can be enhanced if he can threaten to impose costs on a recalcitrant B; that threat can be made credible by making termination costly for B. The relational exchange approach focuses our attention on the reasons why parties might want to erect exit barriers and on the rich array of institutional devices which might be utilized for that purpose.

The organizing theme of much of the new literature is "efficiency." People will adopt certain arrangements because these are more efficient than alternatives, given the opportunities and difficulties confronting them. The analysis need not, however, be an apology for existing institutions: Whatever is, is right. Efficiency is contextual. Given the social context, the parties will attempt to arrange their affairs as best they can. If the context were different, then the efficient structure would also differ. So, to take an extreme example, one might argue that in the best of all possible worlds collective bargaining agreements would be inefficient, but they might be an intelligent (efficient) response in a world characterized by the threat of labor violence. At a different level of analysis, we can take the existence of collective bargaining as given–it is part of the social context. We need not worry about whether it is good, bad, efficient, stupid, or immoral. It simply is. Granted that, we can then ask such questions as: Will increased job security for union members result in predictable changes in the organization of work? For example, will employers now invest more heavily in giving workers firm-specific skills and redesign the production process to take advantage of these skilled workers? Or we might investigate the techniques employed to govern the relationship (less authority, more "due process" or "voice"). Likewise, on the prescriptive level we will be led to search for mechanisms for adjusting ongoing relationships to changing conditions and other problems foreign to the world of conventional economic theory.

* * *

Production functions, transactions costs, and the new institutionalism

VICTOR P. GOLDBERG (1984)

My hostility to [the phrase] *transactions costs* must strike most readers as odd, since the "new institutional economics" and "transactions costs economics" are often thought of as synonymous. My concern in this instance is perhaps more semantic than substantive. It does seem to me, however, that "transactions costs" runs the risk of becoming the "imperfect capital markets" of the 1980s, the all-purpose answer that tells us nothing.

A bit of history. In his early paper on "The Nature of the Firm," Coase [1937], in effect, said: If markets work as well as they do in our models, then no alternative system could do better, and most would probably do worse; why then, he asked, would anything but impersonal markets emerge and thrive? Since firms do exist and do thrive, we must ask how such organizations could be superior to the impersonal markets. The answer – or really the first part of the answer – was that impersonal markets weren't so darn perfect anyway; their imperfection he called "transactions costs." Two decades later, Coase [1960] conducted the same sort of exercise with externalities. Economists were classifying goods in two categories: for normal goods (with zero transactions costs) markets worked perfectly; for externalities (with infinite transactions costs) markets worked not at all. Coase never bothered to give a precise definition of transactions costs because he didn't take the concept very seriously. It was only the name of whatever it was the economists had been ignoring; the intent in both papers was to move analysis away from a world in which market perfection was an all-or-nothing affair.

Reprinted from Victor P. Goldberg, "Production Functions, Transactions Costs and the New Institutionalism." In *Issues in Contemporary Microeconomics*, edited by George Feiwel, 395–402. With the permission of Macmillan Press, Ltd.

Economists have a number of essentially equivalent ways of characterizing the conditions resulting in efficiency. If transactions costs are zero, if all markets exist, if marginal social product equals marginal private product, or if there are no externalities, resources would be allocated efficiently. When there is a shortfall from perfection, as there inevitably must be, there is a tendency to identify its source in terms of the characterization – positive transactions costs, market failure, or whatever. This leap of logic is the source of much of the semantic confusion that has permeated much of the post-Coase discussion of transactions costs.

The phrase "transactions costs" captures the notion that transacting – engaging in economic activity – requires the use of real resources. It embodies two very different meanings. One focuses on identifiable activities involved in transacting. The concept would presumably include the costs associated with bargaining, negotiating, and monitoring performance – costs usually associated with the activities of purchasing agents, lawyers, accountants, and similar functionaries. It is analogous to the Marxist concept of "nonproductive labor." What distinguishes these costs from others (or nonproductive from productive labor)? Is an accountant's bill for $10,000 less painful than a bill for an equal amount from a steel supplier? Firms incur these costs because it is efficient for them to do so. It is cheaper to pay accountants to perform a task than to bear the additional costs of embezzlement that might occur in their absence. As far as the economic actors are concerned, transactions costs are the same as other costs.

The preceding formulation emphasizes the type of activities that might be included under the transactions cost rubric. An alternative formulation better captures Coase's intent. Transactions costs are those costs most likely to differ under alternative institutional arrangements. . . . [They] are the difference between what could have been produced if actual inputs corresponded to efficiency units and what actually happened. The transactions costs are an unobservable residual; they are the opportunity cost of the world not being as nice a place as it otherwise might be. In this formulation, the transactions cost label is a redundancy. If we say the the transactions costs of the worker-controlled gadget-producing firm are higher than its capitalistic counterpart, we mean no more and no less than that it is less efficient in transforming inputs into outputs.

* * *

The transactions cost concept has been particularly misleading because it embodies two very different meanings. On the one hand, it has the natural meaning of costs associated with a set of activities involved

22

in transacting. On the other hand, it can mean a shortfall from what could have been achieved if institutions worked perfectly. There is a strong temptation to join these meanings by attributing the shortfall to a particular set of activities. Much of the confusion involving the transactions cost concept has stemmed from this unfortunate linkage. By explicating this dual meaning, I hope that I have removed one of the barriers to understanding the causes and effects of economic institutions.

CHAPTER 1.4

The market for "lemons": quality uncertainty and the market mechanism

GEORGE A. AKERLOF (1970)

There are many markets in which buyers use some market statistic to judge the quality of prospective purchases. In this case there is incentive for sellers to market poor-quality merchandise, since the returns for good quality accrue mainly to the entire group whose statistic is affected rather than to the individual seller. As a result there tends to be a reduction in the average quality of goods and also in the size of the market. It should also be perceived that in these markets social and private returns differ, and therefore, in some cases, governmental intervention may increase the welfare of all parties. Or private institutions may arise to take advantage of the potential increases in welfare which can accrue to all parties. By nature, however, these institutions are nonatomistic, and therefore concentrations of power – with ill consequences of their own – can develop.

The automobile market is used as a finger exercise to illustrate and develop these thoughts. It should be emphasized that this market is chosen for its concreteness and ease in understanding rather than for its importance or realism.

II. The model with automobiles as an example

A. The automobiles market

The example of used cars captures the essence of the problem. From time to time one hears either mention of or surprise at the large price difference between new cars and those which have just left the show-room. The usual lunch table justification for this phenomenon is the pure joy of owning a "new" car. We offer a different explanation. Suppose (for the sake of clarity rather than reality) that there are just four kinds of cars. There are new cars and used cars. There are good cars and bad cars (which in America are known as "lemons"). A new car may be a good car or a lemon, and of course the same is true of used cars.

The individuals in this market buy a new automobile without knowing whether the car they buy will be good or a lemon. But they do know that with probability q it is a good car and with probability $(1 - q)$ it is a lemon; by assumption, q is the proportion of good cars produced and $(1 - q)$ is the proportion of lemons.

After owning a specific car, however, for a length of time, the car owner can form a good idea of the quality of this machine; i.e., the owner assigns a new probability to the event that his car is a lemon. This estimate is more accurate than the original estimate. An asymmetry in available information has developed, for the sellers now have more knowledge about the quality of a car than the buyers. But good cars and bad cars must still sell at the same price – since it is impossible for a buyer to tell the difference between a good car and a bad car. It is apparent that a used car cannot have the same valuation as a new car – if it did have the same valuation, it would clearly be advantageous to trade a lemon at the price of a new car, and buy another new car, at a higher probability q of being good and a lower probability of being bad. Thus the owner of a good machine must be locked in. Not only is it true that he cannot receive the true value of his car, but he cannot even obtain the expected value of a new car.

Gresham's law has made a modified reappearance. For most cars traded will be the "lemons," and good cars may not be traded at all. The "bad" cars tend to drive out the good (in much the same way that bad money drives out the good). But the analogy with Gresham's law is not quite complete: Bad cars drive out the good because they sell at the same price as good cars; similarly, bad money drives out good because the exchange rate is even. But the bad cars sell at the same price as good cars since it is impossible for a buyer to tell the difference between a good and a bad car; only the seller knows. In Gresham's law, however, presumably both buyer and seller can tell the difference between good and bad money. So the analogy is instructive, but not complete.

III. Examples and applications

A. Insurance

It is a well-known fact that people over sixty-five have great difficulty in buying medical insurance. The natural question arises: Why doesn't the price rise to match the risk?

Our answer is that as the price level rises, the people who insure themselves will be those who are increasingly certain that they will need insurance, for error in medical checkups, doctors' sympathy with older patients, and so on make it much easier for the applicant to assess the risks involved than the insurance company. The result is that the average medical condition of insurance applicants deteriorates as the price level rises – with the result that no insurance sales may take place at any price.* This is strictly analogous to our automobiles case, where the average quality of used cars supplied fell with a corresponding fall in the price level. This agrees with the explanation in insurance textbooks:

Generally speaking policies are not available at ages materially greater than sixty-five. . . . The term premiums are too high for any but the most pessimistic (which is to say the least healthy) insureds to find attractive. Thus there is a severe problem of adverse selection at these ages. [Dickerson, 1959, p. 333]

* * *

Group insurance, which is the most common form of medical insurance in the United States, picks out the healthy, for generally adequate health is a precondition for employment. At the same time this means that medical insurance is least available to those who need it most, for the insurance companies do their own "adverse selection."

This adds one major argument in favor of medicare. On a cost benefit basis medicare may pay off, for it is quite possible that every individual in the market would be willing to pay the expected cost of his medicare and buy insurance, yet no insurance company can afford to sell him a policy – for at any price it will attract too many "lemons." The welfare economics of medicare, in this view, is exactly analogous to the usual classroom argument for public expenditure on roads.

* Arrow's fine article [1963], does not make this point explicitly. He emphasizes "moral hazard" rather than "adverse selection." In its strict sense, the presence of "moral hazard" is equally disadvantageous for both governmental and private programs; in its broader sense, which includes "adverse selection," "moral hazard" gives a decided advantage to government insurance programs.

* * *

C. The costs of dishonesty

The Lemons model can be used to make some comments on the costs of dishonesty. Consider a market in which goods are sold honestly or dishonestly; quality may be represented, or it may be misrepresented. The purchaser's problem, of course, is to identify quality. The presence of people in the market who are willing to offer inferior goods tends to drive the market out of existence, as in the case of our automobile "lemons." It is this possibility that represents the major costs of dishonesty, for dishonest dealings tend to drive honest dealings out of the market. There may be potential buyers of good quality products and there may be potential sellers of such products in the appropriate price range; however, the presence of people who wish to pawn bad wares as good wares tends to drive out the legitimate business. The cost of dishonesty, therefore, lies not only in the amount by which the purchaser is cheated; the cost also must include the loss incurred from driving legitimate business out of existence.

* * *

... [A] major feature of the Indian industrial scene [is] ... the extortionate rates which the local moneylender charges his clients. In India these high rates of interest have been the leading factor in landlessness; the so-called Cooperative Movement was meant to counteract this growing landlessness by setting up banks to compete with the local moneylenders. While the large banks in the central cities have prime interest rates of 6, 8, and 10 percent, the local moneylender charges 15, 25, even 50 percent. The answer to this seeming paradox is that credit is granted only where the granter has (1) easy means of enforcing his contract or (2) personal knowledge of the character of the borrower. The middleman who tries to arbitrage between the rates of the moneylender and the central bank is apt to attract all the "lemons" and thereby make a loss.

This interpretation can be seen in Sir Malcolm Darling's interpretation of the village moneylender's power:

It is only fair to remember that in the Indian village the money-lender is often the one thrifty person amongst a generally thriftless people; and that his methods of business, though demoralizing under modern conditions, suit the happy-go-lucky ways of the peasant. He is always accessible, even at night; dispenses with troublesome formalities, asks no inconvenient questions, advances promptly, and if interest is paid, does not press for repayment of principal. He keeps in close personal touch with his clients, and in many villages shares their occasions of weal or woe. *With his intimate knowledge of those around him he is able,*

27

without serious risk, to finance those who would otherwise get no loan at all.
[Darling, 1932, p. 204, italics added.]

* * *

IV. Counteracting institutions

Numerous institutions arise to counteract the effects of quality uncertainty. One obvious institution is guarantees. Most consumer durables carry guarantees to ensure the buyer of some normal expected quality. One natural result of our model is that the risk is borne by the seller rather than by the buyer.

A second example of an institution which counteracts the effects of quality uncertainty is the brand-name good. Brand names not only indicate quality but also give the consumer a means of retaliation if the quality does not meet expectations. For the consumer will then curtail future purchases. Often, too, new products are associated with old brand names. This ensures the prospective consumer of the quality of the product.

Chains, such as hotel chains or restaurant chains, are similar to brand names. One observation consistent with our approach is the chain restaurant. These restaurants, at least in the United States, most often appear on interurban highways. The customers are seldom local. The reason is that these well-known chains offer a better hamburger than the *average* local restaurant; at the same time, the local customer, who knows his area, can usually choose a place he prefers.

Licensing practices also reduce quality uncertainty. For instance, there is the licensing of doctors, lawyers, and barbers. Most skilled labor carries some certification indicating the attainment of certain levels of proficiency. The high school diploma, the baccalaureate degree, the Ph.D., even the Nobel Prize, to some degree, serve this function of certification. And education and labor markets themselves have their own "brand names."

V. Conclusion

We have been discussing economic models in which "trust" is important. Informal unwritten guarantees are preconditions for trade and production. Where these guarantees are indefinite, business will suffer – as indicated by our generalized Gresham's law. . . . [T]he difficulty of distinguishing good quality from bad is inherent in the business world; this may in fact be one of the more important aspects of uncertainty.

A treatise on the law of marine insurance and general average
Volume I

THEOPHILUS PARSONS (1868)

If we understand the immense utility of insurance, and the grounds, or, as may well be said, the indispensable conditions of this utility, we shall see that these depend upon a few simple principles; and we shall also see that merchants in their practice, and courts in their decisions of the multifarious and complicated questions presented by the law of insurance, constantly regard these principles. And it may be added, that if the sagacity of merchants, stimulated by a sense of direct interest, and gradually taught by experience, has discovered these principles and applied them to practice, it is not less true that courts have been too sagacious to disregard this practice. Since the days of Lord Mansfield, who set a wise example in this respect, the jurisprudence of England and America, in the matter of insurance, has done little else than adopt the usage of merchants, and give to it the force of authority.

What are these principles? They are few and easily stated. And indeed they all rest on one principle. It is, that if insurance be made too costly to the insured, and if it be too difficult for them to obtain indemnity for loss by reason of the narrow construction of the law, or the severe application of technical requirements, the practice of insurance would be checked, and it would be left very much to the wealthiest and the most careful merchants, who are those that need it least, and who would be most disposed – to use a common phrase – to "stand as their own insurers."

On the other hand, if insurance be too cheap, and, when loss occurs, indemnity is so easily recovered as to put the careless and the careful on the same ground, insurers would find themselves losing too much, or, in other words, losing on the whole; and if the business of insurance were conducted on the credit of funds appropriated to it, they would fail, and insurance become in fact no insurance. Or, if to meet these expenses and losses, they raised their premiums high enough to cover them, careful and skillful merchants would avoid insurance when the risks they had to pay for were far greater than the actual risks to which their own property was exposed.

The object, therefore, to be attained by merchants and insurers in their usages, and by the courts in their construction of the laws of insurance, and in the application of them to cases which come before them, is to find if possible the just medium between these extremes.

The ideal perfection of maritime insurance is easily stated. It would become actual, if all maritime property were covered by insurance, and the risks of this insurance were widely distributed, and the cost of it were so accurately proportioned to the real danger that the premiums sufficed to pay all the losses, with only a sufficient surplus to pay the expense of the business when economically conducted, and a reasonable interest on the funds on the security whereof the insurance is effected.

This ideal may never be attained and preserved with precise accuracy; but the departures from it oscillate within narrow limits, and, on the whole, the work is sufficiently well done. At one time premiums run a little too high. Then the business is checked. The best ship-owners and merchants decline to pay more than they think the risk is worth, and insurers are obliged to call them back by lowering the rate of premiums. At another time the premiums run too low: In their desire to do much business, and in the competition for business, insurers take risks at less than they are really worth. The consequence soon shows itself. Losses eat up all the premiums, and something more; and insurers find that the more business they do in that way, the worse it is for them. The mischief cures itself at once. As soon as such a state of things is seen to exist, or rather, as soon as it is seen to threaten, insurers raise their premiums; and, with some check to their business perhaps, conduct it on terms which give them a reasonable profit, and afford security to the insured at reasonable cost. And so it goes on. These fluctuations are inevitable. No law could prevent them, nor could it usefully interfere with them. The necessities of business, and the certain consequences of error in either direction, suffice to keep these alternations within narrow bounds; and the business of insurance, in submitting to them, only follows the universal law of all human actions, and indeed of the movements of the world. Everywhere, nothing is perfectly and permanently right; but aberration in one direction is cured and compensated by aberration in another, and the resultant of the whole is near enough to the right to be practically sufficient.

30

CHAPTER 1.6

The economics of moral hazard: comment

MARK V. PAULY (1968)

...The individual who has insurance which covers all costs demands medical care as though it had a *zero* price, but when he purchases insurance, he must take account of the *positive* cost of that care, as "translated" to him through the actuarially necessary premium. Hence, he may well not wish to purchase such insurance at the premium his behavior as a purchaser of insurance and as a demander of medical care under insurance makes necessary.

The presence of a "prisoners' dilemma" motivation makes this inconsistency inevitable. Each individual may well recognize that "excess" use of medical care makes the premium he must pay rise. No individual will be motivated to restrain his own use, however, since the incremental benefit to him for excess use is great, while the additional cost of his use is largely spread over other insurance holders, and so he bears only a tiny fraction of the cost of his use. It would be better for all insurance beneficiaries to restrain their use, but such a result is not forthcoming because the strategy of "restrain use" is dominated by that of "use excess care."

* * *

It has been recognized in the insurance literature that medical insurance, by lowering the marginal cost of care to the individual, may increase usage; this characteristic has been termed "moral hazard." Moral hazard is defined as "the intangible loss-producing propensities of the individual assured" [Dickerson, 1963, p. 463]. . . . Insurance writ-

Reprinted from Mark V. Pauly, "The Economics of Moral Hazard: Comment," *American Economic Review* 58 (1968): 531–7, with the permission of the author and the American Economic Association.

31

ers have tended very strongly to look upon this phenomenon (of demanding more at a zero price than at a positive one) as a moral or ethical problem, using emotive words such as "malingering" and "hypochondria," lumping it together with outright fraud in the collection of benefits, and providing value-tinged definitions as "moral hazard reflects the hazard that arises from the failure of individuals who are or have been affected by insurance to uphold the accepted moral qualities" [Dickerson, 1963, p. 327], or "moral hazard is every deviation from correct human behavior that may pose a problem for an insurer" [Buchanan, 1964, p. 22]. . . .

The above analysis shows, however, that the response of seeking more medical care with insurance than in its absence is a result not of moral perfidy, but of rational economic behavior. Since the cost of the individual's excess usage is spread over all other purchasers of that insurance, the individual is not prompted to restrain his usage of care.

CHAPTER 1.7

The economics of moral hazard:
further comment

KENNETH J. ARROW (1968)

Mr. Pauly's paper has enriched our understanding of the phenomenon of so-called moral hazard and has convincingly shown that the optimality of complete insurance is no longer valid when the method of insurance influences the demand for the services provided by the insurance policy. This point is worth making strongly. In the theory of optimal allocation of resources under risk bearing it can be shown that competitive insurance markets will yield optimal allocation when the events insured are not controllable by individual behavior. If the amount of insurance payment is in any way dependent on a decision of the insured as well as on a state of nature, then the effect is very much the same as that of any excise tax, and optimality will not be achieved either by the competitive system or by an attempt by the government to simulate a perfectly competitive system. . . .

In this note I would like to stress a point which Mr. Pauly overlooks in his exclusive emphasis on market incentives. Mr. Pauly has a very interesting sentence: "The above analysis shows, however, that the response of seeking more medical care with insurance than in its absence is a result not of moral perfidy, but of rational economic behavior." We may agree certainly that the seeking of more medical care with insurance is a rational action on the part of the individuals if no further constraints are imposed. It does not follow that no constraints ought to be imposed or indeed that in certain contexts individuals should not impose constraints on themselves. Mr. Pauly's wording suggests that "rational eco-

Reprinted from Kenneth J. Arrow, "The Economics of Moral Hazard: Further Comment," *American Economic Review* 58 (1968): 537–8, with the permission of the author and the American Economic Association.

33

nomic behavior" and "moral perfidy" are mutually exclusive categories. No doubt Judas Iscariot turned a tidy profit from one of his transactions, but the usual judgment of his behavior is not necessarily wrong.

The underlying point is that, if individuals are free to spend as they will with the assurance that the insurance company will pay, the resulting resource allocation will certainly not be socially optimal. This makes perfectly reasonable the idea that an insurance company can improve the allocation of resources to all concerned by a policy which rations the amount of medical services it will support under the insurance policy. This rationing may in fact occur in several different ways: (1) there might be a detailed examination by the insurance company of individual cost items allowing those that are regarded "normal" and disallowing others, where normality means roughly what would have been bought in the absence of insurance; (2) they may rely on the professional ethics of physicians not to prescribe frivolously expensive cost of treatment, at least where the gain is primarily in comfort and luxury rather than in health improvement proper; (3) they may even – and this is not as absurd as Mr. Pauly seems to think – rely on the willingness of the individual to behave in accordance with some commonly accepted norms.

The last point is perhaps not so important in the specific medical context, but the author had clearly broader implications in mind and so do I. Because of the moral hazard, complete reliance on economic incentives does not lead to an optimal allocation of resources in general. In most societies alternative relationships are built up which to some extent serve to permit cooperation and risk sharing. The principal–agent relation is very pervasive in all economies and especially in modern ones; by definition the agent has been selected for his specialized knowledge, and therefore the principal can never hope completely to check the agent's performance. You cannot therefore easily take out insurance against the failure of the agent to perform well. One of the characteristics of a successful economic system is that the relations of trust and confidence between principal and agent are sufficiently strong so that the agent will not cheat even though it may be "rational economic behavior" to do so. The lack of such confidence has certainly been adduced by many writers as one cause of economic backwardness.

* * *

CHAPTER 1.8

Efficient rent seeking

GORDON TULLOCK (1980)

... In my article, "On the Efficient Organization of Trials" [1975], I introduced a game that I thought had much resemblance to our court trial, or, indeed, to any other two-party conflict. In its simplest form, we assume two parties who are participating in a lottery under somewhat unusual rules. Each is permitted to buy as many lottery tickets as he wishes at one dollar each, the lottery tickets are put in a drum, one is pulled out, and whoever owns that ticket wins the prize. Thus, the probability of success for A is shown in equation (1), because the number of lottery tickets he holds is amount A and the total number in the drum is $A + B$.

$$P_A = \frac{A}{A + B} \tag{1}$$

In the previously cited article, I pointed out that this model could be generalized by making various modifications in it, and it is my purpose now to generalize it radically.

Let us assume, then, that a wealthy eccentric has put up $100 as a prize for the special lottery between A and B. Note that the amount spent on lottery tickets is retained by the lottery, not added onto the prize. This makes the game equivalent to rent seeking, where resources are also wasted.

How much should each invest? It is obvious that the answer to this question, from the standpoint of each party, depends on what he thinks

Reprinted from Gordon Tullock, "Efficient Rent Seeking." In *Toward a Theory of the Rent-Seeking Society,* edited by James M. Buchanan, Robert D. Tollison, and Gordon Tullock. ©1980 by Texas A&M University Press. With the permission of the author and the publisher.

the other will do. Here, and throughout the rest of this paper, I am going to use a rather special assumption about individual knowledge. I am going to assume that if there is a correct solution for individual strategy, then each player will assume that the other parties can also figure out what that correct solution is. In other words, if the correct strategy in this game were to play $50, each party would assume that the other was playing $50 and would buy fifty tickets for himself, if that were the optimal amount under those circumstances.

As a matter of fact, the optimal strategy in this game is not to buy $50.00 worth of tickets, but to buy $25.00. As a very simple explanation, suppose that I have bought $25.00 and you have bought $50.00; I have a one in three chance of getting the $100.00 and you have a two in three chance. Thus, the present value of my investment is $33.33 and the present value of yours is $66.66, or, for this particular case, an equal percentage gain. Suppose, however, that you decided to reduce your purchase to $40.00 and I stayed at $25.00. This saves you $10.00 on your investment, but it lowers your present value of expectancy to only $61.53 and you are about $5.00 better off. Of course, I have gained from your reduction, too.

You could continue reducing your bet with profit until you also reached $25.00. For example, if you lowered your purchase from $26.00 to $25.00, the present value of your investment would fall from $50.98 to $50.00, and you would save $1.00 in investment. Going beyond $25.00, however, would cost you money. If you lowered it to $24.00, you would reduce the value of your investment by $1.02 and only save $1.00. It is assumed, of course, that I keep my purchase at $25.00.

I suppose it is obvious from what I have said already that $25.00 is equilibrium for both; that is, departure from it costs either one something. It is not true, however, that if the other party has made a mistake, I maximize my returns by paying $25.00. For example, if the other party has put up $50.00 and I pay $24.00 instead of $25.00, I save $1.00 in my investment but reduce my expectancy by only $0.90. My optimal investment, in fact, is $17.00. However, if we assume a game in which each party knows what the other party has invested and adjusts his investment accordingly, the ultimate outcome must be at approximately $25.00 for each party. The game is clearly a profitable one to play, and, in fact, it will impress the average economist as rather improbable. However, it is a case in which inframarginal profits are made, although we are in marginal balance. At first glance, most people feel that the appropriate bet is $50.00, but that is bringing the total return into equality with the total cost rather than equating the margins.

To repeat, this line of reasoning depends on the assumption that the individuals can figure out the correct strategy, if there is a correct strategy, and that they assume that other people will be able to figure it out also. It is similar to the problem that started John von Neumann on the invention of game theory, and I think it is not too irrational a set of assumptions if we assume the kind of problem that rent seeking raises.

But there is no reason why the odds in our game should be a simple linear function of contributions. For example, they could be an exponential function, as in equation (2):

$$P_A = \frac{A^r}{A^r + B^r} \tag{2}$$

There are, of course, many other functions that could be substituted, but in this paper we will stick to exponentials.

It is also possible for more than two people to play, in which case we would have equation (3):

$$P_A = \frac{A^r}{A^r + B^r \ldots n^r} \tag{3}$$

The individuals need not receive the same return on their investment. Indeed, in many cases we would hope that the situation is biased. [The analysis of the case with bias has been omitted (ed.)] For example, we hope that the likelihood of passing a civil service examination is not simply a function of the amount of time spent cramming, but that other types of merit are also important. This would be shown in our equations by some kind of bias in which one party receives more lottery tickets for his money than another.

We will begin by changing the shape of the marginal cost curve and the number of people playing. ... Table 1 shows the individual equilibrium payments by players of the game with varying exponents (which means varying marginal cost structures) and varying numbers of players. Table 2 shows the total amount paid by all of the players, if they all play the equilibrium strategy.

I have drawn lines dividing these two tables into zones I, II, and III. Let us temporarily confine ourselves to discussing zone I. This is the zone in which the equilibrium price summed over all players leads to a payment equal to or less than the total prize. In other words, these are the games in which expectancy of the players, if they all play, would be positive. Although we start with these games, as we shall see below there are cases in which we may be compelled to play games in zones II and III where the expectancy is negative.

37

Table 1. *Individual investments (N-person, no bias, with exponent)*

Exponent	Number of players				
	2	4	10		15
1/3	8.33	6.25	3.0		2.07
1/2	12.50	9.37	4.50	I	3.11
1	25.00	18.75	9.00		6.22
2	50.00	37.50	18.00		12.44
3	75.00	56.25	27.00		18.67
5	125.00	93.75	45.00	II	31.11
8	200.00	150.00	72.00		49.78
12	300.00	225.00	108.00		74.67
		III			

Table 2. *Sum of investments (N-Person, no bias, with exponent)*

Exponent	Number of players					
	2	4	10	15		Limit
1/3	16.66	25.00	30.00	31.05		33.33
1/2	25.00	37.40	45.00	46.65	I	50.00
1	50.00	75.00	90.00	93.30		100.00
2	100.00	150.00	180.00	186.60		200.00
3	150.00	225.00	270.00	280.05		300.00
5	250.00	375.00	450.00	466.65	II	500.00
8	400.00	600.00	720.00	746.70		800.00
12	600.00	900.00	1,080.00	1,120.05		1,200.00
			III			

If we look at zone I, it is immediately obvious that the individual payments go down as the number of players rises, but the total amount paid rises. In a way, what is happening here is that a monopoly profit is being competed away. Note, however, when the exponent is one-third or one-half, even in the limit there is profit of $66.66 or $50.00 to the players taken as a whole. Thus, some profit remains. With the cost curve slanting steeply upward, these results are to some extent counterintuitive. One might assume that with a positive return on investment, it will always be sensible for more players to enter, thereby driving down the profits. In this case, however, each additional player lowers the payments of all the preceding players and his own, and the limit as the number of players goes to infinity turns out to be one where that infinity of players has, at least in expectancy terms, sizable profits.

Throughout the table, in zones I, II, and III, the individual payments go down as we move from left to right, and total payments rise. We can deduce a policy implication from this, although it is a policy implication to which many people may object on moral grounds. It would appear that if one is going to distribute rents, nepotism is a good thing because it reduces the number of players and, therefore, the total investment. This is one of the classical arguments for hereditary monarchies. By reducing the number of candidates for an extremely rent-rich job to one, you eliminate such rent-seeking activities as civil war, assassination, and so forth. Of course, there are costs here. If we reduce the number of people who may compete for a given job, we may eliminate the best candidate or even the best two thousand candidates. This cost must be offset against the reduction in rent-seeking costs.

On the other hand, many cases of rent seeking are not ones in which we care particularly who gets the rent. In such matters as government appointments where there are large incomes from illegal sources, pressure groups obtaining special aid from the government, and so on, we would prefer that there be no rent at all, and, if there must be rent, it does not make much difference to whom it goes. In these cases, clearly measures to reduce rent seeking are unambiguous gains. Thus, if Mayor Richard Daley had confined all of the lucrative appointments to his close relatives, the social savings might have been considerable.

If we go down the table, the numbers also steadily rise. Looking at two players, for example, from an exponent of one-third, which represents an extremely steeply rising curve, to an exponent of two, which is much flatter, we get a sixfold increase in the individual and total payments. This also suggests a policy conclusion. On the whole, it would be desirable to establish institutions so that the marginal cost is very steeply rising. For example, civil servants' examinations should be, as far as possible, designed so that the return on cramming is low or, putting it another way, so that the marginal cost of improving one's grade is rapidly rising. Similarly, it is better if the political appointments of the corrupt governments are made quickly and rather arbitrarily, so that not so many resources are invested in rent seeking.

Once again, however, there is a cost. It may be hard to design civil service examinations so that they are difficult to prepare for and yet make efficient selections. Here again, if we are dealing with appointments to jobs that we would rather not have exist, the achievement of profits through political manipulations and the like, there is no particular loss in moving down our table. Thus, laws that make it more expensive or more difficult to influence the government – such as campaign contribution laws – may have considerable net gain by making the rise in marginal cost steeper. There is a considerable expense involved, however. The actual restrictions placed on campaign contributions are designed in a highly asymmetrical manner, so that they increase the cost for some potential lobbyists and not for others. Whether there is a net social gain from this process is hard to say.

So much for zone I; let us now turn to zones II and III. In zone II, the sum of the payments made by the individual players is greater than the prize; in other words, it is a negative-sum game instead of a positive-sum game as in zone I. In zone III, the individual players make payments that are higher than the prize. It might seem obvious that no one would play games of this sort, but, unfortunately, this is not true.

* * *

For a simple example, consider the game shown on Table 1, in which there are two players, Smith and Jones, and assume that the exponent on the cost function is 3. The individual payment is shown as $75, and the result of the two players putting up $75 is that they will jointly pay $150 for $100. Each is paying $75 for a fifty-fifty chance on $50, which appears to be stupid.

However, let us run through the line of reasoning that may lead the two parties to a $75 investment. Suppose, for example, that we start with both parties at $50. Smith raises to $51. With the exponent of three, the increase in the probability that he will win is worth more than $1 – in fact, considerably more. If Jones counters, he also gains more than $1 by his investment. By a series of small steps of this sort, each one of which is a profitable investment, the two parties will eventually reach $75, at which point there is no motive for either one to raise or lower his bid by any small amount. They are in marginal adjustment, even though the total conditions are very obviously not satisfied.

But what of the total conditions? For example, suppose that Jones decides not to play. Obviously, his withdrawal means that Smith is guaranteed success, and, indeed, he will probably regret that he has $75 down rather than $1, but still he is going to make a fairly good profit on his investment.

. . . If the best thing to do, the rational strategy, in this game is not to play, then obviously the sensible thing to do is to put in $1. On the other hand, if the rational strategy is to play, and one can anticipate the other party will figure that out, too, so that he will invest, then the rational thing to do is to stay out, because you are going to end up with parties investing at $75. There is no stable solution.

Games like this occur many times in the real world. Poker, as it is actually played, is an example, and most real-world negotiations are also examples of this sort of thing; in the case of poker, there is no social waste, because the parties are presumably deriving entertainment from the game. Negotiations, although they always involve at least some waste, may involve fairly small amounts because the waste involved in strategic maneuvering may be more than compensated by the transfer of information that may permit achievement of a superior outcome. But in our game this is not possible. In the real world there may be some such effect that partially offsets the waste of the rent seeking. . . .

In the real world, the solution to rent seeking is rather apt to end up at $75 in our particular case instead of at zero, because normally the game does not permit bets, once placed, to be withdrawn. In other words the sunk costs are truly sunk; you cannot withdraw your bid. For example, if I decide to cram for an examination or invest a certain amount of money in a lobby in Washington that is intended to increase the salaries of people studying public choice, once the money is spent, I cannot get it back. If it turns out that I am in this kind of competitive game, the sunk-cost aspect of the existing investment means that I will continue making further investments in competition with other people studying for the examination or in hiring lobbyists. In a way, the fact that there is an optimal amount – that even with the previous costs all sunk we will not go beyond $75 in the particular example we are now using – is encouraging. Although sunk costs are truly sunk, there is still a limit to the amount that will be invested in the game.

Note that this game has a possible precommitment strategy. If one of the parties can get his $75 in first and make it clear that it will not be withdrawn, the sensible policy for the second party is to play zero; hence, the party who precommits makes, on this particular game, a profit of $25.

Unfortunately, this analysis, although true, is not very helpful. It simply means that there is another precommitment game played. We would have to investigate the parameters of that game, as well as the parameters of the game shown in Tables 1 and 2 and determine the sum of the resources invested in both. Offhand, it would appear that most precommitment games would be extremely expensive because it is necessary to make large investments on very little information. You must be willing to move before other people, and this means moving when you are badly informed. But in any event, this precommitment game would have some set of parameters, and if we investigate them and then combine them with the parameters of the game that you precommit, we would obtain the total cost. I doubt that this would turn out to be a low amount of social waste.

The situation is even more bizarre in zone III. Here the equilibrium involves each of the players' investing more than the total prize offered. It is perhaps sensible to reemphasize the meaning of the payments shown in Table 1. They are the payments that would be reached if all parties, properly calculating what the others would do, made minor adjustments in their bids and finally reached the situation where they stopped in proper marginal adjustment. They are not in total equilibrium, of course.

Once again, the simple rule – do not play such games – is not correct, because if it were the correct rule, then anyone who violated it could make large profits. Consider a particular game invented by Geoffrey Brennan, which is the limit of Table 1 as the exponent is raised to infinity. In this game, $100 is put up and will be sold to the highest bidder, but all the bids are retained, that is, when you put in a bid, you cannot reduce it. Under these circumstances, no one would put in an initial bid of more than $100, but it is not at all obvious what one should put in. Further, assume that the bids, once made, cannot be withdrawn but can be raised. Under these circumstances, there is no equilibrium maximum bid. In other words, it is always sensible to increase your bid above its present level if less than $100 will make you the highest bidder. The dangers are obvious, but it is also obvious that refusal to play the game is not an equilibrium strategy. . . .

Thus ends our preliminary investigation of rent seeking and ways to reduce its social cost. When I have discussed the problem with colleagues, I have found that the intellectually fascinating problem of zones II and III tends to dominate the discussion. This is, indeed, intellectually very interesting, but the real problem we face is the attempt to lower the cost of rent seeking, and this will normally move us into zone I. Thus, I hope that the result of this paper is not mathematical examination of the admittedly fascinating intellectual problems of zones II and III, but practical investigation of methods to lower the cost of rent seeking.

Questions and notes on rent seeking

The arithmetic underlying Tullock's paper is not, numerous law students and faculty have informed me, entirely clear. Herein follow some exercises that might help provide a better understanding of what is going on. I will concentrate on the simplest case in which there are two identical parties, Alan (who buys A tickets) and Bob (who buys B tickets). The central point of the rent-seeking model (an awful name, but we are probably stuck with it) is that the efforts of one party change the rewards to a given level of effort by the other party. In equilibrium each party, in effect, asks the following question: If I had to choose the number of tickets (or level of effort or whatever) first, and the other guy was then going to purchase his tickets knowing what I have done, what should I do? If I assume that the other guy would try to maximize his expected profits, then I can ask myself what would my profits be on the assumption that the other guy makes his best response. Then I choose that level that maximizes my expected profits.

Let us put aside for a moment the question of whether people can actually engage in this type of sophisticated strategic reasoning. (We know by looking in the mirror that they cannot.) There are two central propositions that drive the analytical results. First, as Tullock notes, the payoffs in this game are symmetrical. This means that in equilibrium both sides would buy the same number of tickets and would have a fifty percent chance of winning. Hence, we are interested in Alan's marginal benefit from purchasing an additional ticket at the point at which $B = A$. If the increased probability of winning is high enough, the purchase of an additional ticket would be desirable. Alan would not be content to limit his spending to this amount, and because of the symmetry, neither would Bob.

Second, the sensitivity of the outcome to the purchase of an additional ticket by one of the parties decreases as the total number of tickets rises. If we start at a point at which both Alan and Bob are buying the same number of tickets, the rewards to Alan of "cheating" (of buying an extra ticket) will be smaller, the higher the initial starting point. Thus, if they both started at a single ticket, Alan might find buying a second ticket extremely attractive. If, however, they both started at a point at which they were buying fifty tickets, Alan might find that buying one more would not be worth the cost. It is this feature of the rent-seeking models that makes it possible to attain an equilibrium. The decreased sensitivity is illustrated in problem 1.

1. Consider Tullock's original example in which there are two parties and the exponent is one. The probability of Alan winning the lottery is $A/(A + B)$.
   1.1. Assume that Bob has purchased ten tickets. The probability that Alan will win if he purchases eight tickets is $8/(8 + 10) = 8/18 = 0.444$. What is the probability that Alan will win if he buys ten tickets? Twelve tickets?
   1.2. Assume that Bob has purchased twenty tickets. What is the probability that Alan will win if he purchases sixteen tickets? Twenty tickets? Twenty-four tickets?
   1.3. In Figure 1 the probability of Alan winning is on the vertical axis and the number of tickets purchased is on the horizontal axis. The diagram is drawn on the assumption that Bob purchased ten tickets; twenty tickets; twenty-five tickets. Notice that as the number of tickets purchased by Bob rises, the curves get flatter. That is, the effect of Alan's buying one additional ticket on his probability of winning is less. As the number of tickets purchased by Bob and Alan rises, therefore, the marginal benefit to Alan of buying an additional ticket decreases. At some point Alan (and, by symmetry, Bob) will not find it profitable to continue to buy tickets.
2. The parties are not concerned with the probability of winning as such. Rather they are concerned with the rewards to winning. Suppose that the prize is $100. If Bob has purchased ten tickets, the expected benefits to Alan of spending $10 are $100 \times 10/(10 + 10) = $50. What are the expected benefits to Alan of buying eleven tickets?
   2.1. If Alan's expected payoff to an additional dollar of spending is greater than one dollar, then his incentive is to spend that dollar. What is the marginal benefit to Alan of buying the eleventh

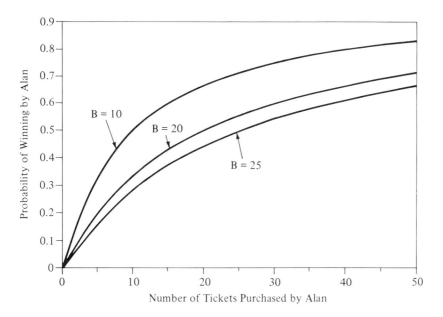

Figure 1

ticket in the preceding example? Given that the cost of the ticket is $1, should he buy the ticket?

2.2. What is the marginal benefit to Alan of buying an additional ticket in the following circumstances? The prize is $100 in all circumstances. In which cases should he buy the ticket?

(a) Bob has ten tickets; Alan has forty.

(b) Bob has twenty-five tickets; Alan has ten.

(c) Bob has twenty-five tickets; Alan has twenty-five.

(d) Bob has twenty-five tickets; Alan has thirty.

Questions 3 and 4 focus on the effects on the outcomes of two parameters: the stakes (or size of the prize) and the exponent r (a measure of the sensitivity of outcomes to the efforts of the parties).

3. In Figure 2 the horizontal axis again measures the number of tickets purchased, but the vertical axis now measures the expected payoff in dollars. With $B = 20$ and the prize $100, find Alan's expected return when he purchases sixteen tickets. Locate this point on the diagram. Now suppose that the prize is $200. What is Alan's expected return if he buys sixteen tickets? Locate this on the diagram.

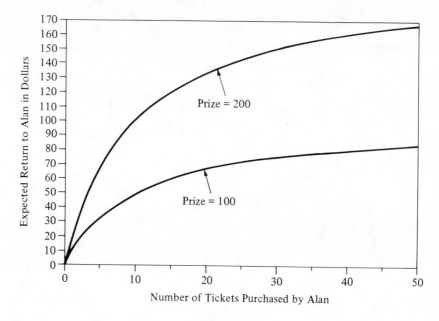

Figure 2

3.1. What is the effect of increasing the stakes on the rewards to Alan for spending an additional dollar on purchasing a lottery ticket?

4. In Figure 3 the prize is fixed at $100 and Bob purchases twenty-five tickets. The diagram shows the expected return for Alan for different values of the exponent r. Notice that when $r = 0$, the line is horizontal. The interpretation of this case is simple. The outcome does not depend at all upon the effort of the parties, and therefore if Alan increases his effort, he reaps no benefits.

4.1. As r increases, what happens to the marginal benefits to Alan of buying a twenty-sixth ticket?

4.2. Figure 4 blows up the portion of Figure 3 between twenty-two and twenty-eight tickets. Would it pay for Alan to buy the twenty-sixth ticket if $r = 8$, or if $r = 1/3$?

4.3. Figure 5 shows the payoff to Alan when the prize is $100 and the exponent is 8 for various values of Bob. What happens to Alan's marginal benefits in equilibrium as Bob's expenditures increase? It is not easy to read the marginal benefits precisely off such a diagram. But it should be clear that the marginal

46

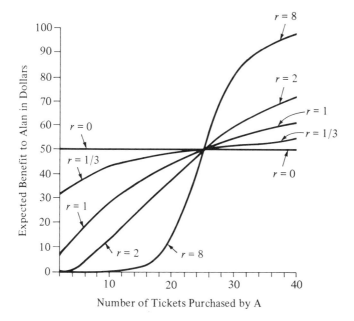

Figure 3

benefits to Alan at the lower values of *B* are considerably greater than the price of a ticket. Spending has to reach•a very high level before either party would find additional expenditures not in his own best interest. As Tullock's tables show, that would entail each party buying 200 tickets.

The preceding questions should clarify some of the analytical conclusions reached by Tullock. Herein follow some remarks on the implications of the analysis. Tullock's result is counterintuitive. Most people would not guess that the correct number of tickets to purchase in his initial example would be twenty-five. But, if that is true, then should we expect people to purchase twenty-five when confronted with the problem? If the answer to that is no, does that mean that the entire analysis is useless for predicting behavior?

The analysis would still be useful for three reasons. First, although the theory might not predict the number of tickets purchased, it could still predict the responses of people to changes in the parameters. That is, if we repeated the experiment changing only the stakes, the data might show that the number of tickets purchased rises as the stakes are

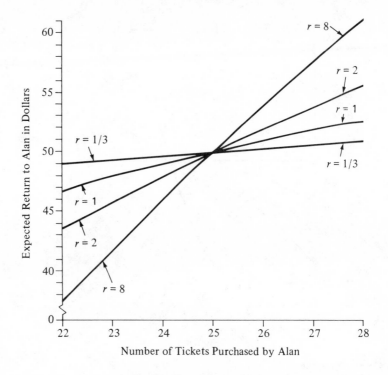

Figure 4

increased. For many purposes we would be more interested in this sort of comparative proposition than we would in the actual number of tickets purchased. Second, even if people do not understand the game, it is possible that external forces might push them toward the equilibrium. Those utilizing good strategies will prosper, and those using poorer strategies will not. Thus, in contexts in which it is reasonable to presume that the environment will weed out poor strategies, the analysis might predict outcomes well, even though the individuals using good strategies could not articulate the basis for their choice of strategies.

Third, the analysis does not necessarily predict that the equilibrium will be achieved in actual situations. Generally, the equilibrium is an unfortunate result that the parties would try to forestall by rearranging their affairs. Thus, in Tullock's original problem the equilibrium is that each party buy twenty-five tickets so that the total available for them is $100 − $25 − $25 = $50. But surely they could do much better if they agreed that one of them would buy one ticket and that they would share the prize. They would then split $100 − $1 = $99, which certainly looks

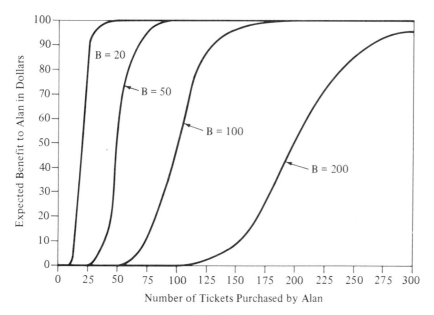

Figure 5

a lot better. Many of the most interesting problems regarding rent seeking will concern the factors that facilitate or impair the parties' ability to move toward superior solutions. Can they make binding agreements to avoid the mutually destructive competition? Can they alter the game by reducing the size of the stakes or reducing the exponents?

The rent-seeking problem is ubiquitous in the law school curriculum. It arises wherever parties have an incentive to expend real resources to capture something of value. For example, people have an incentive to use resources to influence the outcomes of the legislative process. It is possible to view constitutional restrictions on the legislatures – for example, the contract clause, the takings clause, or the commerce clause – as devices for reducing the rewards to rent seeking, thereby increasing the size of the pie available to everyone. The rent-seeking model is a useful characterization of the transformation of an unowned asset to an owned asset – for example, the patenting or copyrighting of intellectual property, the exploitation of wild animals (especially fish), and the development of an oil field where ownership of the oil can only be asserted after it is removed from the ground. And as Tullock's opening comments suggest, the rent-seeking model captures significant elements of the adjudicatory process and could provide insights on the effects of procedural reforms on the resources expended in litigation and on substantive outcomes.

With regard to contracts, rent seeking manifests itself in two classes of problems. First, one party might be vulnerable to a substantial loss if the other party could revise the agreement or breach it; the magnitude of that loss is equivalent to the stakes in a rent-seeking game. The greater the potential loss, other things equal, the more costly the rent seeking would be. This is one aspect of the "*Boomer*" problem discussed in Selection [2.3]; it is a recurring theme of this book. Second, parties can expend resources to obtain information about future prices. Contracting parties might be mutually better off if they could restrict some of this activity. This line of reasoning is developed more fully in Selections [3.2] (a rationale for the enforcement of the executory contract where there has been no reliance) and [9.3] (price adjustment mechanisms in long-term contracts).

PART II

Contract law and the least cost avoider

When two parties enter into a contract, the outcome might ultimately depend upon the subsequent behavior of both of them. The first two selections in Part II begin with this essential insight. Thus, Robert Cooter [2.1] focuses on the harm arising from the breach of a contract and the ability of the parties to avoid that harm – the promisor by reducing the probability that it will breach and the promisee by reducing its reliance on the promisor's performance. Cooter emphasizes the similarity between the problem of controlling the harm arising from a contract breach with that arising from an accident, a nuisance, or a taking of private property by the government. In each context the rules should assign the task of avoiding costs to the party in the best position to do so – the least cost avoider. He points out that the manner in which contract law treats excuses closely parallels the treatment of no liability versus strict liability in torts. He also notes that so long as the victim can influence the magnitude of the harm, a rule of strict liability that places all the avoidance burden on the breacher (or tortfeasor) is inefficient.

Charles Goetz and Robert Scott [2.2] argue that when entering into an agreement the parties rationally attempt to minimize the joint costs of adjusting to prospective contingencies. If that requires them to adjust their behavior over time in response to changed circumstances, then they will want to assign the job of adjusting to particular contingencies to the party in the best position to do so. There is a fundamental tradeoff between explicitly defining the obligations of the contracting parties and allowing the parties to adjust their behavior (and their obligations) in the face of changed circumstances. The problem is exacerbated if the benefits of allowing adjustment are potentially great but permitting adjustment allows one or more parties to engage in opportunistic behavior or rent seeking.

Of crucial importance is the availability of good substitutes – a thick market – at the time of breach. If there is a thick market, that is, if the contract could

51

reasonably be characterized as a discrete transaction, then there is no tradeoff. The cost-minimizing adjustment is for the victim of the breach to cover in the market. The parties do not have to induce the potential breacher to do anything to contain the cost of adjusting to change. The only role the contract serves for discrete transactions is to define the initial obligations. So long as the buyer has available a large number of potential sellers who are reasonably good substitutes at the time of the breach, there is little reason to be concerned about whether the contract is performed by this seller rather than any of the other potential trading partners. The buyer mitigates by purchasing in a timely manner and suing for the difference.

As exchange becomes more relational, the promisor is not always in the best position to minimize the costs of adjustment by acting unilaterally. The law should reflect this by assigning liability for specific costs to the party in the best position to control them – the "least cost avoider." As we move away from the discrete transaction end of the spectrum, the least cost avoider will often be the promisee.

The conventional shibboleth that contract law is a regime of strict liability would, if taken seriously, place responsibility for containing costs on the promisor. Contract law has developed a number of ad hoc devices to avoid this outcome. If one were to take a discrete transaction perspective, these would be aberrations. If instead we take a relational perspective, they can be logically consistent. The tort language of "least cost avoider" and fault, which fits so poorly in the discrete transaction paradigm, is natural in the relational perspective. As in tort law, fault is not exclusively, or even primarily, an ethical concept. It has a large economic component as well.

Selection [2.3] discusses the famous case of *Boomer v. Atlantic Cement*. While this is a nuisance/tort case, *Boomer* illustrates a number of problems that arise in the contract context as well. This treatment should underscore the unity of contracts, property, and torts stressed by Cooter. The issues raised by *Boomer* will surface a number of times in the remainder of the book.

CHAPTER 2.1

Unity in tort, contract, and property: the model of precaution

ROBERT COOTER (1985)

A. Forms of precaution

Even when necessary or unavoidable, an accident, breach of contract, taking, or nuisance causes harm. The affected parties, however, can usually take steps to reduce the probability or magnitude of the harm. The parties to a tortious accident can take precautions to reduce the frequency or destructiveness of accidents. In contract, the promisor can take steps to avoid breach, and the promisee, by placing less reliance on the promise, can reduce the harm caused by the promisor's breach. Similarly, for governmental takings of private property, the condemnor can conserve on its need for private property, while property owners can reduce the harm they suffer by avoiding improvements whose value would be destroyed by the taking. Finally, the party responsible for a nuisance can abate; furthermore, the victim can reduce his exposure to harm by avoiding the nuisance.

Generalizing these behaviors, I extend the ordinary meaning of the word "precaution" and use it as a term of art . . . to refer to any action that reduces harm. Thus the term "precaution" includes, for example, prevention of breach and reduced reliance on promises, conservation of the public need for private property and limited improvement of private property exposed to the risk of a taking, and abatement and avoidance of nuisances. These examples are, of course, illustrative, not exhaustive.

From Robert Cooter, "Unity in Tort, Contract, and Property: The Model of Precaution."
© 1985 by California Law Review. Reprinted from *California Law Review*, Vol. 73, No. 2, January 1985, pp. 1–51, by permission of California Law Review and the author.

B. The paradox of compensation

When each individual bears the full benefits and costs of his precaution, economists say that social value is internalized. When an individual bears part of the benefits or part of the costs of his precaution, economists say that some social value is externalized. The advantage of internalization is that the individual sweeps all of the values affected by his actions into his calculus of self-interest, so that self-interest compels him to balance all the costs and benefits of his actions. According to the marginal principle, social efficiency is achieved by balancing all costs and benefits. Thus, the incentives of private individuals are socially efficient when costs and benefits are fully internalized, whereas incentives are inefficient when some costs and benefits are externalized.

In situations when both the injurer and the victim can take precaution against the harm, the internalization of costs requires both parties to bear the full cost of the harm. To illustrate, suppose that smoke from a factory soils the wash at a commercial laundry, and the parties fail to solve the problem by private negotiation. One solution is to impose a pollution tax equal to the harm caused by the smoke. The factory will bear the tax and the laundry will bear the smoke, so pollution costs will be internalized by both of them, as required for social efficiency. In general, when precaution is bilateral, the marginal principle requires both parties to be fully responsible for the harm. The efficiency condition is called double responsibility at the margin.

One problem with the combination of justice and efficiency, however, is that compensation in its simplest form is inconsistent with double responsibility at the margin. In the preceding example, justice may require the factory not only to pay for harm caused by the smoke, but also to compensate the laundry for that harm. Compensation, however, permits the laundry to externalize costs, thereby compromising efficiency. Thus, a paradox results: If the factory can pollute with impunity, harm is externalized by the factory; if the factory must pay full compensation, harm is externalized by the laundry; if compensation is partial, harm is partly externalized by the factory and partly externalized by the laundry. Assigning full responsibility for the injury to one party or parceling it out between the parties cannot fully internalize costs for both of them. Thus, there is no level of compensation that achieves double responsibility at the margin. In technical terms, when efficiency requires bilateral precaution, strict liability for any fraction of the harm, from zero percent to 100 percent, is inefficient.

* * *

2. Breach of Contract

Yvonne and Xavier enter into a contract in which Yvonne pays for Xavier's promise to deliver a product in the future. There are certain obstacles to Xavier's performance that might arise, and if severe obstacles materialize, Xavier will not be able to deliver the product as promised. The probability of timely performance depends in part on Xavier's efforts to prevent such obstacles from arising. These efforts are costly.

One purpose of contracting is to give Yvonne confidence that Xavier's promise will be performed, so that she can rely upon his promise. Reliance on the contract increases the value to Yvonne of Xavier's performance. However, reliance also increases the loss suffered in the event of breach. The more the promisee relies, therefore, the greater the benefit from performance and the greater the harm caused by breach.

To make this description concrete, suppose that Xavier is a builder who signs a contract to construct a store for Yvonne by the first of September. Many events could jeopardize timely completion of the building; for example, the plumbers union may strike, the city's inspectors may be recalcitrant, or the weather may be inclement. Xavier can increase the probability of timely completion by taking costly measures, such as having the plumbers work overtime before their union contract expires, badgering the inspectors to finish on time, or rescheduling work to complete the roof before the rainy season arrives. Yvonne, on the other hand, must order merchandise for her new store in advance if she is to open with a full line on the first of September. If she orders many items for September delivery and the store is not ready for occupancy, she will have to place the goods in storage, which is costly. The more merchandise she orders, the larger her profit will be in the event of performance, and the larger her loss in the event of nonperformance.

As thus described, the structure of the contractual model is similar to the model developed for tortious accidents. The precaution taken by the potential tortfeasor against accidents parallels the steps taken by the promisor to avoid obstacles to performance. The parallel between the tort victim and the promisee, however, is more subtle. *More* precaution by the tort victim is like *less* reliance by the contract promisee, because each action reduces the harm caused by an accident or a breach. Therefore, the tort victim's precaution against accidents and the contract promisee's reliance upon the contract are inversely symmetrical.*

If Xavier does not perform, then a court must decide whether a breach has occurred or whether nonperformance is excused by circumstances. Among the excuses that the law recognizes are: that the quality of assent to the contract was too low due to mistake, incapacity, duress, or fraud; that the terms of the contract were unconscionable; or that performance was impossible or commercially impractical. If the court narrowly construes excuses, usually finding nonperformance to be a breach, then Xavier will usually be liable. If the court construes excuses broadly, usually finding nonperformance to be justified, then Xavier will seldom be liable.

The incentive effects of a broader or narrower construction of excuses are similar to the effects of strict liability and no-liability rules in tort. If defenses are narrowly construed and perfect expectation damages are awarded for breach, the promisee will rely as if performance were certain. Specifically, Yvonne will order a full line of merchandise as if the store were certain to open on the first of September. A promisee's reliance to the same extent as if performance were certain corresponds to a tort victim's failure to take precaution against harm.

A broad construction of excuses has the symmetrically opposite effect: the promisor expects to escape liability for harm caused by his breach, so he will not undertake costly precautions to avoid nonperformance. Specifically, if Xavier is unconcerned about his reputation or the possibility of future business with Yvonne, and if nonperformance due to a plumber's strike, recalcitrant inspectors, or inclement weather will be excused, say, on grounds of impossibility, then Xavier will not take costly precautions against these events. The promisor's lack of precaution against possible obstacles to performance corresponds to the injurer's lack of precaution against tortious accidents.

As explained, the narrow and broad constructions of excuses for breach of contract affect behavior in ways that parallel no liability and strict liability in tort. Furthermore, the effects of these constructions on cost internalization and efficiency are also parallel. Specifically, if ex-

---

* At this point, it is appropriate to qualify my contracts model. Damage rules for breach of contract influence several types of behavior, such as search for trading partners, negotiating exchanges, drafting contracts, keeping or breaking promises, relying on promises, mitigating damages caused by broken promises, and resolving disputes about broken promises. A complete account of the incentive effects of contract law would model all of these types of behavior. Instead of a complete account, however, this article follows the order of simplification suggested by microeconomic theory and selects two types of behavior from this list for detailed examination: the promisor's precaution against events that may cause nonperformance and the promisee's reliance.

cuses are broadly construed, allowing the promisor to avoid responsibility for breach regardless of his precaution level, the promisor will externalize some of the costs of breach. As a result, his incentives to take precaution against the events that cause him to breach are insufficient relative to the efficient level. If, on the other hand, excuses are narrowly construed and full compensation is available for breach, the promisee can externalize some of the costs of reliance. Insofar as the promisee can transfer the risk of reliance to the promisor, her incentives are insufficient to provide efficient reliance and, therefore, reliance will be excessive.

To illustrate, social efficiency requires Xavier to hire the plumbers to work overtime if the additional cost is less than the increase in Yvonne's expected profits caused by the higher probability of timely completion. Suppose, however, that there are circumstances in which tardiness will be excused regardless of whether or not Xavier hired the plumbers to work overtime. Suppose for example that inclement weather excuses tardiness on grounds of impossibility. In the event inclement weather provides Xavier with an excuse, the extra cost of hiring the plumbers to work overtime, which is valuable to Yvonne, has no value to Xavier. Anticipating this eventuality, Xavier may not hire the plumbers to work overtime, even though social efficiency may require him to do so.

Social efficiency also requires Yvonne to restrain her reliance in light of the objective probability of breach. To be more precise, social efficiency requires her to order additional merchandise until the resulting increase in profit from anticipated sales in the new store, discounted by the probability that Xavier will finish the store on time, equals the cost of storing the goods, discounted by the probability that Xavier will finish the new store late. Suppose, however, that Xavier must compensate Yvonne for her storage costs in the events that the goods must be stored. From a self-interested perspective, Yvonne has no incentive to restrain her reliance in these circumstances. Anticipating this possibility, instead of weighting the cost of storage by the objective probability of breach, Yvonne will weight it by the probability of breach without compensation. Since in this example the probability of breach is greater than the probability of breach without compensation, the weight Yvonne gives to the possibility of storage cost is too small. Therefore, her reliance will be excessive and thus inefficient.

In general, the possibility of successful excuses may externalize the costs of not taking precaution, so that the promisor takes too little precaution and the probability of breach is excessive. Similarly, the possibility of compensation may externalize the costs of reliance, so the promisee relies too heavily and the harm that materializes in the event of breach is excessive. This is an aspect of the paradox of compensation that arises in tort with respect to no liability and strict liability. As with tort law, contract law has a solution to the paradox, but the contract solution is different from the tort solution. To illustrate the characteristic remedy in contracts, consider the liquidation of damages. If the contract stipulates damages for breach requiring Xavier to remit, say, $200 per day for late completion, then the promisor will have a material incentive to prevent breach. Specifically, Xavier may find that paying the plumbers to work overtime is cheaper than running the risk of late completion. If the promisee receives the stipulated damages as compensation, then the level of her compensation is independent of her level of reliance, so she has a material incentive to restrain her reliance. Specifically, if Yvonne receives $200 per day in damages for late completion whether or not she orders the bulky merchandise, she may avoid the risk of bearing storage costs by not ordering it.

Like a negligence rule in tort, liquidation of damages in a contract imposes double responsibility at the margin: The promisor is responsible for the stipulated damages and the victim is responsible for the actual harm. By adjusting the level of stipulated damages, efficient incentives can be achieved for both parties. Stipulated damages are efficient when they equal the loss that the victim would suffer from breach if her reliance were efficient. To illustrate, assume that efficient reliance requires Yvonne to order the compact merchandise and not the bulky merchandise. Furthermore, assume that if Yvonne orders the compact merchandise she will lose $200 in profits for each day that Xavier is late in completing the new store. Under these assumptions, liquidating damages at $200 per day for late completion provides efficient incentives for both Xavier and Yvonne.

Under the stated assumptions, stipulating damages at $200 per day will cause Yvonne to order the compact merchandise and not the bulky merchandise. Consequently, the actual harm that Yvonne will suffer in the event of breach is $200 per day. Thus the stipulation of damages at the efficient level is a self-fulfilling prophecy: The stipulation of *efficient* damages causes the actual damages to equal the stipulation. Since Xavier internalizes the actual harm caused by breach and Yvonne bears the risk of marginal reliance, there is double responsibility at the margin as required for efficiency.

Since liquidation of damages provides an immediate solution to the problem of overreliance, it would seem that liquidation clauses should be found in contracts where efficiency requires restraints on reliance. In fact, rather than liquidating damages, most contracts leave the computation of damages until after the breach has occurred. When damages are not liquidated in the contract and restraint of reliance is required by efficiency, various legal doctrines are available that can accomplish the same end as liquidation of damages. Liquidated damages restrain reliance by making damages invariant with respect to reliance. Courts restrain reliance by applying other legal doctrines that make damages similarly invariant.

To illustrate, the goods supplied by different firms in a perfectly competitive market are, by the definition of perfect competition, perfect substitutes. When the promisor fails to perform in a competitive market, damages are ordinarily set equal to the cost of replacing the promised performance with a close substitute (the replacement-price formula). Specifically, if the seller breaches his promise to supply a good at a specified price, the damages paid to the buyer may include the additional cost of purchasing the good from someone else. In technical terms, damages in such a case will equal the difference between the spot price and the contract price for that particular good. In a competitive market, no single buyer or seller can influence these prices. Consequently, damages computed by the replacement-price formula are invariant with respect to the level of the promisee's reliance. Thus, replacement price damages in a competitive market have the same efficiency characteristics as liquidated damages.

For noncompetitive markets, doctrinal alternatives are available to reduce or eliminate the effects of variations in damages due to reliance. To illustrate, recovery may be limited to damages that were foreseeable at the time the promise was made. It is but a short step to argue that reliance that is excessive in efficiency terms is also unforeseeable. Thus, the foreseeability doctrine can be used to avoid compensation for excessive reliance.

There are other doctrinal approaches to damages that have similar effects. For example, suppose that Xavier fails to complete the building on the first of September as promised, and Yvonne has to rent temporary space elsewhere. The court might award damages based in part on the additional rent, if it finds Yvonne's calculation of lost profits too speculative. If damages are based on the additional rent, and if the additional rent varies less than Yvonne's profits with respect to her reliance, then her incentive to overrely is reduced. As another example, failure to perform on a franchise agreement may result in an award of damages equal to the profit of similar franchise establishments, but not the "speculative profits" lost by the particular plaintiff. The general point of these two examples is that if compensation is restricted to nonspeculative damages, and if nonspeculative damages vary less with respect to reliance than the actual harm, then restricting compensation to non-speculative damages reduces the incentive to overrely.* In other words, although the doctrine of avoidable consequences requires a mitigator to minimize the joint costs of breach, it does not require minimizing the defendant's loss in a way that imposes a still greater loss on the mitigator himself.

* * *

* To avoid confusion, a comment is appropriate concerning the relationship between reliance and mitigation of damages. Mathematically, mitigation and restrained reliance are identical but for time: Reliance occurs before breach is known, whereas mitigation occurs afterwards. . . .

CHAPTER 2.2

The mitigation principle: toward a general theory of contractual obligation (1)

CHARLES J. GOETZ AND ROBERT E. SCOTT (1983)

Most contract rules are permissive, applying only if the parties do not otherwise agree. By providing standardized and widely suitable risk allocations in advance, the law enables most parties to select a preformulated legal norm "off-the-rack," thus eliminating the cost of negotiating every detail of the proposed arrangement. Atypical parties remain free to bargain for customized provisions, much as a person with an unusual physique may purchase custom-tailored garments for a premium rather than accept a standard size and cut available at a lower price.

Ideally, the preformulated rules supplied by the state should mimic the agreements contracting parties would reach were they costlessly to bargain out each detail of the transaction. Using this benchmark raises two separable issues: First, what arrangements would *most* bargainers prefer? And second, what atypical arrangements should be supported as benign alternatives?

The model developed in this article will show that the contractual obligee and obligor would agree in advance to minimize the joint costs of adjusting to prospective contingencies, assigning the responsibility of mitigating to whoever is better able to adjust to the changed conditions. The occurrence of contingencies requiring adjustment, however, may encourage strategic behavior by both parties: The obligor may attempt to evade his performance responsibilities while the obligee may bargain opportunistically whenever his cooperation is requested. Any effort legally to regulate one manifestation of this strategic behavior almost

Reprinted from Charles J. Goetz and Robert E. Scott, "The Mitigation Principle: Toward a General Theory of Contractual Obligation," *Virginia Law Review* 69 (1983): 967–1025, with the permission of Virginia Law Review Association and Fred B. Rothman & Company.

inevitably exacerbates the other. But where a developed market for substitute performances exists, the potential for opportunism is negligible; parties can therefore focus on eliminating evasion of contractual obligations without losing the benefits of cooperation. The tension between performance and mitigation responsibilities is most keen in situations lacking a good substitute market; parties in such environments must balance the costs of evasion and opportunism, knowing that no single solution will eliminate the tension.

A. The principle of joint-cost minimization

1. The readjustment contingency

Formulating the ideal mitigation principle requires one first to identify the kinds of costs contracting parties might want to reduce. The parties recognize many of the costs of promissory activity at the time of contracting and allocate these within the scope of the defined contractual rights and obligations. For instance, they may condition alternative modes of performance or excuse from performance upon the occurrence of certain contingencies. It is one thing, however, to perceive a risk in a manner sufficient to allocate its consequences to one party or the other; it is quite another to work out definitively the optimal responses to all future contingencies. As time passes and information increases, parties reassess the risk associated with certain future contingencies. Such reassessments may follow a change in the probability of an event, the magnitude of its consequences, or both. Inevitably, the party who perceives an increase in prospective cost will regret the initial assignment of risks.

A regretting promisor will react to such a "readjustment contingency" by selecting the least costly of the following alternatives: (1) He may continue to pursue the original performance obligation and absorb whatever loss results from his higher performance costs; (2) he may breach and pay compensatory damages; or (3) he may attempt, by renegotiation or otherwise, to modify the original contract. Although a regretting promisor will naturally seek the least costly alternative, *interparty* cooperation is frequently essential to *minimize* adjustment costs. In other words, both parties may have to adjust in order to exploit fully the net benefits of contracting.

Once a contract has been made, an obligee may seem to have little interest in the obligor's excess costs. But a party who anticipates bearing excess costs will presumably negotiate for a more costly return promise to compensate for those inflated costs. Because the terms acceptable to a risk-bearing obligor will reflect the expected magnitude of his potential regret costs, both parties gain if they agree in advance to provisions that will reduce expected future costs. One can therefore derive a broad principle of mitigation by predicting how contractors would agree to cooperate if charged explicitly with designing a policy to cope with readjustment contingencies. The resulting mitigation principle would require each contractor to extend whatever efforts in sharing information and undertaking subsequent adaptations that are necessary to minimize the *joint* costs of all readjustment contingencies.

2. The doctrine of avoidable consequences and its related rules

The doctrine of avoidable consequences confirms this cost-minimizing conception of the mitigation principle, requiring a mitigator to bear the risk of his failure to minimize losses. It denies a mitigator recovery for losses he unreasonably failed to avoid, but allows him full recovery for costs incurred through any reasonable affirmative efforts to minimize losses. The courts seem implicitly to have adopted a joint-cost minimization construction of "reasonable." In one illustrative case [*Frederick Raff Co. v. Murphy*], breaching subcontractors argued that the plaintiff prime contractor should have mitigated damages by withdrawing from a building contract and forfeiting the one percent bid bond. The court rejected their claim, reasoning that "[t]he duty of the plaintiff to keep the damages as low as reasonably possible does not require of it that it disregard its own interests [in maintaining good will] or exalt above them those of the defaulting defendants." [At 243]

* * *

B. The joint-cost minimization principle in actual practice

1. Ideal readjustment responsibilities in a world of perfect adjudication

Assume that two parties, Seller and Buyer, enter into an executory contract in which Seller agrees to supply for $250,000 an industrial air-conditioning compressor for an office building that Buyer is constructing. Assume further that no preformulated contract rules apply except as the contracting parties specifically agree. The state merely offers standard norms of performance – perfect tender, substantial performance, etc. – and various remedial options as a menu of terms from which contracting parties must make individual selections. In this environment, contractors themselves *choose* the legal rules that will regulate their prospective relationship and the legal system will enforce whatever agreement is reached. Because this model is designed to predict the rules *most* bargainers would select, assume also that neither Seller nor Buyer has any unusual preference for risk or strategic behavior. Finally, to understand the task confronting parties who attempt to create an ideal system of contractual obligations, assume initially that both Seller and Buyer can instantly and costlessly enforce the rules of behavior.

Under such conditions, Buyer and Seller could easily separate the *liability* implied by risk bearing from the *conduct* required for least cost adjustment. For example, suppose that shortly after the parties conclude their contract a labor strike against the principal manufacturer causes the price of industrial compressors to rise to $300,000. Seller, bound by the contract to supply a compressor for $250,000, now faces a possible loss of $50,000. Although the contractual obligation requires Seller to bear the cost of a price increase, it does nothing to encourage behavioral adjustments that minimize Seller's loss. Nonetheless, in a perfect adjudication environment, the parties could assign the adjustment responsibilities after the performance obligations were allocated. Whichever party could better adapt to the readjustment contingency would accept the obligation to do so, although the resultant expense would still be chargeable to the primary bearer of the risk in question. For example, if Buyer can adjust to the price increase at a lower cost than Seller – perhaps by purchasing substitutes, amending specifications, or taking some other action – Seller obviously would prefer to pay Buyer to adjust rather than bear his own higher costs.

2. The problem of evasion in defining contractual obligations

In the real world of costly and time-consuming adjudication, however, neither the performance nor the readjustment responsibilities can be established and enforced except through imperfect rules that reflect a compromise among conflicting concerns. Moreover, the parties to an executory contract are compensated in advance in the form of premiums and discounts to bear any future costs that may arise. Tensions result when conditions such as the price of compressors change unexpectedly, giving the adversely affected party a strong incentive to chisel on his performance obligation by denying that the contract assigned the particular risk to him. He may chisel by contesting facts, exploiting arguably ambiguous terms, or refusing to provide full compensation upon breach. Such attempts to escape performance obligations, together with the other party's efforts to counteract them, create what we shall call evasion costs.

Attempts to evade are, in essence, a method of coercively redefining the performance obligations – of imposing a "new" and more favorable contract on the nonbreacher. Even without legal rules to restrain evasion, however, this behavior is not necessarily costless to the evader. The injured party may retaliate or the evader may damage his commercial reputation. Although the motive to chisel on performance obligations is in principle always present, counterbalancing costs will usually restrain actual attempts to do so. Nevertheless, the same contingencies that trigger readjustments may increase the benefits of evasion above the costs. Because extralegal sanctions will not always deter evasion sufficiently, parties will want to bind themselves to legally enforceable obligations.

Contracting parties could design an unambiguous, categorical assignment of performance responsibilities if reduction of evasion opportunities were the sole concern. An unconditional right of specific performance, for example, would place the full burden of any readjustment contingency, both as to cost and conduct, on the party whose performance was affected by the contingency. Such an arrangement would not only reduce evasion otherwise possible because of ambiguity, but also eliminate the risk that costly mitigation efforts might not be fully reimbursed. Despite its efficacy in reducing evasion, however, it is not clear that contractual parties would actually find such an arrangement advantageous. A contract that relies solely on readjustments by a single contractor will generate substantial costs if the parties lack incentives to readjust cooperatively to subsequent events. To determine the most suitable legal rules, the parties must therefore balance reduction of evasion against the potential costs of relying solely on "autonomous" readjustments.

3. The costs of autonomous readjustments

Autonomous readjustments by the obligor will fail to minimize joint costs because the obligee has inadequate incentives to cooperate in reducing costs. The problem of noncooperation has two components: First, it distorts the obligor's choice among the three readjustment options, and second, it deprives the obligor of information concerning the parties' relative abilities to adjust.

* * *

Parties are not limited to autonomous readjustments. If mutual cooperation is necessary to minimize costs, such cooperation can be achieved consensually through . . . renegotiation. By renegotiation, the parties can reallocate the rights and duties which have become inefficient because of intervening events. For example, Buyer could agree to delay his occupancy until the strike is settled. Seller would thus solicit Buyer's cooperation in making adjustments Seller could not achieve alone. The maximum payment Seller will offer Buyer is the difference between Seller's position with and without Buyer's cooperation.

Renegotiation, however, creates a moral hazard in addition to the obligee's indifference: The obligee may actually threaten to exacerbate damages unless the obligor purchases his cooperation at a premium. For instance, Buyer might engage in opportunistic behavior to extract the full "value" of his cooperation in adjusting to the strike. He could accomplish this goal by foot dragging, by inflating the estimates of mitigation costs, or by manifesting any other sign of reluctance to cooperate. Of course, Seller has analogous motives to induce Buyer's cooperation at minimum cost, perhaps by exploiting the potential for evasion as an implicit or explicit threat.

Would strategic behavior affect renegotiations more than original negotiations? Although both situations involve carving up gains from trade, renegotiations will provoke more costly strategies if parties have become "contractually specialized" and face substantially restricted alternate arrangements. At best, renegotiations impose significant transaction costs on the parties. Especially when opportunism magnifies them, renegotiation costs tend to impede readjustments that offer potential benefits for both parties. Parties will hesitate to trade information necessary for readjustments if bargaining over such transfers may itself alert the potential buyer to all or part of the very information that one might wish to "sell." Moreover, even when the parties ultimately achieve cooperative readjustment, the associated renegotiation costs remain a dead-weight loss reducing the potential benefits of the contractual relationship.

4. The tension between performance obligations and a duty to mitigate

Contracting parties could reduce renegotiation costs by agreeing in advance to a detailed set of alternative rights and duties conditioned upon varying future circumstances. Attempts to provide built-in readjustment within the terms of the original obligation, however, confront a number of serious problems. Increasing the complexity of the obligational definition not only facilitates evasion, but also exposes a party to what we shall call the "breacher-status" problem of contract law. A party who contests the interpretation of his obligation by withholding any part of the disputed performance risks being characterized as a breacher. Obviously, the status of breacher is disadvantageous because the breacher is liable for compensatory damages. Frequently overlooked, however, is the breacher's loss of an accrued interest in what may be extremely valuable rights.

For instance, if our Seller withholds performance based on a plausible claim of excuse due to the labor-caused price increases, he still risks being assigned breacher status by a court. Unlike a deliberate choice of breach, however, this classification does not imply that the consequences of breach were superior to those of performance. Indeed, a court-labeled breacher will frequently view his course of action in retrospect as a serious error. Moreover, a court will assign the burden of interpretation errors exclusively to the first party making a mistake; there is only one breacher and he frequently loses the entire benefit of his bargain.

The breacher-status problem gives parties an additional incentive to select clear, definitive rules of obligation to safeguard the initial allocation of contractual rights. Clear rules of obligation, however, are potentially incompatible with a sufficiently adaptive set of mitigation responsibilities. The parties can reduce both error costs (from insufficient readjustment) and renegotiation costs only by prescribing a more detailed statement of shared responsibilities. Unfortunately, that advantage necessarily accrues at the cost of increased difficulty in enforcing original obligations.

5. The influence of a market for substitute performances

The existence of a market for substitute performance permits parties to reduce the tension between clear performance standards and mitigation responsibilities. Where markets for numerous and close substitute performances exist, the advantages of clear, categorical rules of performance tend to dominate the advantages of elaborate readjustment responsibilities. Such markets eliminate much of the need for mitigation rules because the parties can often make optimal adjustments autonomously by, in essence, purchasing them from the lowest bidder in the marketplace.

In our illustrative case, assume that Seller and Buyer are equally capable of covering by purchasing a substitute compressor on the spot market at the contract price plus the $50,000 premium added by the strike. The market offers both parties the opportunity to readjust autonomously, fixing the cost of doing so at $50,000. Because Seller's access to substitute performance serves as a realistic and effective limit on excessively costly readjustment and renegotiation, the parties can focus on minimizing the difficulties of defining and enforcing the original obligation rather than on mitigation.

Where a specialized market provides fewer substitutes, the strategies for cost-minimization become more varied. As the market for substitute performances thins, the opportunity cost of an alternative performance increases for both parties and the bargaining range is correspondingly expanded. In such an environment, an obligor becomes more vulnerable to an obligee's refusal to readjust. For example, if Seller's additional performance costs amount to $80,000, Buyer may demand a $75,000 premium to readjust even though he may be able to place himself in an equivalent position for $50,000. Buyer, on the other hand, can "sell" his mitigation advantage only to Seller, who may resist paying any premium. The absence of accurate information on the objective "value" of Buyer's readjustment capacity exacerbates this mutual dependence. Both the dependence and informational factors tend to spur opportunism as market accessibility diminishes.

In this more complex environment, therefore, parties must balance the potential evasion and opportunism costs in structuring obligation and mitigation rules. One approach to balancing these costs is to establish a general standard of obligation and mitigation responsibilities such as a "best efforts" or a fiduciary obligation. Ideally, such an inclusive norm will reduce substantially the opportunities for strategic behavior, thus counterbalancing the increased difficulty of determining liability under a general standard of responsibility. Another approach is to design narrower "rules of thumb" which require mitigation in predetermined circumstances. The doctrine of substantial performance in construction contracts, for example, requires the nonbreacher to mitigate by accepting a deficient performance coupled with money damages. Rules of thumb preserve some of the clarity of a market-influenced rule structure, yet they soften the impact of the conventional breacher–nonbreacher distinction. No single solution, however, will fully resolve the dilemma of conflicting performance and mitigation goals. More specialized transacting environments simply require more varied and complex strategies to encourage optimal contractual behavior than do market environments.

* * *

Relational exchange, contract law, and the *Boomer* problem (1)

VICTOR P. GOLDBERG (1985)

Many aspects of relational contract law can be illuminated by examination of a well-known case from outside the realm of contract law: *Boomer v. Atlantic Cement*. The facts of *Boomer* are simple. Atlantic Cement built a large cement plant which produced some pollutants creating a nuisance for some neighboring residents and businesses. The victims sought an injunction to prevent the nuisance. However, the court took into account that the magnitude of damages to the victims was only about $183,000 while if the victims received an injunction, they could conceivably force the cement plant, valued at over $40 million, to shut down.

Shutting down the plant would entail a great social cost and this could be avoided by denying the injunction. Of course, it is highly unlikely that the plant would be closed down even if the injunction were granted. For, if the plant were to close, the victims would receive only a modest benefit: the clean air that removing the nuisance would provide. The clean air might well be worth more to Boomer and friends than the $183,000 price tag assigned it by the court. Nevertheless, the victims could almost certainly do much better if they bargained with Atlantic, selling it the right to continue in business with the same level of pollution. If the plant has no other uses and little scrap value, the victims could conceivably obtain something close to the $40 million that the plant was valued at. The magnitude of the payment would depend upon the bargaining skill and the amount of resources devoted to the bargaining by the two sides.

Reprinted from Victor P. Goldberg, "Relational Exchange, Contract Law, and the *Boomer* Problem," *Zeitschrift für die gesamte Staatswissenschaft/Journal of Institutional and Theoretical Economics* 141 (1985): 570–5, with the permission of the publisher.

Thus, while it is unlikely that the injunction would result in demolishing the plant, there is a real social cost associated with granting the injunction. The injunction creates a large "prize" for the parties to fight over and the resources expended in pursuit of that prize are wasted. The greater the size of the prize, the greater the amount of resources wasted in what economists call "rent-seeking" activity.

Before the plant was built, Atlantic could have acquired easements to pollute at a price much closer to the court-determined damages than to the $40 million. If Boomer and friends refused to sell, the plant would be built elsewhere (or not be built at all). Competition would limit the amount that the residents could extract from Atlantic. Ex ante (before any specific capital had been constructed), Atlantic had a number of options and the price of the easement would reflect this. Ex post, it could buy the easement only from the residents who were in a position to bargain for all the quasi-rents that are associated with the cement plant.

The damage remedy has problems of its own. If the cement company knows that it will only pay court-determined damages, than it need not bargain ex ante. The considerable merits of market-determined prices for directing resource allocation are sacrificed. Encouraging parties to use the market rather than the courts to acquire assets will result in assets gravitating toward their highest and best use.

Boomer presents two interrelated problems which are potentially separable.* First, the parties might be induced to engage in mutually detrimental rent seeking. Other things equal, they would prefer to arrange their affairs to avoid that problem. Second, even if there were no rent-seeking possibilities, there is a temporal problem. Rules that might induce the parties to minimize costs after the cement plant has been built might give incorrect incentives to the parties before the plant is built. Thus, the injunction is an inferior remedy if we begin the analysis with the cement plant a fait accompli. However, if we move the analysis back one step, the injunction encourages the cement company to take the consequences of its action into account when considering whether to construct the plant initially.

The *Boomer* problems arise in a variety of contracts contexts. Con-

---

* A third aspect of the *Boomer* problem arises from the possibility that there might be multiple plaintiffs (or defendants). The larger the number of victims who have to agree on the terms of sale of an easement (ex post or ex ante), the more difficult it will be for the parties to achieve agreement. This would not usually be a problem in contract cases. In those instances where it does matter (for example, a contract between a firm and its employees), the parties at least have an opportunity to devise some sort of voting mechanism to cope with this problem.

sider the matter of the foreseeability of consequential damages suffered by a shipper when a carrier fails to deliver goods in a timely manner as in *Hadley v. Baxendale*. After the goods are placed in the carrier's hands, the efficient mitigator is the breacher, just as Boomer was the least cost avoider after the cement plant was built. But ex ante, before the plant is built or the goods placed in the carrier's hands, there is a lot more that Atlantic and Hadley could do to avoid costs. Would it be cheaper for the shipper to maintain an inventory of shafts or for the carrier to assign special agents to assure that these goods arrive on time with a higher probability than other goods it carries? A finding that the damages were unforeseeable is implicit acknowledgment that the shipper was the best cost avoider. That is, even though contract law might not establish an explicit duty to mitigate damages before a breach, the foreseeability doctrine can create an implicit duty to premitigate. Hadley's "fault" – his failure to control the costs which he was in the best position to control – bars his recovery.

* * *

Hadley illustrates the *Boomer* problem sans rent seeking. "Duress" provides one illustration of the other half of the problem. If, after a contract has been entered into, Smith can impose costs upon Jones by threatening to terminate, he can use that threat to renegotiate the contract and increase his share of the pie. The greater the gains from renegotiation, the more resources would be wasted in that activity. This does not necessarily mean that the law should protect Jones. If it did so, Jones' incentive to avoid the situation in the first place would be attenuated. It might be sensible (efficient) to impose upon Jones a duty not to be too vulnerable or to distinguish degrees of fault. Thus, the likelihood that an injunction would be granted to Boomer might be greater if Atlantic simply built first and asked questions later rather than making a good-faith, but erroneous, projection of the magnitude of the pollution problem. Likewise, a court might be less willing to bail Jones out if his vulnerability were viewed as his own fault.

* * *

71

Questions and notes on the
least cost avoider

1. Consider again Cooter's hypothetical agreement between Xavier and Yvonne. As Yvonne's lawyer, how would you draft the contract to protect against the possibility that the store would not be ready on September 1? Remember that the greater Xavier's potential liability, the higher the original contract price must be to compensate him for bearing that risk. If your contract includes a liquidated damages clause, as Cooter suggests, what sort of damage formula would you include? Would you be willing to accept a disclaimer against consequential damages? Should Xavier's failure to perform be excused if the breach was not his fault (or for any other reasons)?

2. Suppose that one of the items Xavier needs to complete his building is the industrial air-conditioning compressor mentioned by Goetz and Scott. If the compressor is delivered late, Xavier will breach his contract with Yvonne and be liable for damages as specified in the contract you have helped draft. Should Xavier's contract with the supplier shift any or all of these damages to the supplier?

3. Suppose that the compressor manufacturer misfiled Xavier's order. As a result, he ends up installing the compressor six months late and Xavier cannot convey the shop to Yvonne until March 1. Yvonne files a tort suit against the manufacturer claiming that its negligence resulted in lost profits and the incurring of considerable storage costs for inventory purchased in anticipation of the September opening. Should Yvonne be allowed to sue? Note that Yvonne does not have a contractual relationship with the supplier. However, both parties are contractually linked to Xavier. How do you think the supplier's liability to Yvonne under tort law would compare to his liability to Xavier under the contract? How do you think Yvonne's compensation under tort law would compare to her compensation as deter-

72

mined by her contract with Xavier? (For a case in which a tort action was allowed against the supplier under similar facts, see *J'Aire Corp. v. Gregory*.)

4. Economists have put forth the concept of "efficient breach." The concept is useful shorthand, a reminder that the faithful performance of contracts is a means to an end, not an end in itself. Many contracts should be breached, and damage rules can play a useful role in structuring the incentives of the promisor to make the proper decision. However, the concept can easily mislead and should be invoked with caution.

The basic idea is straightforward. If resources would be better allocated if a particular contract were not performed, then the rules regarding remedy should encourage nonperformance. If X has agreed to sell a product to Y, but it turns out that Z values the good more, then the product should end up in Z's hands. This does not, however, mean that X should be encouraged to breach the initial agreement. He could perform and then Y could sell to Z; or Z could just purchase Y's right to buy from X. In either case, the product would end up in the hands of the person who values it most.* It is hard to say much at this level of generality without specifying something about the magnitude of X's costs of resale vis à vis Y's and about the costs associated with the various remedies.

The efficient breach concept is misleading in a more fundamental sense. It suggests that determining the efficient course of action is a unilateral decision. But as the preceding selections illustrate, efficient outcomes will often depend upon the efforts of both parties. Moreover, the possibility that someone will come along who values the good more than the original promisee is only one of the changed circumstances to which the parties will have to respond. "Efficient breach" is only one element of a larger category: efficient adjustment.

---

* This is, essentially, the point Goetz and Scott [2.2] make when they claim that under ideal conditions contracting parties could separate the question of liability (who bears the costs) from what conduct is required to make a least cost adjustment.

PART III

The expectation interest, the reliance interest, and consequential damages

In the event of a contract breach, the victim is entitled to a remedy in the form of money damages, an injunction (specific performance), or sometimes reformation. In Part III we will focus on money damages. Damages are commonly classified as expectation, reliance, and restitution damages. The first would put the victim in as good a position as if the contract had been performed. Reliance damages compensate for expenditures made in preparation for performance of the contract. Restitution damages are equal to the benefits conferred by the victim on the breaching party (in the simplest case a refund of cash to a buyer when the seller refuses to perform). If neither party has yet performed, the restitution remedy is equivalent to rescission: tearing up the contract.

Historically, contract law focused almost entirely on vindication of the expectation interest. The First Restatement of Contracts did not explicitly recognize reliance damages. That has changed in the past half century, and the paper by Lon Fuller and William Perdue, from which Selection [3.1] is taken, played an important role in that change. Indeed, they suggested the primacy of the reliance interest and raised a provocative question: If no one has yet relied upon a promise, why should society bother to enforce it? Their answer is given in Selection [3.1]. Building on their suggestions, I argue in Selection [3.2] that one reason for enforcing such contracts, and for reckoning as damages the difference between the market price and the contract price, is to create a property right in the price. The questions that conclude Part III-A draw out some of the implications of that argument for measurement of damages.

The Fuller and Perdue excerpt should leave the reader with the uneasy feeling that the distinction between expectation and reliance damages may be primarily a semantic one. That feeling should be reinforced by Robert Birmingham's argument in Selection [3.4]. An economic perspective suggests that the two are logically linked. Reliance expenditures are an ex ante measure of expected consequential damages. This somewhat cryptic formulation is expanded on by Birmingham and in the questions and comments that conclude Part III-B.

It is useful to divide the expectation interest into three categories: (a) property in the price, (b) consequential damages, including lost profits and losses incurred in reliance on the other party's performance of its contractual obligations, and (c) imperfect performance. Part III-B deals with consequential damages and the foreseeability doctrine, which limits the breacher's liability. "Imperfect performance" is a catchall category which includes issues such as substantial performance, quasi-contract, nonconforming tender, value of performance versus cost of completion, and warranty. Many of these topics will be covered later in the book.

A. Property in price

CHAPTER 3.1

The reliance interest in contract damages

LON FULLER AND
WILLIAM PERDUE (1936)

Why should the law ever protect the expectation interest?

* * *

In seeking justification for the rule granting the value of the expectancy
... [i]t may be said that there is not only a policy in favor of preventing
and undoing the harms resulting from reliance, but also a policy in favor
of promoting and facilitating reliance on business agreements. As in the
case of the stop-light ordinance we are interested not only in preventing
collisions but in speeding traffic. Agreements can accomplish little,
either for their makers or for society, unless they are made the basis
for action. When business agreements are not only made but are also
acted on, the division of labor is facilitated, goods find their way to the
places where they are most needed, and economic activity is generally
stimulated. These advantages would be threatened by any rule which
limited legal protection to the reliance interest. Such a rule would in
practice tend to discourage reliance. The difficulties in proving reliance
and subjecting it to pecuniary measurement are such that the business
man knowing, or sensing, that these obstacles stood in the way of judicial
relief would hesitate to rely on a promise in any case where the legal
sanction was of significance to him. To encourage reliance we must
therefore dispense with its proof. For this reason it has been found wise
to make recovery on a promise independent of reliance, both in the
sense that in some cases the promise is enforced though not relied on
(as in the bilateral business agreement) and in the sense that recovery
is not limited to the detriment incurred in reliance.

From Lon Fuller and William Perdue, "The Reliance Interest in Contract Damages."
Reprinted by permission of The Yale Law Journal Company and Fred B. Rothman &
Company from *The Yale Law Journal*, Vol. 46, pp. 52–98.

... If we rest the legal argument for measuring damages by the expectancy on the ground that this procedure offers the most satisfactory means of compensating the plaintiff for the loss of other opportunities to contract, it is clear that the force of the argument will depend entirely upon the existing economic environment. It would be most forceful in a hypothetical society in which all values were available on the market and where all markets were "perfect" in the economic sense. In such a society there would be no difference between the reliance interest and the expectation interest. The plaintiff's loss in foregoing to enter another contract would be identical with the expectation value of the contract he did make. The argument that granting the value of the expectancy merely compensates for that loss loses force to the extent that actual conditions depart from those of such a hypothetical society. These observations make it clear why the development of open markets for goods tends to carry in its wake the view that a contract claim is a kind of property. ... He who by entering one contract passes by the opportunity to accomplish the same end elsewhere will not be inclined to regard contract breach lightly or as a mere matter of private morality. The consciousness of what is foregone reinforces the notion that the contract creates a "right" and that the contract claim is itself a species of property.

If, on the other hand, we found the ... explanation on the desire to promote reliance on contracts, it is not difficult again to trace a correspondence between the legal view and the actual conditions of economic life. In general our courts and our economic institutions attribute special significance to the same types of promises. The bilateral business agreement is, generally speaking, the only type of informal contract our courts are willing to enforce without proof that reliance has occurred – simply for the sake of facilitating reliance. This is, by no accident, precisely the kind of contract (the "exchange," "bargain," "trade," "deal") which furnishes the indispensable and pervasive framework for the "unmanaged" portions of our economic activity.*

The inference is therefore justified that the ends of the law of contracts and those of our economic system show an essential correspondence. One may explain this either on the ground that the law (mere super-

* In referring by implication to a species of economic activity which is "managed" we do not have in mind exclusively or even primarily management by the state, but rather those means of organizing economic activity which Commons [1924] classifies as rationing and managerial transactions. As Marx was fond of pointing out, contract has always played a very small role in the internal organization of the factory. The enormous growth of the corporation since his time has meant a further decrease in the importance of contract as an organizing force, since the corporation and vertical integration tend to substitute for an organization resting on contract one resting on the relation of superior and inferior (management) and on "rationing transactions."

structure and ideology) reflects inertly the conditions of economic life, or on the ground that economic activity has fitted itself into the rational framework of the law. Neither explanation would be true. In fact we are dealing with a situation in which law and society have interacted. The law measures damages by the expectancy in part because society views the expectancy as a present value; society views the expectancy as a present value in part because the law (for reasons more or less consciously articulated) gives protection to the expectancy.

* * *

Note on price information and enforcement of the expectation interest

VICTOR P. GOLDBERG

Suppose that on April 1, Able enters into a contract to sell a commodity to Baker at a price of $2.00 per bushel for delivery at Baker's plant on June 1. Five days later, Able changes his mind and says he wants to withdraw the promise. Baker, meanwhile, has done nothing in reliance upon the existence of this particular contract. What functions are served by enforcing this purely executory agreement in the absence of any evidence that Baker has relied upon the existence of the contract? This is the question posed by Fuller and Perdue. The answers to this question can be divided into two categories: practical and conceptual. The former are less interesting and I will get them out of the way quickly.

Three practical reasons for not requiring evidence that the promisee relied in any way on the contract are (a) it would complicate the litigation with a messy fact question of whether the promisee had indeed relied; (b) the promisee might be encouraged to act in a manner that established his reliance to lock in a good deal, even if this action would be inefficient; for example, he might enter into a resale contract specifying delivery of the goods associated with this particular contract rather than promising to sell goods that met certain specifications; (c) requiring reliance might induce the promisor to expend resources to determine whether or not particular promisees did rely, an inquiry that would serve no useful purpose.

With an executory commodity contract, the promisee can avoid the costs arising from untimely contracting. Entering into a contract too close to the performance date can raise costs. Thus, if a buyer of wheat in Buffalo waits until he needs the wheat before entering into the contract, he might find that there is little wheat of the proper quality on hand at that time. Timely contracting avoids the costs associated with last-minute search. Whether this constitutes a "reliance" justification is, I suppose, a semantic problem. In any event, if the seller's breach were early enough for the buyer to cover without incurring these additional costs, this argument would not provide a reason for compensating the buyer for a rise in the commodity price.

To simplify the following discussion, consider Fuller and Perdue's "hypothetical society in which all values were available on the market and where all markets were 'perfect' in the economic sense. . . ." (Selection [3.1], p. 78). Commodities are traded in thick markets (ex ante and ex post), so the promisee can always cover by buying from the market at the current market price. By entering into a forward contract with X, a party incurs the opportunity cost of not entering into a contract at that same time and price with Y. But that still leaves the question of why the parties would find it worthwhile to enter into the executory contract in the first place. Why contract on April 1 to fix the price for a June 1 delivery?

One answer is that by entering into the contract early the parties can reduce the expected joint costs arising from their pursuit of special information on the future course of prices. Before spelling out this argument, a brief digression on the economics of information will be useful.

One well-recognized problem is that people are reluctant to engage in the activity of producing information if they do not receive adequate rewards. Consequently, if there are no property rights in the information, too little information would be produced. A second, less well-known, proposition is that defining property rights in information might result in excessive resources being devoted to information gathering. If the producers are given a property right in the form of, say, a patent, then they have an incentive to convert an unowned resource – knowledge – into an owned one (a patent). In that sense the inventor is like the fisherman or buffalo hunter converting unowned resources (fish, buffalos) into owned ones (dead fish and buffalos). The incentive in this case is to overspend on the activity.

Note that the structure of the problem is very similar to the Tullock rent-seeking model. The patent is the prize and the resources utilized in research are the expenditure on lottery tickets. If the exponents are large, that is, if the private rewards to spending more than the other researchers are high, then a considerable amount of resources can be expended in pursuit of the patent. If it were possible to devise rules that had the effect of reducing the exponents, fewer resources would be wasted.

Ed Kitch (1977) has argued that U.S. patent law has tended to operate in this manner by defining property rights in ideas at a very early stage in their development. Kitch suggests that by assigning the right at this early stage, the patent system induces only a small number of inventors to pursue a particular line of research, and these inventors, he argues, will not have a great incentive to make a "preemptive strike" to beat the opposition to the prize.

Instead of looking at the production of new knowledge, let us consider the production of information on the future course of prices. A commodity's future price is uncertain and there exist potential rewards to people for obtaining information as to what the prices will be. The closer we are to the performance date, the more information there will be about factors that might affect the price. The traders will have an incentive to expend resources to evaluate that information. By making their contract early, the parties reduce the incentive to expend resources on this activity, thereby economizing on their joint search costs. Early contracting enables them to avoid excessive searching for price information just as early assignments of patents could reduce the costs in that context.

Analytically, the problem is an extremely complicated one and I can just hint at some of its features. Other things equal, we would expect that the longer the period between contract formation and the date of execution, the greater the dispersion of price estimates. Hence, the reward to special information (Tullock's prize) should be higher. This would result in greater waste the earlier the contract date. On the other hand, the earlier the contract date, the lower the rewards to special information (Tullock's exponents). This factor would lead to a reduction of wasteful expenditures on information gathering as the length of time between the contract date and performance date increases.

Thus, there are both benefits and costs from increasing the length of time between the performance date of the contract and the time at which the parties enter into the contract. The problem the parties face is determining the optimal lead time. Absent enforceable contracts they would be unable to attain that lead time since the party disadvantaged by a price change in the interval between contract execution and performance would have no reason to honor the original agreement. If the law does enforce these executory contracts, parties will be able to contract in a timely fashion, thereby enabling them to avoid the wastes inherent in the search for price information. I do not mean to imply that businessmen make calculations about the optimal time for entering into a contract or even that they pose the problem in this way. It is reasonable to presume, however, that market forces would sort this out, penalizing those who contract too early or too late and rewarding those who contract in a timely manner.* Enforceable contracts enable the market to perform that function.

In effect, enforcement allows the parties to assert a "property right" in the price just as a patent allows the patentee to assert a property right in an idea. The property language might seem a bit odd in the context of contracts, but it is routine in an area that is virtually indistinguishable – leases. The leasehold interest is recognized as a property interest in many jurisdictions. (See Hicks, 1972.) A fundamental element of that interest, especially in long-term leases, is the "bonus value," the difference between the market price and the contract price. That is, when someone buys a leasehold interest, he buys a property right in the price.

The notion that enforcement of the executory contract enables people to economize on price search costs goes a long way towards illuminating some of the problems arising in the area of contract damages. Should price changes subsequent to the contract performance date be considered when reckoning damages? In the face of an anticipatory repudiation, which market price should be used to reckon damages? What is the relationship between the cover price and the market price remedy? The idea that the parties were attempting to establish a property right in the price suggests that damage measures should be designed to protect that interest.

* The same sort of trade-off is involved with defining the scope of patents. Note that the mechanism for selecting the optimal trade-off is much more likely to work well for the commodity contracts. The choice in the contracts case is made by the two parties who have an incentive to minimize the joint costs at the contract formation stage; the choice of the proper scope of patent claims, on the other hand, is made by outsiders – legislatures and courts. Moreover, the large number of similar transactions for a particular commodity allows the selection mechanism to work effectively. Through trial and error the market is likely to converge on an efficient solution in the long run. The heterogeneity of patents makes that mechanism less effective in determining the optimal trade-off in the patent context.

Questions and notes on protecting the property interest in the price

1. On May 15 shares of Acme Industries are selling at $16 per share. Smith agrees to deliver 1,000 shares to Jones on June 1 at $20. On June 1 Acme is selling at $30 per share and Smith reneges. By June 5 Acme is selling at $12. Jones sues for breach of contract asking for $10,000 – the difference between the contract price and the market price at the time of the breach. Smith argues that Jones might have held the shares rather than selling them immediately and that the market price of $12 should be used in determining damages; consequently, Smith argues, he should not have to pay anything. What is the appropriate measure of damage?

2. In the summer of 1973 X chartered Y's ship for seven years beginning in 1974 at a rental of $1 million per year. After the Yom Kippur War, the demand for shipping soared and Y refused to deliver the ship, renting the ship to someone else for a six-month charter at $3 million. X sued for breach of contract. Justice moves slowly, and by the time the matter reached trial, shipping was in the doldrums. Multiyear charters that were going for $4 million per year in 1974 were available for $200,000 in 1977 when the case finally came to trial. The defendant argued that it did the plaintiff a favor by breaching; since the plaintiff was better off following the breach, Y argued, there were no damages. The plaintiff moved to exclude all evidence on the course of prices following 1974. What should the court do? (See *Compania Naviera Asiatic v. The Burmah Oil Co.*, which is discussed in Simon and Novack, 1979, pp. 1427–36.)

3. On April 1 Farmer Jones agrees to deliver 20,000 bushels of corn to Missouri Elevator on or before October 30 at $1.20 per bushel. On June 1 Jones announces that he will not be able to perform; the market price for corn on that date is $1.25 and the price of corn for

84

October delivery at that time is $1.30. On October 30 the market price of equivalent corn is $1.50. Missouri Elevator argues that it covered on October 30 and that damages should be based on the cover price or the market price on the date that the contract was to be performed: ($1.50 − $1.20) × 20,000 = $6,000. Why is this the incorrect measure of damages? (See *Oloffson v. Coomer.*)

4. Jones has agreed to deliver 1,000 bushels of wheat to Smith. Jones breaches, and on the day that Jones breaches, Smith enters into eight separate contracts (not all at the same price) to take delivery of 1,000 bushels of wheat. How should the court determine which contract was the cover transaction? Does it matter much? Suppose instead that, following the breach, Smith did not buy any more wheat. Does the lack of a cover transaction matter?

5. Richard Posner and Andrew Rosenfield make the following argument in a passage omitted from Selection [9.1]. After the parties enter into a long-term contract to buy coal, the price of coal quadruples and the seller breaches. The damages, they argue, are less than the difference between the market and contract price for coal:

> ... at the current price of coal, oil or natural gas might become an economical substitute. If so, the measure of damages would not be the difference between the contract and current prices of coal; it would be the difference between the contract price of coal and the current price of a substitute fuel, adjusting for any differences in the quality of the substitute.

Is this argument valid?

B. Reliance and consequential damages

CHAPTER 3.3

The contract–tort boundary and the economics of insurance

WILLIAM BISHOP (1983)

In contract cases concerning nonperformance of the promise, the problem of events of very low probability is dealt with mainly under the doctrines of frustration, impossibility, and common mistake. The law of contract also has a doctrine called remoteness of damage, the rule in *Hadley v. Baxendale*. Where nonperformance of the contractual promise is in question, this contract doctrine of remoteness of damage deals most importantly with the adverse selection problem rather than with the problem of low probability events.

Where an event of very low prior probability occurs, should courts hold a promisor to his promise? Performance may have become very expensive or impossible, or the consequences of nonperformance may be very much more expensive than was contemplated when the contract was made. In general a promisor is excused performance where an uncontemplated event of very low prior probability having expensive consequences has occurred, as noted, chiefly under the headings of common mistake and frustration (or impossibility). The main distinction between frustration and common mistake is a formal one. Common mistake deals with cases where both parties make and act on an incorrect assumption about facts existing at the time the contract is made; the usual consequence is that such a contract cannot be enforced. Frustration deals with events arising subsequent to the time of contracting; the usual consequence here is that a contract is discharged from the time of frustration. Unilateral mistake, as we shall see, deals with a different problem, with adverse selection and not with events of low probability.

Reprinted from William Bishop, "The Contract–Tort Boundary and the Economics of Insurance," *Journal of Legal Studies* 14 (1983): 299–320, with the permission of the author and The University of Chicago Press.

To illustrate, consider an agreement on April 10 by A to deliver a cargo of wheat to B when the ship carrying it arrives, both parties believing the cargo to be in transit at that date. If the ship had sunk and the cargo been lost before April 10, the case is one of mistake and no rights or liabilities are created by the contract. If the ship sinks after April 10, then the case is one of frustration and such rights and obligations as accrued before sinking are enforceable, but those scheduled to accrue thereafter are not. The sinking has made performance of the promise much more costly for A, and he is excused. Now B bears his own losses, just as he would in tort law if he were the victim of a freak accident caused by A.

However, frustration and common mistake do not deal with all possible events of very low probability. They concern only events that make performance costly to the promisor. Where the event increases the victim's loss, the rule in *Hadley v. Baxendale* applies.

The rule in *Hadley v. Baxendale* must deal with two distinct classes of case: first, cases where both victim and "injurer" are equally ignorant of the abnormal risk, and second, cases where the victim is better informed about the possibilities than is the "injurer" (i.e., the performing party). Cases of unusually heavy loss arising from an accident usually fall into the first category. Such cases typically arise in claim under a contractual warranty of quality or a contractual duty of care. Here the contract remoteness doctrine in *Hadley* is and ought to be equivalent to the remoteness doctrine in tort. This is most clearly seen by considering the contractual duty of care. Here the basis of liability is the same in contract as in tort. The duty is almost always implied by the parties' actions rather than explicitly bargained over. The question, "What would they have agreed to if . . . ?" is the spectral guest at the feast in contract as well as in tort. This identity of purpose leads to a rule that is identical.

However, the second class of case, where the victim is better informed about the likelihood of unusually large losses, leads to a different analysis. It raises adverse selection possibilities and requires different rules. Once the adverse selection problem has been examined it will become plain that the contract remoteness rules in *Hadley* deal in different cases with two quite distinct problems. In effect, two quite different "rules" are embodied in a single verbal formulation.

* * *

The classic formulation of the doctrine of remoteness in contract was that of Alderson, B. in *Hadley v. Baxendale*:

Where two parties have made a contract which one of them has broken, the damages which the other party ought to receive in respect of such breach of contract should be such as may fairly and reasonably be considered either arising naturally, i.e., according to the usual course of things, from such breach of contract itself, or such as may reasonably be supposed to have been in the contemplation of both parties, at the time they made the contract, as the probable result of the breach of it. [At 354]

The "first rule" of *Hadley* has been considered in numerous cases. In...[*C. Czarnikow Ltd. v. Koufos (Heron II)*] the court held that damages could be recovered if there were a "serious possibility" or "real danger" of their arising from the breach, but not if (as in tort) they were merely "foreseeable" as one of many possibilities. Lord Reid also used the expression "not unlikely" as a test. Lord Reid gave as reason for the difference between tort and contract the fact that "in contract, if one party wishes to protect himself against a risk which to the other party would appear unusual, he can direct the other party's attention to it before the contract is made.... But in tort there is no opportunity for the injured party to protect himself in that way...." [At 386] Reid's view is widely, and correctly, regarded as the normal explanation for the difference. It has, however, ramifications so far not generally appreciated, which are pursued here.

The line of cases *Hadley v. Baxendale, British Columbia Sawmill Co. v. Nettleship, Victoria Laundry [(Windsor) v. Newman Industries]*, and *Heron II* concerns a matter that is usually irrelevant in tort (at least as between strangers): the efficient transfer of information. The law of contract denies recovery to the plaintiff when four conditions are met:

1. The plaintiff possessed information unknown to the defendant.
2. The defendant, had he possessed that information, might have altered his behavior so as to make his breach less likely to occur.
3. The plaintiff could have conveyed the information to the defendant cheaply. (This condition is not mentioned in the cases, though it is clear that it is assumed by the courts to be fulfilled. Of course it is normally *not* fulfilled in tort.)
4. The plaintiff did not do so.

A good example of these rules in operation is the *Victoria Laundry* case. The defendant manufacturer of boilers contracted to supply them to the plaintiff laundry. In breach of contract the manufacturer delivered late. The laundry sought to recover damages for profit lost on an unusually lucrative dyeing contract. The court limited the plaintiff to such damages as would be normal in a case of this kind.

Less clear is *Heron II*. There the plaintiff charterer under a charterparty to transport sugar to a well-known sugar market complained that the shipowner had in breach of contract delayed arrival in port by ten days. In the interim the price of sugar fell. The court held the shipowner liable for the loss. Lord Reid thought that the circumstances (that the charterer might well wish to sell on arrival) ought to have been so clear to the shipowner that the latter ought to have realized the risk without explicit warning. This case is near the line, with everything depending on the circumstances the parties were in. If the circumstances were clear, then to require an explicit warning of the obvious would be wasteful of resources (here labor and time).

I take no position on the doctrinal controversy about whether affirmative assumption of risk or merely notice of risk is needed to found liability. I doubt that it really matters very much. Sometimes merely receiving notice, particularly notice of strikingly unusual risks, will be tantamount to affirmative assumption and sometimes not. It is unlikely that a uniform general rule for such cases would be appropriate. It seems that courts treat this, sensibly I think, as depending on the facts of each case.

The central point here is that where the four conditions above are met, the value of the information to the defendant is greater than the cost to the plaintiff of conveying that information to him. To encourage such efficient transfers of information is the purpose of the contract remoteness rule of *Hadley v. Baxendale*.

Note that the first limb of the rule in *Hadley* fits easily into this scheme. The normal case is one in which no information needs to be conveyed, since the defendant, knowing normal business conditions, already knows as much as the plaintiff. To require the plaintiff to inform the defendant of normal conditions would be inefficient, because the cost of transactions here, though low, is not zero. Any expenditure on information transfer is only wasted.

It might seem that there is a casus omissus. Consider the case where the consequence of the defendant's breach normally would be a certain loss but in fact is less. Then it seems the plaintiff has no incentive to transfer the information, even though the information would be valuable in that it would allow the defendant to spend less in essential reliance. Such transfer would be efficient: The marginal social value of expenditure on breach avoidance is lower and so less should be spent. But in fact there is no casus omissus. The plaintiff has sufficient incentive to inform the defendant, wholly without legal compulsion, if such information transfer is in fact cost justified. The reason is that the plaintiff can obtain a lower price for the defendant's performance if he informs the defendant of the limited damages for breach. The price is lower because such a contract is cheaper to perform than is a "normal" contract. This incentive will induce parties to act efficiently in the case of unusually inexpensive breach as well as in the case of unusually expensive breach.

It should be clear that the function of remoteness in the *Hadley v. Baxendale* line of contract cases is very different from the function of remoteness in tort. The tort measure of foreseeability seeks to define as too remote an event that no one would anticipate at all – one to which the ordinary observer would assign near zero probability. The contract measure of foreseeability will include as too remote many consequences which are merely unusual – ones that have quite substantial probabilities of occurring. The defining characteristics of an event that is too remote for the purposes of contract are those set out in conditions 1–4 above. These conditions have nothing to do with unforeseeability in the sense of very low probability. If this analysis is correct, it follows that Lord Scarman was wrong to suggest, as he did in *Parsons v. Uttley*, that the differences between contract and tort remoteness are semantic only. Rather they are distinctions of substance with a coherent purpose behind them.

The promisors or defendants in *Hadley*, *Victoria Laundry*, and *Heron II* were insurers. Like all insurers they charged a price for that service. Like all insurers they wished to guard against "adverse selection," against high-risk promisees obtaining low-priced insurance. This is not just a distributional matter between promisor and promisee. If such adverse selection occurs, promisors will make fewer promises and ask higher prices for them. In consequence, planning becomes harder and more costly. So long as planning for the future is of value, this form of adverse selection will be disadvantageous for society.

In sum then, analytically the rule in *Hadley v. Baxendale* is a rule designed to minimize adverse selection. As we have seen, cheap information is the best antidote to adverse selection problems. So in contract the promisor is entitled to assume "usual risks" unless he is notified to the contrary, whereupon he can demand and obtain a high price.

In cases of nonperformance of the promise the contract doctrine of unilateral mistake (that is, a plaintiff cannot hold a defendant to his contractual promise if the plaintiff knew or ought to have known that the defendant entered into the contract under a mistake) is also in a sense addressed to the adverse selection problem. Again, where we label the case as one of mistake the crucial circumstance is one existing at the time the contract was made, and not some subsequent event. But this is only a matter of doctrinal classification, for again the important point concerns information transfer. Where one party to the knowledge of the other is mistaken, information transfer is cheap; where information is valuable to the pricing of the contract, other things equal, it should be transferred. Exceptions to the disclosure requirement can be explained as attempts to overcome the inefficiency arising from the nonappropriability characteristic of information – thus the right to enforce a contract creates a property right in the information, giving people an incentive to invest in generating valuable information.

In cases of a contractual warranty of quality the adverse selection problem is similarly dealt with by the doctrine of fitness for purpose. Under the law of sale in common-law countries the seller can be liable to the buyer for buyer's loss when the goods are unfit for the buyer's purpose, even if the purpose is unusual, provided the buyer notified the seller of that purpose. Again, efficient information transfer is the gist of the rule.

Finally, problems of adverse selection under contractual warranties of quality are catered for by special clauses limiting liability or excluding it in cases of certain specified kinds of loss. These limitations prevent the highest-risk (or highest-cost) customers from undermining the economic viability of warranties given to the lower-risk customers. Such low-risk warranties are undermined if adverse selection makes warranties expensive for all.

Notes on the reliance interest

ROBERT BIRMINGHAM (1985)

We will try to get some mileage out of *Security Stove & Manufacturing Co. v. American Railway Express Co.*, hardly the latest thing. The defendant broke its promise to deliver the plaintiff's gas furnace to Atlantic City to be exhibited at the American Gas Association Convention. The plaintiff intended to display, not sell, the particular furnace token it shipped. Profit would have come by increased sales and was uncertain. If exhibited, the furnace might have malfunctioned so the plaintiff would have sold fewer furnaces than it actually did. Or the plaintiff might have sold every furnace it could manufacture anyway.

With respect to the broken promise, the plaintiff sought reliance damages. . . . The defendant argued the plaintiff should get expectation damages or nothing (besides shipping charges refunded). The defendant complained the plaintiff was "endeavoring to achieve a return of the status quo in a suit based on a breach of contract," thereby committing a conceptual error that the defendant invited the court not to endorse. The defendant said the plaintiff was "trying to recover what he would have had, had there never been any contract of shipment," rather than correctly "seeking to recover what he would have had, had the contract not been broken." Apparently, the defendant put squarely before the court the choice between protecting the expectation interest and protecting the reliance interest.

The court awarded reliance damages. The plaintiff had rented a booth at the convention. It had transported a workman and its president to Atlantic City and back and had maintained them there throughout the convention, waiting respectively to assemble the furnace and to point

Reprinted from Robert Birmingham, "Notes on the Reliance Interest," *Washington Law Review* 60 (1985): 217–66, with the permission of the publisher and the author.

to it. That the workman and the president had a good time in Atlantic City did not benefit the plaintiff. Giving out-of-pocket expenses as reliance damages, as the court did, is ordinary. . . . I will call cases like *Security Stove* where profit is uncertain 'type I reliance cases'.

The usual way we read *Security Stove* is illustrated by Murray's [1983, p. 19] classifying the case under "The Protection of the Reliance Interest." We get:

Hypothesis 1 (conventional wisdom): The court in type I reliance cases protects the reliance interest as such.

There are a couple of problems that disturb us early on about hypothesis 1.

The first problem is that the language of the court (by Bland, J.) seems slightly incongruent with hypothesis 1. The court was *unhappy* giving reliance damages but could not give expectation damages or could not do this directly. It admitted the defendant got "the general rule" of damages right, but said this rule is not "inconsistent with the holdings that, in some instances, the injured party may recover expenses." We should expect more of this consistency than that the general rule is not general enough to apply here. Taken more vigorously, 'consistent' suggests the rules are related. The court professed to award the damages it did lest the plaintiff "be deprived of any substantial compensation for its loss." A court doctrinally at ease does not talk this way.

The second problem with hypothesis 1 is that Security Stove's damages are only implausibly reliance damages. . . . [W]e [define] reliance damages as putting the nonbreaching party where [it] should have been had the parties not contracted. Consider then the counterfactual: 'had the parties not contracted'. Imagine that Security Stove had not contracted with American Railway Express Company (*A*). It would have not just stayed home but contracted with another carrier (*B*). If *B* would have delivered the furnace on time, and *A* was required to, the consequents of the counterfactuals for reliance damages and expectation damages are identical except for the name of the carrier, ' . . . the furnace parts would have arrived on time, delivered by ____', the blank to be filled '*A*' or '*B*'. In *Security Stove*, reliance and expectation damages are identical and include lost profits because the plaintiff would have obtained these had the furnace been delivered on time regardless of who delivered it. Consequently, the court by giving expenses protected neither interest exactly.

There is a terminological awkwardness because we naturally apply the phrase 'reliance damages' to recoveries calculated counterfactually and to recoveries calculated by expenditure and these may diverge. How we use 'reliance damages' in *each* instance (and the distinction matters) will be indicated whenever its usage is not clear from the context.

It is worth entertaining a different reading of *Security Stove*:

Hypothesis 2: Courts in type I reliance cases award the expectation interest as best they can.

We would support hypothesis 2 by citing what troubles us about *Security Stove* (its weak endorsement of reliance damages and then its not giving them) and arguing: The court's "fundamantal premise" is that contract law should protect the expectation interest. The court could have calculated damages many ways. It could have given Security Stove the sum of the ages of its president's children plus $1,000, etc. But it wanted not to be arbitrary. The court was not arbitrary if (whatever it recognized as) the reliance interest is related to the expectation interest so that by awarding the first, it awarded approximately the second.

Security Stove is perfectly compatible with both hypotheses. We ordinarily test competing hypotheses by finding contexts where their consequences diverge. Here, the consequences diverge in two kinds of cases. Paradigmatically, *L. Albert & Son v. Armstrong Rubber Co.* is the first kind. Armstrong contracted with Albert to buy four refiners – machines to recondition old rubber – and constructed foundations for them. Albert delivered two of the machines late. Armstrong justifiably rejected all four and sought the cost of the foundations. The difficulty in *Albert* was not that profits were uncertain as they were in *Security Stove*. Armstrong we imagine could calculate its profits too well. World War II was winding down; nobody wanted reconditioned old rubber; the profits would have been negative.

Learned Hand, deciding *Albert*, observed the case law was inconsistent. But [Fuller and Perdue's] *The Reliance Interest* endorsed what Hand called a "very simple formula": "We will not in a suit for reimbursement for losses incurred in reliance on a contract knowingly put [the relying promisee] in a better position than he would have occupied had the contract been fully performed." Hand liked this. "On principle," Hand concluded, "the proper solution would seem to be that the promisee may recover his outlay in preparation for the performance, subject to the privilege of the promisor to reduce it by as much as he can show that the promisee would have lost, if the contract had been performed." I will call cases like *Albert*, characterized by the plaintiff's declining to prove profits because there are losses, 'type II reliance cases'.

Fuller recognized type I reliance cases by his category 1 – contracts having uncertain expectancies. He lacked a category corresponding to type II reliance – evidently because courts do not, and he believed they should not, give reliance damages in type II cases. After all, it was Fuller's formula that Hand liked. Types I and II have in common that the promisee in a paradigmatic bargaining context has requested reliance damages. They are unique or nearly unique in this. Courts are in the business of protecting the expectation interest in promises belonging to bargains if they can identify it (type I problem). If both interests are identified, a promisee would ask a court to protect the reliance interest instead of the expectation interest only if the reliance interest is larger (type II problem).

I added the optional 'nearly' before 'unique' in the preceding paragraph to account for a response to the rule in *Hadley v. Baxendale*. A court does not protect unnatural and unanticipated parts of the expectation interest. A promisee might instead seek reliance damages. In *Hadley* itself we would calculate damages indifferently using expectation or reliance – we imagine if Hadley had not contracted with Pickford, he would have shipped the shaft by another carrier expected to be equally fast. Section 90 says the promisor must reasonably expect the promise to be relied on. Here, 'reasonably' reads the rule in *Hadley* to be that a promisee cannot do better than recover her expectation interest, recalculated to exclude unnatural and unanticipated losses.

The law might have been that the reliance and the expectation interests are unconnected. Then a promisee could sue on either independently. The holdings (although not always the dicta) of type I reliance cases are consistent with the law being this way. Nevertheless, type II cases indicate that the law is not (in bargaining contexts). By these cases, a court gives a promisee only her expectation interest when both interests have been proven. Hand's rule clarifies Fuller's rule by having its result depend on the burden of proof (this dependence is probably implicit in Fuller's 'knowingly'). The promisee makes out a prima facie case for recovering her reliance interest (sometimes understood as her expenditures) by proving this loss. The promisor may then reduce this recovery by the amount that he can prove her expectation interest falls short of her reliance interest so understood. Briefly, if anybody proves the expectation interest, the promisee gets it exclusively.

We attend again to the counterfactual aspects of the definitions of the interests. In type I reliance cases, the court protects the expectation interest indirectly. A promisee mostly proves her expectation interest directly: 'If *Y had* delivered the widgets under the contract, I *would* have had them for ____ dollars less'. But pretend her expectancy is uncertain so she cannot do this. She may still prove it indirectly by showing how much she has relied; 'If I *had* not contracted with *Y*, I *would* not have built this widget-using machine'. We contract expecting

95

to be at least as well off as if we had not contracted, the argument goes. (Fuller appreciated this: "Plainly it is this divergence between the cost of giving and the gain realized by receiving that makes possible the reciprocal advantages that can result from a properly negotiated exchange.") Our reliance loss consequently gives the *minimum* gain we expect. We might be disappointed of course. But it is up to the promisor – this being only a matter of the burden of proof – to show we would have been.

The second kind of case by which we can compare hypotheses 1 and 2 includes *Chicago Coliseum Club v. Dempsey* and *Anglia Television Ltd. v. Reed*. These cases go oppositely, so we support either hypothesis by picking sides. I have never like *Dempsey*. Dempsey broke his promise to fight and the Club sought its expenses. The court decided it could not recover those incurred before it contracted with Dempsey because it could not, *at that time*, reasonably have been relying on the contract. So it was pretty obviously protecting the reliance interest. *Dempsey* is like a type I reliance case because profits are uncertain. But in *Dempsey*, or *Dempsey* unadulterated, there is no reliance, the plaintiffs having spent what they spent before contracting.

In *Anglia*, Anglia contracted with Reed for the latter to act in its filmed play. Reed repudiated (apparently) a day later. Anglia did not contract with another actor and did not produce the play. It could not prove its profits and consequently claimed for what the court called 'wasted expenditure'. Lord Denning gave expenditures wasted *both* after *and* before contracting, all expenditures "as would reasonably be in the contemplation of the parties as likely to be wasted if the contract was broken."

Murray [1983, p. 543], not a hero here, classifies *Anglia* with *Security Stove* under "The Protection of the Reliance Interest." This appears wrong. Given Denning's reasoning, the result would have been insensitive to Reed's having repudiated anytime, regardless of how short, after agreement. But then we get an unadulterated case of no reliance. Denning's term 'contemplation of the parties' is expectation measure talk. The brief *Hadley* opinion uses forms of 'contemplate' five times. Denning put Anglia where it would have been had Reed performed the contract, not where it would have been had Anglia and Reed not contracted. That is, Denning did this to the extent Anglia's proof permitted it: As did Bland in *Security Stove*, Denning had to estimate Anglia's expectation from its expenditures. *Anglia* is unequivocally a case in which the court chose the expectation measure over the reliance measure where this choice mattered not just doctrinally but to the result. . . .

Hoffman v. Red Owl Stores, Inc. is a good reliance case. . . . In *Hoff-*

man, the defendant promised the plaintiffs to build and let them operate a grocery store. The plaintiffs relied on the defendant's promise by selling their bakery, etc. The court appealed to section 90 [of the Restatement of Contracts] to establish liability, then awarded reliance damages. . . .

The result in *Hoffman* is ordinary, but its language is atypically direct. The court, in working up to not protecting the expectation interest, denies it is doing contract law. It says: "We deem it would be a mistake to regard an action grounded on promissory estoppel as the equivalent of a breach-of-contract action." Still more explicitly it says: "Plaintiffs contend that in a breach-of-contract action damages may include loss of profits. However, this is not a breach-of-contract action." . . .

Except for damages, *Walters v. Marathon Oil Co.* is like *Hoffman v. Red Owl Stores, Inc.* Relying on Marathon's promise (which Marathon broke) to sell gas to them, Walters and wife bought property for a gas station/food store. The district court found Marathon liable by promissory estoppel *and* awarded Walters and his wife lost profits. Marathon argued on appeal that, its liability being based on promissory estoppel, "loss of profits is not a proper measure of damages"; instead, damages ought to be the "expenditures in reliance on the promise," calculated by subtracting the then present value of the property Walters bought from what he paid for it. Conveniently for Marathon, the calculation yielded a negative number.

Applying Indiana law, the circuit court affirmed, awarding lost profits. Feinman [1984, pp. 687–8] cites the case first to support a claim that "the typical damage remedy applied in promissory estoppel cases is measured by the expectation interest." But the *Marathon* court does not appear to be applying this remedy. It said, "[i]t is unreasonable to assume" Walters and his wife "did not anticipate a return of profits from this investment of time and funds, but, in reliance upon [the] promise, they had forgone the opportunity to make the investment elsewhere"; consequently they "suffered a loss of profits as a direct result of their reliance upon the promise." *Obviously*, this talk is not about the expectation interest.

The *Marathon* court asked, 'Where would Walters and wife have been if they had not contracted with Marathon?', and answered, 'Getting equal profits elsewhere'. The court protected the reliance interest, but gave just what it would have given had it been protecting the expectation interest. Its doing this should not surprise us because Fuller warned that reliance damages *often* equal expectation damages, if we regard opportunity cost (as we should). . . . The line between not recovering and recovering profits, or between expenditures and other reliance, may itself by significant. But classically, 'reliance interest' and 'expectation interest' do not draw it.

Walters' reliance recovery ought to include the profits Walters would have made investing elsewhere, not (as such) the profits he would have made if Marathon had kept its promise. But Walters proved only the latter. Because the market for capital is approximately competitive, the profits either way should be the same modulo risk. Or Walters, by proving his profits if Marathon had kept its promise, established a prima facie case of the extent of his reliance, shifting to Marathon the burden of proving he could not have gotten these profits elsewhere. This latter result is symmetrical with that reached by Hand in *Albert*.

* * *

Questions and notes on fault, consequential damages, and reliance

1. As Bishop notes, the foreseeability doctrine in contracts has little to do with the possible occurrence of low-probability events. It concerns the ability of the parties to control the magnitude of the damages that actually occur. Bishop emphasizes one device for doing so: providing notice of the special circumstances. An alternative, which he does not consider, is for the parties to arrange their affairs so that the magnitude of the damages would not be so great if the other party failed to perform. That is, in *Hadley v. Baxendale* the shipper could have reduced the expected cost of a breach by informing the carrier of the consequences of a failure to deliver or by carrying a greater inventory of shafts so that the plant would not have to remain idle in the event of a delay (breach) by the carrier.*

The possibility that Hadley could have held a larger inventory of shafts (an input) has been widely recognized. Less attention has been given to other ways in which the costs of the failure could have been limited by timely effort on the part of Hadley. Hadley could have held a larger inventory of flour (the output). After the shaft was delivered and the mill again operating, Hadley could have made up for some of the lost output by running at a higher level of output than he otherwise would have. (In effect, that entails having a larger inventory of productive capacity – another input – than Hadley might otherwise carry.)

In tort language, Hadley's vulnerability to Baxendale's failure to perform constituted a "thin skull." The thinness of the skull was not,

---

* Actually, although the decision is couched in terms of a lack of notice, Danzig (1975, p. 254) points out that Hadley's agent did communicate his urgency to Baxendale's agent, but the court chose to ignore this fact.

however, inexorable. There is, loosely speaking, a duty not to have too thin a skull. By barring recovery for at least some portion of the consequential damages, the foreseeability doctrine encourages the promisee to behave efficiently before the promisor breaches.

2. *Hadley* represents, as noted in Selection [2.3], one aspect of the *Boomer* problem. It highlights the fault of the "victim," the reasonableness of its behavior, which made it vulnerable to a subsequent large loss. The reasonableness of the other party will also come into play. Thus, a carrier's failure to deliver on time can result from (a) factors beyond the carrier's control, (b) the carrier's error (as in *Hadley*), or (c) a deliberate choice by the carrier – diverting from the initial path to pick up another profitable freight order. The likelihood that a court would find the damages foreseeable would be greatest for (c) and least for (a).

The parties do not have to rely upon the courts to make this decision for them. They can specify in their contract whether the carrier's liability will depend upon his fault. Contracts to transport goods typically include *force majeure* clauses that excuse a party if factors beyond its control preclude performance. What is the economic rationale for taking the carrier's fault into account?

3. Bishop treats *Heron II* as a close case with the outcome depending upon the issue of whether the shipper informed the carrier of the specific risk – that the shipper would suffer if the sugar were delivered late and the price of sugar fell in the interim. This seems strange at first blush since it is obvious that if delivery is delayed, the price of a commodity could fall. Why would anyone need to be informed about so obvious a fact? There are circumstances in which, even though the price of sugar fell, the shipper would suffer no damage. Suppose, for example, that the shipper sold his cargo to a buyer at the port of delivery and transferred title while the ship was still at sea. It is possible that under such circumstances, the shipper would not be injured at all. Should this possibility matter in determining the liability or the damages? Does it make sense to make liability for the damages for the price decline depend upon the shipper's timely conveyance to the carrier of information regarding the ownership and disposition of the sugar?

   3.1. The general rule in the United States is that in the event of an unexcused delay, the carrier is liable for the decrease in price. Can you develop a rationale for holding the carrier liable regardless of whether the shipper conveyed any information to the carrier about his vulnerability to price changes at the destination? If the price of the commodity at the destination increased, should the shipper compensate the carrier for the windfall?

3.2 Suppose that Smith agrees to deliver one ton of sugar to Jones in Liverpool on June 1. (Shipping contracts rarely promise delivery on a specific date; the assumption of a specific date just serves to simplify the hypothetical problem.) On May 15 he announces that he will not deliver. The damages would be the difference between the contract price and the forward price on May 15 of sugar for June 1 delivery. Now suppose that Smith contracts with Heron Shipping to have one ton of its sugar delivered to Liverpool by June 1. On May 15 Heron informs Smith that it is deviating from its original route to pick up additional cargo and that it will not arrive until well after June 1. Damages in this instance are not measured as of May 15; instead, they are measured by the difference between the price on June 1 and the price on the actual date of delivery. Why the difference?

4. Suppose that a contract has been breached and that the market price of the subject matter has remained unchanged. Damages could be reckoned by the amount spent by the plaintiff on which he failed to reap the anticipated benefit because of the breach (reliance) or on the benefit he did not receive (consequential damages). These are closely related. A firm makes a particular expenditure because it expects to earn at least a normal rate of return on it. The expected benefits (with the expectation being measured at the time the expenditures are made) are equal to the costs plus a normal rate of return (reliance damages including prejudgment interest). These expected benefits are also equal to the anticipated consequential damages – that is, in the event of a breach, the expected benefits would not be obtained.

Of course, expected consequential damages need not be equal to actual consequential damages. The expected damage (or benefit) is a weighted average of outcomes depending upon which future state of the world occurs, while the actual damage (or benefit) is determined by which one actually did occur. *Heron II* (discussed by Bishop) provides an example of a case in which actual damages exceeded expected damages; *Albert* discussed by Birmingham) provides an example of a case in which actual damages fell short of expected damages.

The essential similarity between the two concepts is often obscured by the way the facts are stated. Thus, compare *Security Stove* with *Hadley*. Both involve damages incurred because of the carrier's delay in delivery. In the former case, the furnace was an input into selling

101

more furnaces. Delay resulted in a reduction in value of the funds invested in selling furnaces (reliance). The loss could also be viewed as the value of the sales that would have occurred had the contract actually been performed. The expected value of these two measures would be the same (if we could measure accurately). In *Hadley* the delay resulted in the plant being shut down for a few days. As a consequence, earnings were below what they would have been had the contract been performed. The loss could also be viewed as a decline in value of the specific assets of the firm. The expected value of the two measures is, again, equal.

The former case involves lost out-of-pocket costs and the latter a temporary decline in the value of an existing stock of assets. This distinction doesn't matter. We could just as easily turn the problem around. Security Stove could have owned a house in Atlantic City that it used for housing its executives during the many trade shows and conventions that occurred there. And Hadley could have rented most of his plant, rather than owning it. The basic problem remains the same regardless of whether the plaintiff owns the assets or rents them.

The cases can be distinguished on the pragmatic ground of ease of measurement. It is easier to add up Security Stove's expenses than it is to project the outcome of their selling effort; it is easier to determine Hadley's normal rate of output than to ascertain the change in value of its assets that are not traded on a public market. This is not a matter of principle, merely one of convenience. It is, essentially, Birmingham's hypothesis II.

5. In both *Hadley* and *Security Stove* losses were suffered because a carrier failed to deliver on time. Assuming that the carriers' behavior in the two cases was equally negligent, is there any basis for distinguishing between the two cases and compensating more liberally in the latter?

6. Suppose that Jones, Inc., had entered into a one-year contract with Baxendale Freight (BF) for transporting goods to Consolidated Industries (CI). The contract with CI turned out to be an exceptionally good one for Jones, and it became clear that CI was looking for grounds to claim that Jones had breached so that CI could be free of its onerous obligation. Jones informed BF of the situation and urged it to be especially careful to meet all its shipping schedules to CI. BF failed to do so; CI claimed that Jones had breached and refused to accept further deliveries. Jones lost its suit against CI alleging a breach of contract and then sued BF to recover the benefit of its bargain with CI. Should it be allowed to recover?

7. Acme, Inc., submitted a bid for a contract. All submissions had to be in by noon on June 30. Acme's arrived 15 minutes late and was disqualified. It would have been the low bidder, and evidence shows that the failure to get the bid cost it $100,000 and that it had spent $15,000 in preparing the bid. Acme's bid was delivered by an express company that promises all its customers that it gives overnight delivery with arrival before 10:30 A.M. Acme sued the express company for the $100,000 it lost by not winning the contract or, alternatively, the $15,000 that it spent in bid preparation. What should be the outcome? Since such problems are likely to arise frequently for firms in the express delivery business, they probably stipulate a remedy in the contract. What do you think that remedy would look like?

   7.1 Suppose that the president of Acme had decided to submit the bid personally. Unfortunately, his plane was delayed for five hours and he arrived ten minutes late. He sued the airline for the damages incurred. How should that suit be resolved?

8. Birmingham presented two hypotheses. There is a third hypothesis, which Birmingham alludes to, that we might label the cynical or realist hypothesis:

> *Hypothesis III*: to avoid the rigidity of classical contract law, courts fudge.

If the court thinks the *Hadley* result too harsh, it can avoid it by talking of reliance damages rather than consequential damages. Instead of restricting the outcome of a trial to two damage awards – the contract price or the costs arising from the plant being shut down – a number of intermediate outcomes can be achieved by manipulating various doctrines. Labeling some damages too conjectural in some contexts but not in others is one way to do this. Measuring out-of-pocket reasonable reliance costs in such a way as to be considerably less than measured consequential damages would be another. In the words of Fuller and Perdue (p. 375):

> What is principally revealed in the actual application of the standard of certainty is a judicial disinclination to impose on the defendant liability for those injurious effects of his breach which do not result "directly," but are due to the internal structure of the plaintiff's business. This disinclination finds a number of distinct doctrinal formulations, of which the requirement of "certainty" [that damages not be conjectural] is only one, the others being the test of foreseeability, ... and the theory that liability rests on a tacit assumption of risk.

103

8.1 In a part of his article not reproduced here, Birmingham (p. 238) provides a good example of such manipulation in discussing the remedies in *Hoffman* and *Marathon*. In *Hoffman* the court refused to compensate for lost profits, while in *Marathon* it did. The different treatment is not related to any difference in the basic facts or to doctrinal changes. Rather, Birmingham attributes the different treatment to the fact that the inflation rate was considerably higher when the latter was decided. Question: Why does this matter?

8.2 Invocation of doctrines like foreseeability and certainty of damages makes the law more flexible and enables judges to fine-tune the outcomes. Do you see any problems with this sort of ad hoc approach?

9. If a party incurred costs in anticipation of entering into a contract but the contract never materialized, should that party be compensated? The American rule prior to *Hoffman* was that if the parties did not enter into a contract, the disappointed party could not recover its costs. Continental law, under the doctrine of *culpa in contrahendra* (fault in negotiating), often did allow the disappointed party to recover. Why might a rule that at least creates a strong presumption against compensation make good economic sense? Could you state a rule such that cases like *Hoffman* and *Marathon* might overcome that presumption?

PART IV

The lost-volume seller puzzle

The lost-volume seller problem is a very confusing one that has been incorrectly analyzed by numerous commentators and has been a constant source of confusion to the courts. The issue is this: If a buyer breaches a purchase contract for a manufactured item and the seller subsequently resells the product at the same price, has the seller suffered any damage, and if so, should he be compensated for it? In cases in which the seller is a retailer, the conclusion is (a) yes, the seller does suffer damages, (b) the damages are the market price of the service of selling the goods, (c) the market price of selling is approximately the gross margin, (d) even though the damages are incurred, full compensation would probably be inefficient, and (e) the law ought to encourage the parties to use nonrefundable deposits as liquidated damages. This argument is developed in Selection [4.1], one of the few papers in this book that considers contracts between businessmen and consumers.

While that argument is of interest in its own right, it serves as a useful introduction to the lost-volume problem that arises in contracts between business firms. The line of argument is somewhat different, but the basic conclusion remains the same: Although the damages are real, the law should deny recovery and facilitate customized remedies via liquidated damages clauses. The treatment of the lost-volume problem in the nonretail case is explored in the notes and questions at the end of Part IV.

105

CHAPTER 4.1

An economic analysis of the lost-volume retail seller

VICTOR P. GOLDBERG (1984)

Suppose that a customer agrees to buy a boat and before it is delivered, he reneges. The dealer subsequently resells the boat to another customer at the same price. Has the seller suffered damages (aside from incidental damages) and, if so, should he be compensated? This question, dubbed the lost-volume seller problem, has been the subject of considerable legal analysis, usually in the context of explicating section 2-708(2) of the Uniform Commercial Code (U.C.C.)....

* * *

[I will use the case of *Neri v. Retail Marine Corp.* as a vehicle for analysis.] Professors Goetz and Scott [1979, p. 332] ... summarize the *Neri* facts and decision concisely:

Retail Marine, a dealer in marine equipment and supplies, contracted to sell a new boat to Neri for $12,500. Marine then ordered and received the boat from its supplier. Six days after the agreement Neri repudiated the contract. Four months later Marine sold the boat to another buyer for the same price. When Neri sued to recover his downpayment, Marine counterclaimed for lost profits of $2,500 under U.C.C. 2-708(2), arguing that absent Neri's default it would have earned two profits rather than one. The New York Court of Appeals sustained Marine's lost-volume claim, holding that "the conclusion is clear from the record – indeed with mathematical certainty – that [market damages are] inadequate to put the seller in as good a position as performance ... and hence ... the seller is entitled to its [profit]." The court categorized Retail Marine's situation as that of a dealer with an "inexhaustible" supply of boats; consequently, the second buyer did not replace the first.

From Victor P. Goldberg, "An Economic Analysis of the Lost-Volume Retail Seller," *Southern California Law Review* 57 (1984): 283–297. With the permission of William S. Hein & Co., Inc.

* * *

Suppose that once Neri has placed his order, he is legally bound to take the boat for his own or to arrange for its resale to another buyer. In Calabresi-Melamed terminology, Neri's placement of the order gives Marine an entitlement protected by a property rule. Conceivably, Neri could sit outside Marine's showroom and try to convince potential buyers to purchase his boat rather than the dealer's boat. Obviously, this is costly to Neri, but it would be feasible. Alternatively, Neri could pay a retailer to resell the boat for him. If Neri could choose from a number of equally attractive dealers, he would pay a fair market price for the reselling service. Whether that price is 1 percent, 10 percent, or 20 percent of retail price depends upon the anticipated costs of retailing. Thus, even if Neri has access to a competitive market of resellers, he could find disposing of the boat a very expensive proposition. Neri's situation is complicated if the initial seller – Marine – is better situated than others to resell the boat. This would be so, for example, if Neri's purchase and resale converts the boat from a new to a used one and results in instant depreciation of, say, 20 percent.

Initially, when buying his boat, Neri has a choice from a number of boat retailers, some of whom carry brands that he prefers. After he has placed the order with one, however, that dealer has an advantage that it could exploit in bargaining to determine the price of reselling. The legal damage rule – if unmodified by the initial contract – serves as a backdrop for bargaining to determine the price of the reselling services. That price would depend upon such considerations as Neri's vulnerability to Marine's opportunism (the costs of the next best alternative), Marine's interest in maintaining customer good will, the costs of using the legal system (the status quo determines whether one party must invoke the costly legal system), the existence and amount of any down payment, and the like.

Alternatively, Marine's entitlement could be protected only by a liability rule (damages rather than specific performance). This is the more customary rule for breach of contract. What are Marine's damages? A reasonable approximation would be the competitive price for the service of renegotiating the sale of a new boat. This damage rule would not permit the retailer to take advantage of his unique ex post situation in the postbreach bargaining. The competitive price of the reselling service is, roughly, the gross margin (retail minus wholesale price) of the dealer. This measure of damages is precisely what the drafters of the U.C.C. had in mind under section 2-708(2):

The provision of this section permitting recovery of expected profit including reasonable overhead where the standard measure of damages is inadequate . . . [is] designed to eliminate the unfair and economically wasteful results arising under the older law when fixed price articles were involved. This section permits the recovery of lost profits in all appropriate cases, which would include all standard priced goods. The normal measure there would be list price less cost to the dealer or list price less manufacturing cost to the manufacturer. [U.C.C. 2-708, comment 2 (1978).]

It would appear then that the arguments of the proponents of the lost profit notion are vindicated. This conclusion, however, would be premature. The following section considers other aspects of the economics of retailing and relates them to the damages problem.

The economics of retailing and lost profits

Why would a manufacturer choose not to sell directly to consumers? The simple answer is that it would cost too much. Retailers provide services to manufacturers and customers, reducing the costs of distributing the goods. The retailer's revenue minus the costs of goods sold will compensate for the costs of retailing, including a normal rate of return on the retailer's investment. While it would be possible for a retailer to sell retailing services separately (for example, by charging an admission fee or by selling a catalogue), the typical retailer's compensation is directly tied to the sale of its output. The gross margin is set high enough so that the costs will be covered by sales revenue. Thus, regardless of which customers use the retail services, the retailer's compensation comes solely from the buyers of his goods. If Mr. Jones buys, he pays for the product and for a share of the retailing service; if Mr. Smith does not buy, he pays nothing for the retailing services, regardless of how much selling effort was exerted on his behalf. If Mr. Neri orders a boat and then reneges, should he bear any of the costs of retailing in the absence of specific contract language on this point? If we hold him liable for lost profits, then the answer is yes.

A. The price of options

When Neri orders the boat, he can be viewed as purchasing an option. If the boat is delivered, he pays the contract price, which, of course, includes a share of the overall costs of retailing. If between the contract date and the delivery date Neri changes his mind, the option is cancelled (i.e., the contract is breached). Neri would then pay the price of the option (i.e., contract damages). What would be a reasonable measure of the value of the option? The retailer's gross margin is one possibility. If one has doubts that reasonable customers know or ought to know the extent of their commitment when making an option contract, then one should be uncomfortable about assessing the customer for lost profit damages. Most buyers of boats and cars probably would be shocked to learn that the price of their option exceeds 15 percent of the retail price. Fortunately, there exists a relatively simple device to determine an accurate measure of the value of the option: a nonrefundable deposit. The law should encourage the parties to use this device, by denying recovery for lost profits in the absence of explicit contract language to the contrary.

This policy conclusion is not inevitable. Reasonable people might agree with the analytical approach, yet conclude that a different policy is in order. The remainder of this section develops the argument in more detail. . . .

B. A fish story

A retailer can influence his sales volume by his price or his selling effort. To simplify the discussion, assume that price is fixed. Selling effort includes a broad mix of activities: advertising, maintaining high ratios of inventory or salespeople to sales, locating in places that generate a high volume of foot traffic, maintaining elegant facilities, providing high-quality service departments, developing high levels of consumer good will, and so forth. Diminishing returns to selling effort reflect the increased difficulty of reaching additional customers. For example, an advertisement targeted to an audience within a one mile radius of a boat dealership is likely to result in a larger percentage of recipients responding to the ad than would one aimed at customers within a 100 mile radius. With the retail and wholesale prices fixed, the profit-maximizing firm sets marginal selling costs equal to the gross margin [Figure 1].

Suppose that one customer, Neri, breaches. What are the effects on the dealer's sales and costs? The seller, Marine, loses the sale and his costs are reduced roughly by the wholesale price of the boat – his loss from the breach is approximately the gross margin. Goetz and Scott [1979, pp. 333–5], however, would argue either that another sale would replace the Neri sale, or that Marine's cost saving would be the marginal cost, which is equal to the retail price. Hence, there would be no lost profit. The difference lies in the interpretations of the marginal cost concept. Marginal cost should not relate to actual output, ex post, as Goetz and Scott's analysis implies; rather, it concerns planned output, ex ante.

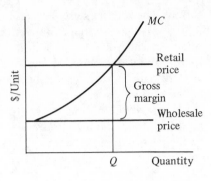

Figure 1

An analogy is helpful. Think of the customers as fish and the retailer as a fisherman. The fisherman makes decisions on boat size, crew, equipment, et cetera on the basis of the relationship between these inputs and expected catch. For a given combination of inputs (a given level of fishing – or retailing – expense) on a normal day the fisherman might anticipate a catch of, say, 1,000 pounds. On a good day he might land 2,000 pounds and on a bad day he might do no more than drown a lot of worms. The fisherman's optimal level and mix of expenditures depends upon the distribution of expected outcomes and their relationship to the input mix. There is no unique marginal cost concept in this formulation. But if we had to have a single, summary marginal cost measure, it would almost surely be the cost of increasing the *expected* catch by one pound. Thus, if on a particular day, a fish is hooked and then is lost, the fisherman loses the revenue from that fish and avoids virtually no costs – the ex post marginal costs are roughly zero. The fish that got away, like Neri, constitutes a net loss of revenue for the business. So long as the probability of a fish getting away is not positively correlated with the probability of hooking the next fish, the lost fish constitutes a net loss to the fisherman. Likewise, so long as the customer's reneging does not increase the likelihood of making the next sale, the breach results in a net loss of revenue to the business.*

This analogy captures the notion that the lost profits proponents were trying to convey – the typical retailer can expand sales in the short run with little cost beyond the wholesale price in the sense that, if he has a

---

* If the probabilities are negatively correlated, then the problem is exacerbated. This is, in fact, likely. Deteriorating economic conditions would result in an increased probability of buyer breach and would also result in lower demand; finding a new customer would be harder.

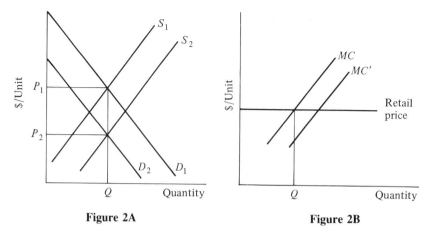

Figure 2A   **Figure 2B**

lucky month, then he could fill the additional orders. Commentators, however, have used awkward terminology, such as an ability to "supply all probable customers" and the "seller has an unlimited supply of goods," to describe this concept.

C. Who should bear the loss

By now the reader should be convinced that the breach does impose a loss upon the retailer and that the gross margin is an approximation of the magnitude of that loss. That does not mean, however, that the breacher should be held liable. In the absence of a nonrefundable deposit or explicit contract language to the contrary, the retailer ought to bear the loss.

Suppose initially that the customer's decision to breach was a random event. In Figure [2A], the industry supply and demand curves (S_1 and D_1) are drawn on the assumption that the customer pays no damages if he breaches. The supply curve reflects the sellers' costs of doing business, including the expected costs of buyers breaching. Compare the equilibrium price/quantity combination with what would happen if customers were liable for damages arising from the breach. Under the new liability rule, represented by D_2 and S_2, the supply curve shifts to the right since the firm no longer bears the expected costs of breach. On the other hand, since the buyers now bear the costs, they are willing to pay less for the good; the demand curve shifts to the left. If the expected level of breach is independent of the legal regime, if attitudes toward the risk of breach are the same for buyers and sellers, and if the perceived likelihood of breach is the same on both sides of the market, then the

111

demand shift would completely offset the shift in the supply curve. The quantity would be the same in both regimes and the price difference $(P_1 - P_2)$ would be exactly equal to the expected unit cost of breach. The rule does not matter. This might appear surprising at first glance, but, in fact, it is nothing more than Demsetz's variation on the Coase Theorem.

Now, consider the hypothetical with the retail price constant (Figure 2B). (In Figure [2A] the price is allowed to adjust, while in Figure [2B] the retail price is held constant; the basic analytical result remains unchanged). The typical firm's marginal costs are shown by MC, drawn under the assumption that the firm bears the costs of breach. Shifting liability to the customers has two effects. First, it lowers the firm's costs in the same manner as in Figure [2A], to MC'. Second, since the customers now value the good less than before, the firm will have to work harder to persuade customers to buy the good at the constant price; this results in a shift in the marginal cost curve in the opposite direction back to MC.

The idealized conditions posited above do not hold. Information about the probability of breach is not the same for buyers and sellers at the formation stage of the contract. The individual customer has more knowledge about his own tendencies to adhere to contracts, and some scholars are inclined to emphasize this information asymmetry. I, however, would be inclined to put more weight on the dealer's superior ability, gathered from his business experience, to assess the probability that an individual customer will back out of a deal. Dealers are in a better position to know the magnitude of damages in the event of a breach, as noted in the discussion of options. Dealers also would appear to be in a better position to spread the risk of a breach over similar transactions than would a customer. Moreover, both Figures [2A] and [2B] are drawn on the assumption that enforcement of the law is equally costly regardless of which way the right is assigned, which is not the case. . . .

A nonrefundable deposit has considerable attraction. First, it is cheap to arrange, given that the parties are already entering into a contract. Second, it provides evidence that the customer has been apprised of the extent of his liability in the event that he fails to take delivery. Third, it forces the customer to value explicitly the option he purchases. Conversely, it induces the seller to state ex ante the price he is willing to put on that option. Finally, a policy of finding no damages in the absence of a nonrefundable deposit has low enforcement costs. Other things equal, a policy of leaving the losses where they lie is very attractive.

A nonrefundable deposit is, in effect, a prepaid penalty. It would not be fruitful to explore here the courts' historic distaste for contractual penalties. It is sufficient to note that a proper resolution of the legal issues involving the lost-profit puzzle will inevitably involve some of the same questions raised in the debates about the enforceability of penalty clauses. The best policy would probably be to have no liability for lost profits unless the agreement so provides. The provision would probably take the form of a nonrefundable deposit, but there is no a priori reason to restrict the parties' choice to this device.

The *Neri* contract did utilize a deposit, and its fate was interesting. Neri's initial deposit was only $40, but when the dealer arranged for "immediate delivery on the basis of 'a firm sale' " the deposit was increased to $4,250, even though the dealer's margin was only around $2,500. On the back of the contract, in small print, the following term appeared: "If the within agreement is canceled by mutual consent, the seller shall retain the deposit paid hereunder, whether paid in cash or other consideration, as liquidated damages." In his complaint, the plaintiff alleged: "The said provision of the contract appeared on the reverse side in fine print and is fraud." The trial court judge did not agree but did rule that "[t]he liquidated damage clause ... does not apply to the instant case since the contract was not canceled by the mutual consent of the parties. Accordingly an assessment of damages must be had, at which time it may be determined whether the plaintiffs are entitled to the return of any portion of the down payment previously made." This ruling was not appealed. Consequently, the magnitude of the deposit was not a relevant factor in the determination of damages. The court only allowed Marine to keep the $2,579, expected profit plus an additional $674 for incidental expenses of storage, upkeep, finance charges, and insurance.

* * *

Questions and notes on the seller's lost profits

1. The analysis in the last part of the preceding paper invokes a variation on the Coase Theorem. This argument is extremely important in both tort and contract analysis and the reader should reflect upon it carefully. The central point is this: If the law changes so that the seller bears a particular cost instead of the buyer, sellers will in the long run have to charge a price to cover the higher cost. At the same time, buyers, who no longer bear the cost, will be willing to pay more for the good in question. Under idealized conditions, the final outcome is the same. The argument is developed in Demsetz (1973). The invariance of the outcome to the legal rule is not, however, the moral one should draw from the exercise. Rather, it suggests the factors one should consider when analyzing the impact of legal rules.

2. Suppose that Mr. Heery placed orders for delivery of a boat (that is, he signed a contract) at six different dealers. When the first boat came in, he immediately canceled the other orders (that is, he breached the contracts). Should he be able to cancel without penalty, or should the law discipline such breachers? Should the law distinguish between such a breacher and an innocent breacher, like Mr. Neri, who was hospitalized after signing his contract and no longer wanted the boat?

   2.1. Should Heery be liable regardless of the contract language? If so, what damages should be assessed?

   2.2. If the Heery and Neri contracts included "nonrefundable" deposits, should the courts treat them the same when deciding whether the deposits should be refunded? Should the courts accept evidence on the reasons for the breach when deciding whether the deposits should be refunded?

3. UCC 2-708(2) reckons damages as "the profit (including reasonable

114

overhead) which the seller would have made from full performance by the buyer. . . . "Does this measure make sense if the lost-volume seller is a manufacturer? Consider the following fact situation.

3.1. Mr. Beery orders a customized boat. The standard model costs $9,000, of which amount $2,000 is the retailer's margin and $1,000 the manufacturer's margin. The price for the customized boat is $12,000, even though the additional costs of customizing to the manufacturer are only $500 and the manufacturer charges the retailer $1,500 for the customization. The retailer accepts the offer and transmits the order to the manufacturer. That is, the retailer enters into contracts with both Mr. Beery and the manufacturer. Before the manufacturer performs any work on the boat, Beery cancels his order. The retailer sues Beery claiming as damages (a) the $2,000 margin on the standardized boat, (b) the $1,500 for the lost profits on the customization, and (c) the $2,000 the manufacturer did not receive after the order was canceled.

3.2. Should all three properly be reckoned as lost profits arising from the breach?

3.3. Should the manufacturer have an action against the retailer for the $2,000 lost profits arising from the breach?

3.4. Suppose that the manufacturer was vertically integrated into retailing. That is, a single entity claims that it lost (a),(b), and (c). Should it be able to recover for all three?

3.5. For the lost-volume retailer I argued that the damages would be the market price of reselling the product. The market price in that context is easily observable – it is the difference between the wholesale and retail prices. That corresponds closely to the notion of "reasonable overhead." Outside the retailing context, however, there is no relation between the reasonable overhead and the market price of resale. For manufacturers, the difference between the market price and marginal production costs includes many items in addition to the expected costs of selling. It includes the fixed plant, research and development expenditures, general management costs, and so forth. These costs could be a substantial portion of the selling price and their measurement could depend critically on how particular accounting rules assign overhead costs. In *Teradyne v. Teledyne* for example, the nonvariable costs were reckoned at about 75 percent of a $95,000 contract. Thus, if manufacturers are to recover their reasonable overhead, it would have to be on very different grounds.

4. The relationship between a seller's capacity and damages is compli-

cated. Capacity utilization is related both to the cost of resale and the narrow expectation damages: the change in the price.

4.1. In the analysis of *Neri* I treated the market price of resale as fixed. However, that is not strictly correct. If demand is high, selling is easy and the price to be paid for it should be low. It doesn't take much effort to sell Cabbage Patch dolls when people are lining up for them. On the other hand, if demand is weak, selling requires greater than normal effort. The level of capacity utilization might serve as a proxy for the market conditions. When demand is great, the firm has a high rate of capacity utilization (little excess capacity), and a relatively low cost of selling. Conversely, when demand is low and the firm has substantial excess capacity, its selling costs will be relatively high. Would you expect to observe large nonrefundable deposits when industry conditions are bad (demand is low, excess capacity high) and small deposits when times are good?

4.2. Rather than change the quoted price, sellers sometimes will change the terms of sale instead. In particular, when demand tightens, rather than raising the price, they might increase the expected delivery lag. A car to be delivered tomorrow at a given price is more valuable than the same car at the same price to be delivered one month from now. The delivery lag can be viewed as a separate component of price. A seller can give its buyers the equivalent of a price cut by holding the price constant, but speeding up deliveries. Since the delivery lag will be greater if capacity utilization is higher, this provides a second link between the level of capacity utilization and damages.

The relevant concern is not the level of capacity utilization itself, but rather the *change* in the level. Thus, if a seller had substantial excess capacity when the contract was formed and that same rate existed at the time of breach, no adjustment to the market price measure of damages is necessary. If, however, conditions had changed adversely for the sellers so that the level of excess capacity had increased, the change in market price would understate the damages. The value of a piece of paper that said "bearer will receive the tenth unit produced" would decline. Similarly, if conditions had improved so that the delivery lag had increased, the change in market price would overstate the damages. The breaching buyer in effect gives up a claim that has increased in value. The likelihood that a buyer would want to cancel an order (breach a contract) would, of

116

course, be higher when conditions had changed adversely.

The delivery lag component of market price is generally not directly observable. However, in some instances explicit markets will develop. Thus, an airline might pay $50,000 for the option to buy the fourth Boeing 767 while the price of the tenth slot might only be $20,000. These options could be resold to other airlines with the prices of the options changing to reflect shifting market conditions. If a purchaser were to breach, incorporating the change in the market value of the option in the damage measure would be a relatively simple task.

The preceding discussion is hard going. But it is very useful in clearing up a puzzle. As delivery lags lengthen (as capacity utilization increases), buyers will be willing to pay more to be near the front of the line. They will be willing to pay higher deposits. Thus, even though the selling costs are higher when there is substantial excess capacity, the deposit that the parties will agree to is likely to be lower for reasons that have nothing to do with the "market price of selling services."

5. Alpha promises to deliver one million pounds of customized aluminum rods per month to Beta for a three-year period beginning six months after the order has been placed. Shortly after placing the order, Beta decides to cancel. Alpha then uses the capacity that it would have otherwise allocated for fulfilling this order to produce a standardized aluminum ingot. It claims that the contract price of the rod is twenty-eight cents per pound and its costs of producing it are seventeen cents. The market price of the standardized product is only twenty-two cents and its costs, it claims, would be sixteen cents. Its loss, it argues, is the reduced profit (five cents per pound) on the entire order, or $1.8 million.

To isolate the essential features of the problem, let us assume that Alpha has done nothing in reliance upon the contract. It has made no expenditures and incurred no obligations in anticipation of performing. Nor is there any evidence that there had been any change in the market conditions for either aluminum product. For what damages, if any, should Alpha be compensated?

To analyze this problem it is convenient to reframe the original contract as two separate contracts. In the first, Alpha agrees to sell the standardized aluminum to Beta. In the second, Alpha agrees to provide customization services to convert the aluminum to rods.

5.1 In the ingot contract, there are no damages (by assumption) arising from a change in market conditions. Unless Alpha can invoke 2-708(2), it will recover nothing from the breach of this contract (except, perhaps, for incidental damages). The normal treatment of this problem would be to deny Alpha compensation. Notice, however, that the argument developed with regard to *Neri* would apply here as well. We need not worry about whether Alpha would have sold ingot to Delta and Gamma even if Beta had not canceled his order. It is enough to say that Beta would pay Alpha the fair market value of the reselling service and that these represent the damages. Does it make sense to hold Alpha liable for these damages? Do you think that sellers would be tempted to add clauses to their contracts making breachers liable for these damages?

5.2. The customization contract presents a harder case. Alpha has not, by assumption, incurred any expenses in reliance on this contract. The market conditions for its primary input (ingot) have not changed. Nor has there been a change in the demand for the customized rod. What is Alpha's loss? It has lost the "benefit of its bargain." Contract law would compensate Alpha, giving the additional profit that would have been earned if it had carried out the customization. In this particular example, that would be the five cents per pound ($1.8 million).

But should Alpha be compensated? What does the five-cent differential represent? If all it represents is creative accounting on the part of Alpha's expert witness, then no purpose is served by compensating. If the differential represents the sale of customization services at a particularly good price, then the case for enforcing the "property in the price" (see Part III. A) is stronger. Macaulay's observation (Selection [1.1]) that buyers usually consider themselves free to cancel an order without liability if the seller has not yet incurred expenditures in reliance is consistent with the proposition that compensation for this interest is unwarranted.

5.3. The problem becomes more difficult when (a) conditions have changed somewhat and quoted prices do not fully reflect those changes; (b) the seller has incurred some costs in preparing to perform this contract; and (c) it is difficult to disentangle these costs from others incurred by the seller in filling other orders.

There is an element of truth in 2-708(2)'s treatment of the manufacturer's lost profits in this case. The seller's usual remedy, the difference between contract and market price, is inadequate. The parties might well want to compensate for at least some of the losses arising from changed conditions and reliance, but identifying such losses might prove to be extremely difficult and pre-specifying damages might present problems. There is, however, little reason to believe that 2-708(2)'s alternative remedy, profit including reasonable overhead, would be particularly good at tracking these compensable losses.

Where does this leave us? The remedies provided by the Uniform Commercial Code are probably wrong. Whether that matters much is a different question. Where there has been little change in market conditions and little reliance by the seller, the parties will generally ignore the contract and contract law and allow the buyer to cancel without cost (except, perhaps, compensation for easily observable costs incurred by the seller). If the contract is a large one in which the seller is likely to incur considerable contract-specific costs before delivering the goods to the buyer, then the contract will probably provide for this by including progress payments, liquidated damages, or some other mechanism for assuring the seller some compensation prior to delivery. Between these two extremes, the Code's default rule might be significant.

This suggests two types of empirical questions to which we do not have answers. First, do parties typically contract to avoid 2-708(2)? If buyer's forms generally waive liability for the seller's lost profits arising from a cancellation and the seller's form holds otherwise, which term wins? Second, where the buyer would be legally liable, under what circumstances will sellers pursue their legal remedies? Are sellers protecting their reliance interest? Are they reacting to buyers who breached to take advantage of a better offer? Are they responding to the possibility of a large windfall? To what extent does reputation with the trade suffer when sellers seek to recover lost profits?

PART V

Specific performance and the cost of completion

The standard remedy for breach of contract is monetary damages. However, under certain circumstances – notably, when the subject matter of the contract is "unique" – the victim of a breach can obtain specific performance. There has been considerable debate about the appropriate scope of the specific performance remedy and about its efficacy relative to damages in varying contexts. Anthony Kronman (1978) argues that the uniqueness distinction is an appropriate one for demarcating the domain of the specific performance remedy. Steven Shavell (1984) emphasizes the distinction between contracts "to do" and contracts "to give." Alan Schwartz (1979) and Thomas Ulen (1984) argue that the specific performance remedy should be routinely available to promisees. All of these invoke economic analysis to justify their conclusions. In Selection [5.1], William Bishop provides another economic analysis that proposes a slight modification of Shavell's distinction. I present some further thoughts on the specific performance remedy in Selection [5.2]. Part V concludes with Timothy Muris's [5.3] analysis of the merits of two alternative damage measures: the cost of completion versus diminution of value. Analytically, the problem turns out to be nearly the same as the specific performance versus damages question.

CHAPTER 5.1

The choice of remedy for breach
of contract

WILLIAM BISHOP (1985)

French contract law distinguishes between contracts "to do" and contracts "to give," with damages as the normal remedy for the former and
specific performance as normal remedy for the latter. A contract to
design an aircraft is a contract to do. A contract to sell an aircraft is a
contract to give. A contract to build an aircraft to a certain design, and
then to transfer ownership of it, is a contract both to do and to give.
The distinction corresponds to the commonsense distinction between
contracts for services and contracts for conveyance of land or chattels,
with an intermediate area where goods are to be made in accordance
with customized terms.

Steven Shavell has built a formal economic model of contract remedies that suggests that the French solution is the appropriate one,
though he notes that the common law (damages as the general remedy)
and German law (specific performance as the general remedy) in practice
reach much the same solution by different routes, at least in the most
important cases. Shavell's mathematical approach will make his paper
impenetrable to most lawyers, yet its core is really fairly simple and
analytically not very different from the informal models used by Kronman and Schwartz.

Shavell considers the case of a buyer who after contract must undertake some fixed reliance (to abstract from a difficult problem) and
a seller who is subject to uncertainty about the cost of his contractual
promise, only learning about the true cost of performance after the
buyer has relied. Where the true cost exceeds the buyer's expectancy it

Reprinted from William Bishop, "The Choice of Remedy for Breach of Contract," *Journal
of Legal Studies* 14 (1985): 299–320, with the permission of the author and The University
of Chicago Press.

is not in the parties' joint interest to proceed, since the seller would save so much by not performing that he could compensate the buyer by a sum equivalent to the expectancy and still have something left over, constituting a net social gain. The central problem for contract remedies is the usual one: to devise a system that *both* avoids breaches of contracts that are worth performing and avoids performances of contracts that are not worth the cost.

Consider first the contract to do where the seller faces uncertainty about production cost. If the buyer is protected by a damages rule and if the court awards the buyer accurate expectation damages, then the seller will breach when and only when it is efficient for him to do so. But if the court underestimates the buyer's expectation, then there will be excessive breach. If the buyer is protected by specific performance, then there will be no danger of excessive breach but there will be a danger of excessive performance. Regardless which rule is in force the parties can negotiate to reduce such problems . . . though there will still be some cost since negotiations themselves are costly. For contracts to do these problems are intractable. It is not possible wholly to avoid both costs, only to keep them to a minimum. Common-law courts evidently consider the potential costs of excessive breach to be less serious than the costs of excessive performance, since they confine the buyer to a damages remedy.

The contract to give, however, can be entirely different. Here the uncertainty faced by the seller is not about production cost but about later offers of purchase at a higher price. Often these offers will be available to the buyer just as easily as to the seller. If so and if the buyer is protected by specific performance, then there is no danger of excessive performance, because where the value to the third party is higher than the buyer's expectancy the third party will offer a price that induces the buyer to resell to the third party. (The analysis assumes that transfer costs for the subsequent transactions are unimportant.) By contrast, if the buyer is protected by damages, given that the courts can make mistakes, a potentially costly problem of excessive breach remains. So it seems that for contracts to give, the efficient remedy is specific performance.

Note that the crucial assumption is that in contracts to give seller and buyer have equal access to the bids made by third parties. This is reasonable for land transactions when potential purchasers have no difficulty in finding owners with whom to deal. It is far less appealing for sale of goods where, if one party is a dealer and another a user, the dealer usually will be more visible to potential alternative offerers. Shavell might just as plausibly have concluded that the common-law rule of automatic specific performance for land sales is more appealing than the civilian rule of general specific performance for all contracts of sale.

* * *

An important lacuna in Shavell's analysis is opened up by his concentration on seller's breach to the exclusion of buyer's breach, for in buyer's breach cases the relevant considerations are rather different. In Shavell's model the only uncertainty is about seller's production cost (in the case of contracts to do) or about alternative bids (in the case of contracts to give). Consider the converse case of no seller's uncertainty at all, but some buyer's uncertainty about the value to himself of the contract at date of performance. Assume initially that complications of variable reliance can be ignored. What remedial term is in the antecedent interest of the two parties to the contract?

Consider sale of goods and suppose that the buyer decides before time of delivery that he does not need the goods. For concreteness suppose the good is to be a component in some more complex manufactured good, the market for which has just collapsed. Here instead of *two* wanting to buy at or above the contract price (the original buyer and the third party) there is often *no one* who wants to buy at that price. Here any automatic assumption of equal access to bids will be very implausible. Sometimes the buyer might be just as good at making an alternative sale as the seller, but often, perhaps usually, he will not be as good at it. This is especially so where the seller is a dealer and the buyer a consumer or an occasional user. The efficient complete contingent contract would exploit this cost advantage by having the *seller* seek resale. The parties would fail to do this only if the saving in doing so is outweighed by a very serious problem of inefficient breach arising from the courts' underestimation of the seller's expectancy. As always, we are ultimately concerned only with transaction costs magnitudes since the buyer could purchase from the seller a release from his obligation to take goods still undelivered, or even pay the seller to take back the goods for resale, as circumstances require.

On the other hand, where the seller has no advantage over the buyer in reselling, the complete contingent contract would allow him specific performance. Once the seller has completed all substantial steps toward performance, any tradeoff between the problem of excessive breach and the problem of excessive performance disappears. For once the seller has finished committing resources to performance, by definition, there can no longer be any perverse incentive for excessive use of resources. What does remain is the possibility of excessive breach by the buyer, and this can be avoided by allowing the seller specific performance once he has substantially performed his side of the bargain.

124

* * *

The foregoing analysis of sales cases applies also to cases of contracts to do. The only real difference is this. In many cases of sales contracts, completion costs, in the sense of expenditure needed to make the good, are very small or even nonexistent because the goods are held in inventory. Therefore such contracts will often be those in which specific performance rights for the seller are necessarily efficient from the moment the contract is concluded. This will *not* necessarily be true (though sometimes on balance it is true) in cases of contracts to do, where the tradeoff between excessive breach and excessive performance is always relevant, since the "doing" can waste resources.

To sum up, the choice between expectation damages and specific performance turns on the following ... crucial variables: (1) the expected cost of excessive breach due to court's errors under expectation damages; (2) the expected cost of excessive performance under a specific performance rule. ... The critical point is this: The value of the second of these variables will diminish as the contract performance moves from the purely executory stage to the stage of substantially complete performance. Since the tradeoff between this cost of excessive performance and the cost of excessive breach is at the core of the policy choice the law must make, it will be efficient to switch from damages to specific performance depending on how complete performance is ...

The essence of Shavell's case for a distinction between contracts to do and contracts to give is that for contracts to give there is no loss from inefficient performance, since the contract is purely a contract to transfer *title*. This requires little use of resources and hence potential costs of wasteful performance are small. The essence of the case for specific relief on substantial completion of a contract of sale or of a contract to do rests on the same logic: Once all resources are committed, there remains in these contracts one issue only, and that is the same issue, the transfer of title.

125

CHAPTER 5.2

Relational exchange, contract law, and the *Boomer* problem (2)

VICTOR P. GOLDBERG (1985)

The specific performance remedy provides...[an] illustration [of the *Boomer* problem]. Confining a buyer to a court-determined measure of damages short-circuits the market mechanism preventing the buyer from registering his true preferences. On the other hand, if after a seller's breach, performance is expensive and is of little value to the buyer, granting the buyer an injunction would result in "economic waste." The waste will not, except by accident, entail actual performance of the obligation. Rather, as in *Boomer*, it would entail excessive rent seeking by the two parties.

Suppose that the costs that a buyer would incur if the contract were breached exceeded the damages that he could collect. In that case the seller would have an incentive to use the threat of termination to redefine the contract on more favorable terms. The buyer can be shielded from this threat by granting him specific performance so that the seller could not legally carry out his threat. This is very similar to allowing the buyer to invoke duress to disallow the contract modification that the threat produced. In both cases, the costs of rent seeking are avoided.

But avoidance of these costs itself involves costs. It encourages buyers to get into such situations in the first place.* The routine granting of specific performance (just as a policy of liberal acceptance of the duress excuse or routine compensation of consequential damages) would in

---

* In the absence of a specific performance remedy, parties can achieve the same result by going beyond contract, a mere exchange of promises, and instead transferring title. In the commercial context this might entail shifting from a supply contract to vertical integration.

Reprinted from Victor P. Goldberg, "Relational Exchange, Contract Law, and the *Boomer* Problem, *Zeitschrift für die gesamte Staatswissenschaft/Journal of Institutional and Theoretical Economics* 141 (1985): 570–5, with the permission of the publisher.

many instances provide perverse incentives to promisees inducing over-reliance on the contract. They could maintain tiny inventories, build machines that require inputs from a single supplier, and so forth, knowing that the specific performance remedy would bail them out.

This is not to say, of course, that specific performance would inevitably be a poor remedy. In many instances the incentives to over-rely on the other party's performance will be minimal and they will easily be outweighed by the discouragement of opportunistic rebargaining by the promisor. In other instances, however, this will not be the case. Making specific performance a remedy available at the discretion of the court rather than of the promisee is one way of achieving the distinction. The court could exercise its discretion when the probability that perverse incentives would exist is quite low or even when the probability is high, but the promisee has avoided making itself excessively vulnerable. Put another way, when the promisee argues that assessing damages would give it an inadequate remedy, the court can ask whether the inadequacy was the fault of the promisee. The greater its responsibility for its present position, the greater the likelihood that the court would confine it to a money damages remedy.

* * *

Cost of completion or diminution in market value: the relevance of subjective value

TIMOTHY J. MURIS (1983)

In contract cases – typically construction or mining cases – courts frequently measure the damages of the innocent party either by the diminution in the market value at the time of breach from less than perfect performance or by the cost of rendering performance perfect. The diminution measure is objective; that is, observers external to the contract, such as the judge or jury in a lawsuit, can ascertain its amount with reasonable accuracy at a tolerable cost. Yet this objective measure can undercompensate the aggrieved party, thereby contradicting contract law's principle that damages should place the injured party in the same position as if the contract were performed. For example, consider construction of a family dwelling that deviates from the contract specifications by changing the location and size of some of the rooms while leaving the total square footage of the house unchanged. This breach need not diminish market value: Preferences for housing style vary considerably, and the builder might simply sell the house to another buyer at the price the original purchasing party had offered. Nevertheless, the original purchaser may value the house promised more highly than the house actually delivered. Because market value did not decrease, there is no damage by the objective measure. Nevertheless, damage does exist, albeit of a nonpecuniary or subjective nature.

* * *

Any decision to ignore subjective value cannot rest on the ground that such damages are either unreal or frivolous – this argument is patently false. Instead, the decision must rest on more prudential con-

Reprinted from Timothy J. Muris, "Cost of Completion or Diminution in Market Value: The Relevance of Subjective Value," *Journal of Legal Studies* (1983): 379–400, with the permission of the author and The University of Chicago Press.

siderations, namely, that the costs of determining subjective value exceed any allocative benefits that the determination might yield. This conclusion assumes that fact finders can only guess at the appropriate award, thereby reducing the costs of inaccurate (i.e., noncompensatory) awards little, if at all. The increased costs from litigating over subjective value could be substantial, particularly because nonbreachers would have an incentive to claim subjective losses even when they did not exist. If these costs produce no benefit in increasing the accuracy of damage awards, then direct recognition of subjective value is unwarranted.

* * *

[Suppose that P agrees to build a house for N.]... Assume that... part way through construction... N discovers that P is not making the agreed-upon changes, perhaps because his employees misread the plans or because the employees deliberately diverted resources elsewhere. To make the change at this stage, P would have to undo some of the work already done at an expense of $3,000. If the house is completed per the original specifications, the market value will not drop. Thus, at this stage in the contract, cost ($3,000) exceeds diminution ($0).

The question arises whether cost or diminution best protects N's subjective value, if any. The answer is complex, depending upon how the parties will act under the alternative awards. The cost award protects subjective value, because cost is equivalent to awarding specific performance. Awarding cost, however, may cause expenses that make protection of subjective value not worth the effort. To understand this point, one must first realize that... the cost of completion does not necessarily measure subjective value. Indeed... cost could greatly exceed the amount necessary to protect subjective value even if the diminution award is inadequate, as cost may vary with factors unrelated to subjective value, such as how much work must be redone.

Similarly, if N has no subjective value or if cost would overcompensate N's subjective value, the cost award will cause costs of its own. Assume for the sake of illustration that $500 would make N indifferent between receiving the revised performance or the money. N and P then have an incentive to negotiate a settlement of N's claim against P for some amount between $3,000 and $500. N has no incentive to reveal the true amount for which he will settle, and, to force negotiations, P may have to threaten to complete performance. However the process occurs, settlement negotiations could be quite costly, particularly given that no legal principles determine the expected judicial damages award. Indeed, it is now an elementary principle in economics that such forced bargaining can lead to significant costs.

Another cost of an overcompensatory award is that P will take more

129

care to perform according to specifications. Because the cost award will increase liability (relative to the diminution award) by the negotiation costs plus the amount the settlement exceeds diminution, P will increase expenditures to prevent breach up to the expected savings, which equal these extra costs discounted by the probability of breach. For example, P may exercise more supervision over his employees or he may negotiate a stipulated damage clause to limit his damages upon breach. Whether these expenditures are significant will vary with the factual circumstances. The full amount of these expenditures by P are not merely added to the forced bargaining costs, however, because their existence reduces the need for forced bargains. If P negotiates a limit on damages, the risk of being subjected to forced bargaining would be eliminated.

The cost-of-completion award thus has costs as well as benefits. The relevant issue for protecting subjective value, therefore, involves comparing these costs and benefits with those that would occur with the diminution award. Awarding the diminution in market value avoids forced bargaining, but it sometimes underprotects subjective value. With diminution, innocent parties who value specific performance more than the market have an incentive to protect themselves. For example, they can increase expenditures on investigating those with whom they contract, or they can negotiate stipulated damage clauses for the amount of subjective value. If stipulated damages are used, N has the incentive to set the damages at the proper level, for he has no desire to pay for protection that he does not in fact want. Yet if diminution is the judicial standard, there is some risk that the clause itself – if far above the diminution level – will be challenged (at least under current doctrine) as an illegal penalty clause, thus inviting a costly and uncertain legal proceeding.

In contrast, cost as a presumptive benchmark has one clear advantage given the current judicial attitudes to penalty clauses. Even with cost as the presumptive judicial measure, the parties should wish to calculate subjective value properly. With cost, then, any negotiated clause will be normally for a lesser amount than the law itself allows. Legal challenges to the validity of the clause will therefore be more difficult to mount, given that these limitations upon damages are routinely enforced, while estimated damage clauses are subject to far greater scrutiny. A second advantage of cost over diminution is that the cost of completion may often be easier to calculate than the drop in market value. Although resources spent on determining diminution will be limited by the spread between the reasonable high and the reasonable low estimate for that measure, parties can simply venture into the market to calculate cost. To calculate diminution, they must use costly expert testimony.

. . . Many courts and some commentators argue that, in construction cases, the nonbreaching party should receive the cost of completion unless that award will result in excessive "economic waste." The concern is that awarding cost would mean undoing, and therefore wasting, work already completed. As has been noted elsewhere, in this form the argument is erroneous. . . . [U]ndoing of work would occur only if it is beneficial. If N values exact performance at less than cost, he will offer P a settlement between cost and his own subjective value if P insists upon performing to specification. Nor will N spend the money received on completing performance under this assumption. Only if N values exact performance at or above the cost of completion will the work be redone. Under this assumption, rework is not wasteful in the sense of producing value not worth the expense to the buyer.

Nonetheless waste can occur, at least if that term is not confined to the meaning given it in the decided cases. As before, expensive negotiations are the culprit, as the parties try to settle the case at some figure between cost and subjective value. The greater the gap between these two numbers, the greater the expenses incurred upon breach, and so too the economic waste. At least two factors are relevant in determining that the cost award is so excessive as to indicate that settlement costs from awarding cost are likely to exceed any benefits from protecting subjective value. First is the reason that the cost of completion exceeds the drop in market value. If market value has dropped and the cost has not changed over time (meaning that the original purchase price still reflects the cost of the entire job), cost is probably not an excessive award, because the original price reflects N's subjective value. The second factor is the amount of undoing and redoing work that comprises the cost figure. Because these factors are not correlated with N's subjective value, the higher the percentage they comprise, the more likely it will be that the cost of completion greatly exceeds N's subjective value, all else equal.

To summarize this discussion . . . it appears that neither measure of damages dominates the other under all circumstances. It remains to be asked, therefore, what judicial strategy should be adopted in the face of this uncertainty. One possibility is to adopt a single rule for all circumstances. This approach reduces the costs associated with judicial fine-tuning. It also cuts down the errors in judicial application and provides parties with a certain baseline, should they wish to draft damage provisions for themselves. Exceptions might be desired in those cases in which the parties themselves would wish to escape the consequences of the uniform rule, but these should be kept simple and easy to understand, as appears to be the case with the consumer/business distinction and with the economic waste exception already discussed.

* * *

Questions and notes on specific performance and cost of completion

1. Suppose Smith enters into a contract selling a unique antique chair to Brown for $500. Along comes Jones who was totally unaware of the contract with Brown. Jones offers Smith $800. Note that this is a case in which the subject matter of the contract is unique and the contract is one "to give," both of these being conditions that most commentators say favor granting of specific performance.

   1.1. Should Brown be granted an injunction?

   1.2. If Jones gave Smith the $800 and took the chair home with him, should Brown be granted specific performance? What would that entail? Would it require voiding the Jones–Smith transaction? Or would Smith have to buy back the chair from Jones?

   1.3. If he were denied specific performance, what would Brown's damage remedy be? How would the market price be measured?

   1.4. If specific performance is infeasible after Jones has taken possession, the only circumstances in which the remedy would be feasible would be when Brown learned of a not-yet-executed substitute contract that he could then enjoin. Notice that Brown could have easily gotten a stronger remedy than specific performance by taking title instead of simply entering into a contract. If Smith then sold the chair to Jones there would be a civil action in conversion, and probably a criminal action as well. Why then would an antique dealer ever enter into an executory contract rather than simply exchanging title?

   1.5. People dealing in antiques will rarely take the time to negotiate the precise terms of a sale. What remedy do you think reasonable parties would choose if they were to take the time to draft carefully an appropriate contract?

2. Relate the *Boomer* problem to Bishop's concept of "excessive performance," and Muris's discussion of "economic waste."

3. A grower of carrots has a contract to deliver his entire crop to a canner. There is a shortage of this particular type of carrot and the market price rises to three times the contract price. The seller threatens to sell elsewhere unless the contract price is renegotiated. The canner's loss in the event of breach could be much greater than the price difference. If he has to buy an inferior variety of carrot as a substitute, he might have his reputation for quality harmed and suffer a loss of consumer good will. Or he might choose not to can products that required a special quality of carrots. This might entail producing a product mix that is not as profitable or it might entail keeping some production lines idle for part of the canning season. Even if these damages could be accurately reckoned by a court, the seller might end up judgment-proof and the buyer would be out of luck.* Should the seller be granted specific performance? (See *Campbell v. Wentz.*)

4. One criterion for granting specific performance adopted by the courts is "uniqueness." In consumer contracts, the notion is that the individual might value certain items at much more than their market price; to make the consumer whole it would be necessary to compensate him for the loss of this idiosyncratic value. In commercial contracts it is reasonable to presume that firms want particular items not for sentimental reasons, but because they expect that the items will contribute to profit. Uniqueness in this context means that the buyer is especially reliant on this particular seller. If the contract were terminated it would incur considerable costs. To turn this around, if the buyer can cover simply by purchasing identical goods from another supplier, the goods are not unique. In such a case, the damage remedy is perfectly adequate and the only reason for wanting the option of specific performance would be the relative cost of the remedies. For unique goods, since the buyer would incur considerable costs if it had to replace this particular seller, it is not indifferent. If the subject matter of the contract is unique in this sense, should the promisee be granted specific performance? How does this question relate to the issue of the compensability of consequential damages?

---

* The possibility that a promisor would go bankrupt and not be able to pay a damage claim is present even in the simplest of discrete transactions. A grant of specific performance to a promisee who would otherwise be an unsecured creditor has the effect of changing the promisee's priority vis à vis other creditors. The merits of granting specific performance to counter the possibility that the promisor will be unable to pay damages cannot be judged independently of the policy considerations underlying the system of assigning claims to secured and unsecured creditors. That question, while fascinating, is beyond the scope of this book.

5. The often-raised practical objection to the specific performance remedy is that it presents the court with a problem of supervision. A similar problem arises, however, with a damage rule and it is not at all obvious that the problem would be more serious for specific performance. Develop an alternative to Shavell's explanation of the French distinction between contracts "to do" and "to give" that rests on the relative ease of supervising the latter.

6. In the dispute between N and P in Muris's hypothetical, if the court orders the defaulting builder to pay the cost of completion, would there be any opportunity for strategic bargaining? Why does Muris treat this as one of the costs of overcompensation?

7. Suppose a plastic surgeon promises a client an improved nose. The operation, however, makes the nose worse than it was before. What should the damages be?
    (a) The doctor's fees (restitution)?
    (b) The costs incurred by the client, including, in addition to the doctor's fees, hospital fees, and pain and suffering (reliance)?
    (c) The expected value of the promised nose?
    (d) The cost of producing the promised nose (cost of completion)?
    The first three options are considered in *Sullivan v. O'Connor* and *Hawkins v. McGee.*

8. The National Computer Company (NCC) sold a computer system to Chapman Products for $50,000. The system was purchased for the express purpose of handling Chapman's payroll and inventory control functions. The equipment and programs never worked properly, however, and after a year of trying to work things out, Chapman sued for breach of contract. It asked for consequential damages (the costs of not having the promised system in place) and the costs of replacing NCC's system with one that would perform the functions as originally promised. It introduced testimony by an expert witness that such a system would cost $200,000. (See *Chatlos Systems Inc. v. National Cash Register Corp..*)

8.1. Should Chapman be awarded consequential damages?

8.2. Should it be awarded the $200,000 that would enable it to put in a system that would do what NCC had originally promised?

8.3. Suppose that NCC was held liable for the $200,000. What do you think the effect would be on future contracts entered into by computer firms?

8.4. Try to draft a limitation on liability for the computer company that would be acceptable to a knowing buyer. Recall that the lower the seller's liability, the less a buyer would be willing to pay.

8.5. Suppose that performing the task wasn't feasible. Even if one spent $10 million, a computer would not be able to perform the task. Should the court give an award in excess of $200,000? Should it declare performance impossible and excuse NCC?

9. NCC promised a system that would perform certain functions. Suppose that instead it had promised to install a computer system that was intended to solve Chapman's problems. This would be analogous to the doctor promising to perform an operation intended to improve the patient's nose. That is, the seller promises only *the delivery of inputs* not *the quality of the outcome*. How should that effect the seller's liability?

9.1. If it is unclear as to whether the seller is promising delivery of inputs or a specific outcome, what should the default rule be? Do you think that as a general rule parties would promise a specific outcome?

PART VI

Power, governance, and the penalty clause puzzle

In a discrete transaction, the parties need not rely upon performance by a particular trading partner. For many exchange relationships, however, that is not the case. Having entered into a contract with a particular supplier, a buyer will find that the costs of leaving this contract and dealing with an alternative supplier are high. The buyer's dependence on continued dealing with this supplier gives the supplier power over the buyer in the sense that the seller can threaten to impose costs on the buyer unless it acted in a certain way.

The first two selections are concerned with some issues regarding power within the contractual relationship. While Klein [6.1] focuses primarily on franchise contracts and I [6.2] focus on the employment relationship, much of the analysis is relevant to a broader class of contracts. The crucial point is that the power is not necessarily bad; rational parties often want to set up their relationship so that one party will be able to exercise power over the other. At the same time, they often want to utilize some devices for governing the exercise of that power. This might entail reliance on reputation with the trade, public enforcement, explicit contract terms, establishment of a private dispute resolution apparatus, or some combination of these.

Klein's central point is that it will often be the case that the most efficient arrangement will entail apparently unfair contracts. One party will be able to impose a substantial penalty on the other. The penalty might sometimes be explicit in the form of a penal bond or a liquidated damages clause, but often it would only be implicit, a sacrifice of some relation-specific assets upon termination of the agreement. Courts, he argues, should be very careful about second-guessing such arrangements. Apparently unfair contracts might, when looked at ex ante, have very desirable features.

In the next selection, I discuss (but do not resolve) a puzzle. Protection from termination is valuable to workers (and franchisees). If they act individually, they are rarely able to get such protection in contracts with employers (or franchisors). However, they have pursued the goal through collective action and have achieved substantial success. If job security is not worth the price in one-on-one contracts, why are the workers and franchisees willing to pay the price when they act collectively?

Richard Posner (1979, p. 290), who argues that the common law tends toward efficiency, views the judicial hostility to penalty clauses as a puzzle: "[T]he refusal of the common law to enforce penalty clauses . . . , which apparently promotes inefficiency, remains a major unexplained puzzle in the economic theory of the common law." Clarkson, Miller, and Muris [6.3] attempt to provide an efficiency-based explanation and claim that it reflects the pattern of decisions. While they identify an interesting problem, they have not fully explained the judicial hostility to penalty clauses and forfeitures. In the final selection, I suggest that although there might be plausible economic grounds for not enforcing certain penalty clauses, hostility to penalty clauses goes well beyond what economic analysis would suggest is appropriate.

Transaction cost determinants of "unfair" contractual arrangements

BENJAMIN KLEIN (1980)

Terms such as "unfair" are foreign to the economic model of voluntary exchange which implies anticipated gains to all transactors. However, much recent statutory, regulatory and antitrust activity has run counter to this economic paradigm of the efficiency properties of "freedom of contract." The growth of "dealer day in court" legislation, FTC franchise regulations, favorable judicial consideration of "unequal bargaining power," and unconscionability arguments, are some examples of the recent legal propensity to "protect" transactors. This is done by declaring unenforceable or illegal particular contractual provisions that, although voluntarily agreed upon in the face of significant competition, appear to be one-sided or unfair. Presentation of the standard abstract economic analysis of the mutual gains from voluntary exchange is unlikely to be an effective counterweight to this recent legal movement without an explicit attempt to provide a positive rationale for the presence of the particular unfair contractual term. This paper considers some transaction costs that might explain the voluntary adoption of contractual provisions such as termination at will and long-term exclusive dealing clauses that have been under legal attack.

I. The "holdup" problem

* * *

Given the presence of incomplete contractual arrangements, wealth-maximizing transactors have the ability and often the incentive to renege

Reprinted from Benjamin Klein, "Transaction Cost Determinants of 'Unfair' Contractual Arrangements," *American Economic Review, Papers and Proceedings* 70 (1980): 356–62, with the permission of the author and the American Economic Association.

on the transaction by holding up the other party, in the sense of taking advantage of unspecified or unenforceable elements of the contractual relationship. Such behavior is, by definition, unanticipated and not a long-run equilibrium phenomenon. Oliver Williamson [1975] has identified and discussed this phenomenon of "opportunistic behavior," and my recent paper with Robert Crawford and Armen Alchian [1978] attempted to make operational some of the conditions under which this holdup potential is likely to be large. In addition to contract costs, and therefore the incompleteness of the explicit contract, we emphasized the presence of appropriable quasi-rents due to highly firm-specific investments. After a firm invests in an asset with a low-salvage value and a quasi-rent stream highly dependent upon some other asset, the owner of the other asset has the potential to hold up by appropriating the quasi-rent stream. For example, one would not build a house on land rented for a short term. After the rental agreement expires, the landowner could raise the rental price to reflect the costs of moving the house to another lot.*

* * *

II. Contractual solutions

Since the magnitude of the potential holdup may be anticipated, the party to be cheated can merely decrease the initial price he will pay by the amount of the appropriable quasi-rents. For example, if an employer knows that an employee will cheat a certain amount each period, it will be reflected in the employee's wage. Contracts can be usefully thought to refer to anticipated rather than stated performance. Therefore the employee's behavior should not even be considered "cheating." A secretary, for example, may miss work one day a week on average. If secretary time is highly substitutable, the employer can cut the secretary's weekly wage 20 percent, hire 20 percent more secretaries, and be indifferent. The secretary, on the other hand, presumably values the leisure more than the additional income and therefore is better off.

---

* This problem is different from the standard monopoly or bilateral monopoly problem for two reasons. First, market power is created only after the house investment is made on a particular piece of land. Such postinvestment power can therefore exist in many situations that are purely competitive preinvestment. Second, the problem we are discussing deals with the difficulties of contract enforcement. Even if some preinvestment monopoly power exists (for example, a union supplier of labor services to harvest a crop), if one can write an enforceable contract preinvestment (i.e., before the planting), the present discounted value of the monopoly return may be significantly less than the one-time postinvestment holdup potential (which may equal the entire value of a crop ready to be harvested).

Rather than cheating, we have a voluntarily determined, utility-maximizing contractual relationship.

In many cases, however, letting the party cheat and discounting his wage will not be an economical solution because the gain to the cheater and therefore his acceptable compensating wage discount is less than the cost to the firm from the cheating behavior. For example, it is easy to imagine many cases where a shirking manager will impose costs on the firm much greater than his personal gains. Therefore the stockholders cannot be made indifferent to this behavior by cutting his salary and hiring more lazy managers. The general point is that there may not be perfect substitutability between quantity and quality of particular services. Hence, even if one knew that an unspecified element of quality would be reduced by a certain amount in attempting the holdup, an ex ante compensatory discount in the quoted price of the promised high-quality service to the cost of providing the anticipated lower-quality supply would not make the demander of the service indifferent. Individuals would be willing to expend real resources to set up contractual arrangements to prevent such opportunism and assure high-quality supply.

The question then becomes how much of the holdup problem can be avoided by an explicit government-enforced contract, and how much remains to be handled by an implicit self-enforcing contract. This latter type of contract is one where opportunistic behavior is prevented by the threat of termination of the business relationship rather than by the threat of litigation. A transactor will not cheat if the expected present discounted value of quasi-rents he is earning from a relationship is greater than the immediate holdup wealth gain. The capital loss that can be imposed on the potential cheater by the withdrawal of expected future business is then sufficient to deter cheating.

... [O]ne way in which the future-promised rewards necessary to prevent cheating can be arranged is by the payment of a sufficiently high-price "premium." This premium stream can usefully be thought of as "protection money" paid to assure noncheating behavior. The magnitude of this price premium will be related to the potential holdup, that is, to the extent of contractual incompleteness and the degree of specific capital present. In equilibrium, the present discounted value of the price–premium stream will be exactly equal to the appropriable quasi-rents, making the potential cheater indifferent between cheating and not. But the individual paying the premium will be in a preferable position as long as the differential consumer's surplus from high-quality (noncheating) supply is greater than the premium.

One method by which this equilibrium quasi-rent stream can be achieved without the existence of positive firm profits is by having the potential cheater put up a forfeitable-at-will collateral bond equal to the discounted value of the premium stream. Alternatively, the potential cheater may make a highly firm-specific productive investment which will have only a low-salvage value if he cheats and loses future business. The gap between price and salvageable capital costs is analytically equivalent to a premium stream with the nonsalvageable asset analytically equivalent to a forfeitable collateral bond.

III. "Unfair" contractual terms

Most actual contractual arrangements consist of a combination of explicit- and implicit-enforcement mechanisms. Some elements of performance will be specified and enforced by third-party sanctions. The residual elements of performance will be enforced without invoking the power of some outside party to the transaction but merely by the threat of termination of the transactional relationship. The details of any particular contract will consist of forms of these general elements chosen to minimize transaction costs (for example, hiring lawyers to discover contingencies and draft explicit terms, paying quality-assurance premiums, and investing in nonsalvageable "brand name" assets) and may imply the existence of what appears to be unfair contract terms.

Consider, for example, the initial capital requirements and termination provisions common in most franchise contractual arrangements. These apparently one-sided terms may be crucial elements of minimum-cost quality-policing arrangements. Given the difficulty of explicitly specifying and enforcing contractually every element of quality to be supplied by a franchisee, there is an incentive for an individual opportunistic franchisee to cheat the franchisor by supplying a lower quality of product than contracted for. Because the franchisee uses a common trademark, this behavior depreciates the reputation and hence the future profit stream of the franchisor.

The franchisor knows, given his direct policing and monitoring expenditures, the expected profit that a franchisee can obtain by cheating. For example, given the number of inspectors hired, he knows the expected time to detect a cheater; given the costs of low-quality inputs, he knows the expected extra short-run cheating profit that can be earned. Therefore the franchisor may require an initial lump-sum payment from the franchisee equal to this estimated short-run gain from cheating. This is equivalent to a collateral bond forfeitable at the will of the franchisor. The franchisee will earn a normal rate of return on that bond if he does not cheat, but it will be forfeited if he does cheat and is terminated.

In many cases franchisee noncheating rewards may be increased and short-run cheating profits decreased (and therefore franchisor direct policing costs reduced) by the grant of an exclusive territory or the enforcement of minimum resale price restraints. . . . [T]he franchisor may require franchisees to rent from them short term (rather than own) the land upon which their outlet is located. This lease arrangement creates a situation where termination implies that the franchisor can require the franchisee to move and thereby impose a capital loss on him up to the amount of his initial nonsalvageable investment. Hence a form of collateral to deter franchisee cheating is created.

It is important to recognize that franchise termination, if it is to assure quality compliance on the part of franchisees, must be unfair in the sense that the capital cost imposed on the franchisee that will optimally prevent cheating must be larger than the gain to the franchisee from cheating. Given that less than infinite resources are spent by the frenchisor to monitor quality, there is some probability that franchisee cheating will go undetected. Therefore termination must become equivalent to a criminal-type sanction. Rather than the usually analyzed case of costlessly detected and policed contract breach, where the remedy of making the breaching party pay the cost of the damages of his specific breach makes economic sense, the sanction here must be large enough to make the expected net gain from cheating equal to zero. The transacting parties contractually agree upon a penalty-type sanction for breach as a means of economizing on direct policing costs. Because contract enforcement costs (including litigation costs which generally are not collectable by the innocent party in the United States) are not zero, this analysis provides a rationale against the common-law prohibition of penalty clauses.

The obvious concern with such seemingly unfair contractual arrangements is the possibility that the franchisor may engage in opportunistic behavior by terminating a franchisee without cause, claiming the franchise fee and purchasing the initial franchisee investment at a distress price. Such behavior may be prevented by the depreciation of the franchisor's brand name and therefore decreased future demand by potential franchisees to join the arrangement. However, this protective mechanism is limited by the relative importance of new franchise sales compared to the continuing franchising operation, that is, by the "maturity" of the franchise chain.

More importantly, what limits reverse cheating by franchisors is the possible increased cost of operating the chain through an employee operation compared to a franchise operation when such cheating is communicated among franchisees. As long as the implicit collateral bond put up by the franchisee is less than the present discounted value of this cost difference, franchisor cheating will be deterred. Although explicit bonds and price premium payments cannot simultaneously be made by both the franchisee and the franchisor, the discounted value of the cost difference has the effect of a collateral bond put up by the franchisor to assure his noncheating behavior. This explains why the franchisor does not increase the initial franchise fee to an arbitrarily high level and correspondingly decrease its direct policing expenditures and the probability of detecting franchisee cheating. While such offsetting changes could continue to optimally deter franchisee cheating and save the real resource cost of direct policing, the profit from and hence the incentive for reverse franchisor cheating would become too great for the arrangement to be stable.

Franchisees voluntarily signing these agreements obviously understand the termination-at-will clause separate from the legal consequences of that term to mean nonopportunistic franchisor termination. But this does not imply that the court should judge each termination on these unwritten but understood contract terms and attempt to determine if franchisor cheating has occurred. Franchisees also must recognize that by signing these agreements they are relying on the implicit market-enforcement mechanism outlined above, and not the court, to prevent franchisor cheating. It is costly to use the court to regulate these terminations because elements of performance are difficult to contractually specify and to measure. In addition, litigation is costly and time consuming, during which time the brand name of the franchisor can be depreciated further. If these costs were not large and the court could cheaply and quickly determine when franchisor cheating had occurred, the competitive process regarding the establishment of contract terms would lead transactors to settle on explicit governmentally enforceable contracts rather than rely on this implicit market-enforcement mechanism.

The potential error here is, after recognizing the importance of transaction costs and the incomplete "relational" nature of most real-world contracts, to rely too strongly on the government as a regulator of unspecified terms. While it is important for economic theory to handle significant contract costs and incomplete explicit contractual arrangements, such complexity does not imply a broad role for government. Rather, all that is implied is a role for brand names and the corresponding implicit market-enforcement mechanism I have outlined.

IV. Unequal bargaining power

An argument made against contract provisions such as termination-at-will clauses is that they appear to favor one party at the expense of another. Hence it is alleged that the terms of the agreement must have been reached under conditions of "unequal bargaining power" and therefore should be invalid. However, a further implication of the above analysis is that when both parties can cheat, explicit contractual restraints are often placed on the smaller, less well-established party (the franchisee), while an implicit brand-name contract-enforcement mechanism is relied on to prevent cheating by the larger, more well-established party (the franchisor).

If information regarding quality of a product supplied by a large firm is communicated among many small buyers who do not all purchase simultaneously, the potential holdup relative to, say, annual sales is reduced substantially compared to the case where each buyer purchased from a separate independent small firm. There are likely to be economies of scale in the supply of a business brand name, because in effect the large firm's total brand-name capital is put on the line with each individual sale. This implies a lower cost of using the implicit contract mechanism, that is, a lower-price premium necessary to assure non-breach, for a large firm compared to a small firm. Therefore one side of the contract will be relatively more incomplete.

For example, in a recent English case using the doctrine of inequality of bargaining power to bar contract enforcement, an individual songwriter signed a long-term (ten-year) exclusive service contract with a music publisher for an agreed royalty percentage. Since it would be extremely costly to write a complete explicit contract for the supply of publishing services (including advertising and other promotion activities, whose effects are felt over time and are difficult to measure), after a songwriter becomes established he has an incentive to take advantage of any initial investment made by a publishing firm and shift to another publisher. Rather than rely on the brand name of the songwriter or require him to make a specific investment which can serve as collateral, the exclusive service contract prevents this cheating from occurring.

The major cost of such explicit long-term contractual arrangements is the rigidity that is created by the necessity of setting a price or a price formula ex ante. In this song publishing case, the royalty formula may turn out ex post to imply too low a price to the songwriter (if, say, his cooperative promotional input is greater than originally anticipated). If the publisher is concerned about his reputation, these royalty terms will be renegotiated, a common occurrence in continuing business relationships.

If an individual songwriter is a small part of a large publisher's total sales, and if the value of an individual songwriter's ability generally depreciates rapidly or does not persist at peak levels so that signing up new songwriters is an important element of a publisher's continuing business, then cheating an individual songwriter or even all songwriters currently under contract by refusing to renegotiate royalty rates will imply a large capital cost to the publisher. When this behavior is communicated to other actual or potential composers, the publisher's reputation will depreciate and future business will be lost. An individual songwriter, on the other hand, does not generally have large, diversified long-term business concerns and therefore cannot be penalized in that way. It is therefore obvious, independent of any appeal to disparity of bargaining power, why the smaller party would be willing to be bound by an explicit long-term contract while the larger party is bound only implicitly and renegotiates terms that turn out ex post to be truly divergent from ex ante, but unspecified, anticipations.

However, the possibility of reverse publisher cheating is real. If, for example, the songwriter unexpectedly becomes such a great success that current sales by this one customer represents a large share of the present discounted value of total publisher sales, the implicit contract enforcement mechanism may not work. Individuals knowingly trade off these costs of explicit and implicit-enforcement mechanisms in settling upon transaction cost-minimizing contract terms. Although it would be too costly in a stochastic world to attempt to set up an arrangement where no cheating occurs, it is naive to think that courts can cheaply intervene to discover and "fix up" the few cases of opportunistic behavior that will occur. In any event, my analysis makes it clear that one cannot merely look at the agreed-upon, seemingly "unfair" terms to determine if opportunism is occurring.

* * *

A relational exchange perspective on the employment relationship

VICTOR P. GOLDBERG (1984)

Suppose that none of the work performed for a large firm required firm- or job-specific skills. Further, assume that all the paperwork costs associated with labor turnover were nil. Even in these extreme circumstances there would still be good reason for the large firm to establish an elaborate governance structure for employees and for the employees to achieve considerable de facto job security.

To direct workers to perform certain tasks and to discourage behavior that impairs performance, the firm requires devices which impose costs on the worker for noncompliance. The ability to impose costs is enhanced by making quitting expensive for the worker. If the worker could simply walk away without cost, any particular punishment (say a suspension or fine) could be ignored; if, however, quitting imposed a substantial loss on the worker, he would be vulnerable to the threat of punishment and thus the deterrents become credible. Further, a high exit cost can be a powerful deterrent in its own right. The firm can use the threat of termination to influence the worker's behavior.

The firm has available a number of devices with which to penalize exit, or what amounts to the same thing, reward continuation. One device is to pay a premium wage (like Ford's five-dollar day), the sacrifice of that premium being a cost of leaving borne by the worker. Note that the premium is not paid "up front"; it is deferred so that the payment is contingent upon the worker's continued satisfactory (from the employer's viewpoint) performance. Deferral enables the firm to enforce the agreement without recourse to the expensive judicial system; if legal

Reprinted from Victor P. Goldberg, "A Relational Exchange Perspective on the Employment Relationship." In *Organization and Labor*, edited by Frank Stephens. With the permission of Macmillan Press, Ltd.

enforcement were free, then up-front payment would suffice. Nonwage compensation (in the form of pensions, health insurance, company-provided housing, and so forth) and internal promotion ladders are more complex variations on this. Firms (and employees) will not be indifferent between the forms the compensation takes. The penalty or reward structure can be fine-tuned to achieve specific purposes. For example, a pension which can be collected only if the worker remains with the firm makes for a very high penalty in the employee's final years on the job. If the worker's ability to perform the task decreases after a certain age, the deferred compensation might take the form of providing a lower-paying, less-demanding job.

It should be clear that the larger the deferred payment, the greater is the employer's incentive to cheat. If worker distrust were sufficiently high at the formation stage, the contingent reward would be heavily discounted; the strategy would not be viable. Assuming that that hurdle has been surmounted, the effect of such opportunistic termination on a firm's good will (i.e., the reaction of its other employees and its future employees) would be a significant deterrent. *Ceteris paribus*, the firm's credibility would be a declining function of the gap between the deferred compensation and the expected future output of the worker (or group of workers); for example, if a firm alleged that a worker had been careless or performed a bit too slowly, other workers would have cause to be dubious if by firing that worker the firm avoided paying a large pension. Turning this around, to maintain a given level of good will, the firm would have to offset the increased gap by meeting a higher standard of proof in justifying a termination. If termination were the firm's only sanction, then, paradoxically, raising the penalty could reduce its ability to discipline the work force. This suggests that a natural extension of deferred compensation arrangements in large firms is a system of lesser penalties (fines, suspensions, bad evaluations) to discipline lesser transgressions and a fact-finding procedure which workers might reasonably perceive as fair for identifying violations.

* * *

While firms generally want to encourage the presumption that a job is to be a long-term affair, they have historically been opposed to granting the workers formal job security. The typical employment agreement of fifty years ago could easily be terminated by the firm. Notice requirements were short, employees received little or no compensation for their reliance, and the employer was not required to show cause. If the law had initially given potential employees the right to tenure, they would have voluntarily "sold" it to the employer as a condition for entering into the agreement (or else they would have remained potential employees). The benefits to the employees afforded by job security, such as protection of "investments" made outside the employment relationship but in reliance on its continuity (for example, in a home, in a neighborhood, or in establishing roots), protection from arbitrary dismissal, protection of the surplus of their deferred compensation over their expected future value to the firm, protection of job-specific human capital, and so forth, were not, in general, sufficiently attractive to outweigh what employers would offer them to accept a contract without protection of job security.

As argued above, a system relying heavily on the carrot of deferred compensation will entail considerable de facto job security. Procedures for appealing disciplinary actions, including outright terminations, are natural accompaniments of such systems. The cost to the firm of converting the de facto protection to de jure are likely to decline as deferred compensation becomes a more prominent element in the total package. Nevertheless, although the cost to the firm of formal recognition declines, it is still considerable. Without collective action by employees, the de jure protection would not, in general, have been forthcoming.

The preceding two paragraphs entail some bold generalizations, but I believe that they are in accord with the facts for the period preceding passage of the Wagner Act. Experience in a closely related area, franchising, tends to confirm this. Even though the franchisee's relation-specific investment would appear to make de jure protection more valuable than in the labor context, minimal protection has remained the norm. Unless franchisees succeeded in obtaining legislation to the contrary or judges extended extracontractual protection to franchisees, the agreements remained terminable at will. The similarities between the franchise and employment relationship suggest that similar forces were at work. Why then have workers (and franchisees) pursued the goal of increased security through collective action when they did not find it sufficiently valuable in a one-on-one contract? The answer is by no means clear, but some plausible conjectures can be put forth.

Collective action (whether through collective bargaining, political action or extralegal channels including the threat of violence) can plausibly influence the level of job security achieved in a number of different ways. With individual choice of contract terms, the nature of the contract will be determined by the marginal man: The earnings/security combination will be chosen so that the last employee is indifferent between his contract and the next-best alternative. With collective action, the interests of the average existing employee are the relevant concern. If the differences between the marginal and average employee are systematic, the resultant contracts will differ. In the employment context (and

149

no doubt others) such divergences are likely. Average existing employees are likely to be older, have higher moving costs (for example, uprooting a family), and have more deferred compensation to lose than the marginal employee. All these influences would lead to a greater demand for security when the employees act collectively.

If by collective action employees can attain a larger compensation package, then so long as job security is not an inferior good, we should expect them to get more of it. That is, collective action causes the individual's budget constraint to shift outward. While plausible, I doubt the explanatory power. Casual empiricism suggests that there is little relationship between income and formal security for workers or franchisees in the absence of collective action. Of course, if collective action yields future rewards to members of an organization (deferred compensation contingent upon continued membership), then the individuals will want to increase the likelihood that they will be able to capture these rewards. Termination protection can be a means for achieving the rewards of collective action as well as an end in itself.

Collective action can, in effect, lower the "relative price" of formal security. In the absence of a union or specific legislation, individual workers would find the opportunity cost of de jure job protection (higher wages, better working conditions, etc.) excessive. It would, in effect, grant them a "hunting license" – the right to sue in court for damages or reinstatement. Given the penurious nature of contract remedies (including the general rule that the plaintiff bear his own legal expenses), the hunting license is of little value. Collective action alters this. For one thing, it facilitates pooling of these costs since the union, not the individual, would bear them. Also, by providing a governance structure which supplants the rules of the common law, the union can lower the costs of pursuing redress. Moreover, linking a relationship to other similar ones can reduce the costs of extrajudicial enforcement. Thus, while the individual worker acting alone is in no position to impose significant costs upon the employer, the collective ability to impose costs (for example, with the strike or boycott threat) could be used to protect the individual's security.

To the "shift of the budget constraint" and "change in relative prices" it is natural to add the remaining element of the textbook diagrams: altered preferences. The great efforts to raise or otherwise alter workers' consciousness have undoubtedly had an impact. My failure to pursue this line of enquiry further here is not based on a conviction that such pursuit would be fruitless; it simply means that I have little to contribute. I shall, however, suggest one plausible conjecture. It is quite likely that unions would be induced to err systematically by providing "too much" job security. Collective action is facilitated by framing issues in an "us versus them" manner and by building worker solidarity: my brother, right or wrong. The lower the level of trust (or the greater the benefits to the union of maintaining distrust), the more likely it is that the union would support a worker with a dubious case in a termination dispute. The survivability of the union would be enhanced by backing the worker. Extension of this protection imposes real costs on the group of workers; decreased ability to discipline the labor force results in decreased productivity which would be reflected in compensation packages. Nevertheless, the misperception might still enhance the probability that the union survives (and thrives).

* * *

CHAPTER 6.3

Liquidated damages versus penalties: sense or nonsense?

KENNETH W. CLARKSON,
ROGER LEROY MILLER, AND
TIMOTHY J. MURIS (1978)

... [T]here are substantial benefits from stipulating damages. When these benefits exceed the costs of negotiating them, the parties will stipulate damages, adjusting the contract price accordingly. With such clauses, both parties reach preferred positions, economic activity is increased, and goods are produced at lower costs. Since the net benefits appear to be positive, it seems difficult to explain why stipulated damage clauses are not strictly enforced. Are the courts in error? Alternatively, are there costs associated with these clauses that we have yet to consider?

An important cost of stipulated damage clauses ... results from activities that may induce breach and from activities to prevent breach inducement, both of which waste scarce resources. Consider, for example, a contract to build a bridge with a stipulated damage clause of $500 for each day of delay beyond a specified completion date chosen to correspond with the first day that the purchaser expects to use the bridge. If the clause is carefully drafted, the $500 will closely approximate the expected damage to the purchaser from actual delay. Suppose, however, that during construction (or, for that matter, even at the time of the initial contract) the cost of delay to the purchaser becomes zero because the bridge could not be used until much later than originally planned. Since the producer's breach would now actually improve the purchaser's position, the purchaser has an incentive to undertake activities to cause delay as long as the additional expected revenues from creating delay ($500 multiplied by the number of days of delay) exceed the additional costs.

From Kenneth W. Clarkson, Roger LeRoy Miller, and Timothy J. Muris, "Liquidated Damages Versus Penalties: Sense or Nonsense?" *Wisconsin Law Review 1978* (1978): 351–90. © 1978 by the University of Wisconsin. With the permission of Wisconsin Law Review and the authors.

. . . [E]ven if all stipulated damage clauses are enforced, the incentive to induce breach would exist only when the potential breach-inducer knows that actual damages will be less than the stipulated amount. This may occur either at the time of initial contracting or, more likely, at some time during performance when circumstances change, affecting the likely amount of damages upon breach. When the incentive for breach inducement is present, a further cost could be incurred since the producer might devote time and resources to detect and prevent possible breach-inducing activities. This may entail additional personnel to acquire information about the purchaser or to monitor activities of the purchaser.

Resources spent both on breach-inducing activities and on detecting and preventing breach inducement are wasteful. They do not produce any real good or service that the contracting parties value, nor do they move resources to production of goods and services whose value to others is greater than to the contracting parties. Accordingly, the value of *all* resources expended in inducement is wasted and increases the costs of forming, completing, and monitoring the contract. Such expenditures, like those employed to defraud others, are merely necessary inputs in obtaining the benefits from induced breach and, again like resources spent to defraud, contribute to overall costs without producing real products. If these costs could be avoided while retaining the desirable outcomes of stipulated damage clauses (and without incurring any new costs), contracting parties as a group, and hence society, would gain.

Besides incentive, the potential breach-inducer needs opportunity before he will induce breach. Since detected inducement would result in nonenforcement of the clause, thereby removing the incentive to waste resources, breach inducement will present special difficulties only when the courts are unable to detect it easily. The opportunity to induce breach does arise, however, in situations where inducement is exceedingly costly to detect, particularly where the producer's performance depends at least in part upon the purchaser's cooperation and assistance. For example, a party may intentionally withhold useful information for a critical period of time, yet still comply with the contract. Thus, in our bridge hypothetical, the purchaser may withhold certain information whose existence or source is not known to the producer, such as information about difficult construction conditions. Further, if the contract calls for close cooperation with respect to the building specifications, the purchaser may delay (or become unexpectedly "fussy") in providing the assistance necessary to complete construction on time. It may also be possible to supply information or resources that are clearly inferior, but within the limits of the contract. Purchasing parties may even provide misleading or erroneous data, such as on the condition of the river bed soil in the bridge case.

Perhaps more importantly, breach inducement can occur in ways more subtle than those just mentioned. Unless the purchaser will receive more from the clause than from performance, it has no incentive to be uncooperative. When, however, the purchaser will be better off with the clause than with performance, as in the changed circumstances of the bridge hypothetical, it does have reason not to cooperate. This lack of cooperation may be as innocent as following the precise rules and regulations of the purchasing enterprise for supplying information to the producer. Anyone who has had experience in a large corporation or government bureau knows that not breaking "red tape" can significantly delay action. If red tape is not broken, delay can also occur by simply slowing down the normal activity through regular channels. Even if red tape is broken, delay can occur by slowing down the speed of this activity.

* * *

Further, when inducement is possible, the producer has incentive to monitor the purchaser. For example, in the bridge hypothetical, the contractor-producer may incur substantial costs in determining the probability that the purchaser will engage in different breach-inducing activities. The contractor may, prior to entering into a contract, interview some of the purchaser's employees, review previous contracts between the purchaser and outside parties, as well as seek information from current suppliers to the purchaser. Once the contract is made, the producer may also use resources to detect possible breach inducement since detection will result in nonenforcement of the clause. Thus, to the extent that producers do stipulate damages, increased negotiating and monitoring costs may increase the total costs of resources used to produce the commodity.

* * *

One can derive at least three principles for an optimal rule from the analysis . . .

(i) *When contracting parties can covertly increase the probability of breach and when they might have incentive to do so, the courts should closely scrutinize the relation of the amount of the stipulated damage clause to damages from the breach.* Under this principle, courts should ask whether the clause is "reasonable." If the amount of the clause does not exceed the damages from the breach, that is, if it is reasonable, then there is no incentive to induce breach, and the courts should enforce it. In defining reasonableness, our theory predicts that two considerations will be paramount. The first concerns changed circumstances. If circumstances have changed to make the clause clearly unreasonable ex post (i.e., as measured by damages from the actual breach), the clause should not be enforced even if it is reasonable ex ante (i.e., at the time of contracting). Otherwise, changed circumstances can create an incentive both to induce wasteful breach and to monitor for breach inducement, as in the bridge hypothetical above. Further, if the changed circumstances make the clause reasonable ex post where it may have been unreasonable ex ante as to some possible breaches, there is no reason to deny enforcement.

Second, reasonableness must not be so narrowly defined as to include only damages that are provable under normal court rules. Otherwise, beneficial clauses would be prohibited where there is no incentive to induce breach because the clause was in reality reasonable. To prevent parties from wrongfully claiming that unprovable damages make the clause reasonable, courts could enforce clauses where the fact of damage is demonstrable, even if the amount of a clause is only at best approximately reasonable. For example, if the clause allows for recovery of lost profits that would be unrecoverable in the absence of the clause because they are too speculative, it should be enforced if there is good reason to believe that the nonbreacher was in fact damaged and if the amount of the clause appears as a roughly reasonable estimate of the lost profits. If the court knows that the damage exists, there is no rational reason to deny recovery as too speculative or uncertain when the trier of fact no longer has to guess at the appropriate sum of compensation.

Although retaining the benefits of the all-enforcement rule, the some-enforcement rule would not be optimal if it resulted in increased costs that more than offset the savings from the elimination of breach inducement. Of the relevant costs, litigation expenses are those most likely to increase under the some-enforcement rule. Although one might contend that these litigation costs would be substantially higher than under the all-enforcement rule, three considerations undermine this argument. First, litigation costs under the some-enforcement rule could be reduced if the economic rationale underlying the liquidated damage/penalty distinction were clearly understood and explicitly applied. For example, clauses clearly no longer reasonable in light of ex post damages normally would not be litigated, nor would clauses where the opportunity or incentive to induce breach was lacking. Second, under an all-enforcement rule, the courts may turn to fraud, unconscionability, or other grounds to scrutinize stipulated damages, thereby minimizing that rule's potential for reducing litigation. Third, to the extent that attacks upon stipulated damages accompany other legal challenges, the marginal reduction in litigation costs from a shift to an all-enforcement rule will be reduced. For these reasons, any increase in litigation costs from employing a some-enforcement rule could be very small. On the other hand, our analysis suggests that the costs of covert breach inducement could be significant, particularly given frequent changes in circumstances from the time of contract to the time of breach. Hence, the benefit of the some-enforcement rule could be large.*

(ii) *When contracting parties clearly cannot covertly increase the probability of breach or when they have no incentive to do so, stipulated damage clauses should be enforced regardless of reasonableness.* . . . [I]f breach requires a positive step rather than mere nonperformance, such as in the case of a breach of a covenant not to compete, the nonbreacher usually cannot covertly induce breach. Another example is the case in which the clause limits damages below those that actually result. Since there is no incentive to induce breach, these clauses should be routinely enforced.

Finally, our theory implies that:

(iii) *Enforcement of penalty clauses (that is, clauses for which stipulated damages are clearly much greater than actual damages and induced breach is possible) will increase overall costs of economic activity.* Enforcement of all clauses implies that, where contracting parties have the opportunity and incentive to increase the probability of breach, wasteful activities will occur. Consequently, producers will increase their contract prices to cover the expected cost of detecting and preventing wasteful activities plus the expected costs resulting from the actual higher probabilities of breach.

. . . [S]ome versions of the reasonableness standard refer only to reasonableness at the time of the formation of the contract (reasonableness ex ante), while economic theory implies that reasonableness at the time of breach (reasonableness ex post) will be relevant in at least two situations: one when the clause is reasonable ex ante but not ex post; the other when the clause is reasonable ex post but was not reasonable ex

---

* Besides avoiding the costs of breach inducement, there are three other costs that the distinction avoids. One is the cost of renegotiation . . . which would be avoided in cases in which the clause was unreasonable. Another is the increased contracting costs to avoid the problems of inducement. . . . The third is the cost incurred to identify, and to draft around, exogenous events that might require payment of stipulated damages under an all-enforcement rule. The current liquidated damages/penalty distinction, however, causes one cost that an all-enforcement rule would avoid, namely the cost to parties who more carefully draft their clauses when the possibility of nonenforcement is high. Since the present confusion over the basis for distinguishing liquidated damages from penalties is a major reason why parties engage this expense, this cost should be significantly reduced if the principles espoused in this article are understood.

ante as to all possible breaches that might have occurred (this is the so-called blunderbuss clause). We will consider each situation in turn.

When circumstances have so changed that breach would cause no injury, or injury greatly less than the value of the clause, the nonbreacher can profit from inducing nonperformance, even if the clause was reasonable ex ante. Decisions that enforce stipulated clauses in such situations may be inconsistent with our theory. Although there are dicta to the contrary, and a few cases even hold on their facts that absence of actual damages will not bar enforcement, beyond doubt the majority of the cases support the analysis on this crucial point. In most cases that declared actual damages to be irrelevant, the court could not have accurately measured damages even with full knowledge of the events surrounding breach. On their facts, then, these cases hold that the clauses were reasonable ex ante and, given the difficulty in measuring actual damages, not unreasonable ex post. Further, in numerous cases where the clause was clearly no longer reasonable ex post, the court refused enforcement.

* * *

The second situation where reasonableness ex post should control concerns the blunderbuss clause, in which the parties provide a single amount for various possible breaches. If it is reasonable as measured by the actual breach, the clause should be enforced since the non-breacher could not have benefitted from spending resources to induce breach. The *Restatement*, however, adopting the reasoning of the well-known 1829 case of *Kemble v. Farren*, states that blunderbuss clauses are invalid regardless of their ex post reasonableness. The rationale (which is inconsistent with the rejection of intent as the test for enforceability) is apparently that a clause with a single amount designed to cover various breaches with possibly great differences in damages cannot be truly intended to liquidate damages. Fortunately, the cases are not as harsh on this issue as the *Restatement* would have them be. Many clauses are routinely enforced where a lump sum is provided for breaches of varying severity, a notable example being clauses for breach of a covenant not to compete. Indeed, given the extreme difficulty in foreseeing the nature and extent of damages from every possible breach, a literal application of the blunderbuss principle would void many clauses that are now enforced. Further, some decisions that pay lip service to blunderbuss theory are on their facts consistent with our analysis since the clause is unreasonable in light of the breach that actually occurred. Finally, other cases allow enforcement of the clause if it is reasonable by construing it to apply only to major breaches. To avoid confusion, the *Restatement* rationale should be openly dropped, as most commentators have urged. The U.C.C. and the preliminary draft of the *Restatement (Second)* [Section 339] have taken this step by defining reasonableness in "light of the anticipated *or* actual harm caused by the breach."

* * *

Although the reasonableness of the clause (including reasonableness ex post) explains most cases, our analysis implies that courts will enforce clauses regardless of their reasonableness when there is clearly no opportunity or incentive to induce nonperformance. An examination of stipulated damage clauses as they arise in several of their most common settings appears to verify this implication. When there is no opportunity or incentive to induce breach, most courts routinely enforce the clauses; when there is opportunity or incentive to induce breach, courts closely scrutinize the clauses under the reasonableness test. . . . Although the cases can largely be explained on the basis of whether or not incentive and opportunity to induce breach were present, the opinions have not articulated this distinction. This failure has contributed significantly to the confusion over the law of stipulated damages.

Clauses clearly without incentive or opportunity to induce nonperformance

At least four important types of clauses are relevant here: limits on damages, accords after breach, clauses for breach of a covenant not to compete, and clauses where the sole relation between the parties is that of borrower and lender. When the nonbreaching party will not benefit from nonperformance, he has no incentive to induce it. Accordingly, limits are not subject to the economic objection against penalties, and should be freely enforced. A review of the cases reveals that, although courts occasionally say that the normal rules apply, the effect of the decisions is to enforce limits freely. . . .

After breach has occurred, the parties may agree to stipulate an amount that the breacher will pay in satisfaction of the duty he failed to perform. Since such settlements do not provide an opportunity for the nonbreaching party of the original contract to induce breach, they should be enforced without inquiry into whether or not they are penalties. This appears to be the rule that courts follow.

Clauses stipulating damages for breach of a covenant not to compete are the third type that should not be measured by the reasonableness test for liquidated damages. Unlike most contracts, breach of these covenants requires more than mere nonaction; instead, one party must take the affirmative step of competing with the other. Since it seems extremely difficult covertly to induce someone into such action, these clauses do not ordinarily present an opportunity for wasteful activity. Because of the lack of that opportunity, there is no need to scrutinize them under normal liquidated damages/penalty rules. Again, the law is consistent with our analysis as most courts routinely enforce these clauses. Of those clauses that are not enforced, at least some can be explained on grounds consistent with economic theory. For example, in some cases, there may have been no competition, hence no violation of the purpose of the covenant. In others, the nonbreaching party received an injunction where the intent of the parties was probably that he could obtain enforcement of the clause or an injunction, but not both.

* * *

Clauses where the sole relation between the parties is that of borrower and lender arguably present a fourth type of stipulated damage clause that should be freely enforced. When the borrower stipulates an amount that he will pay upon breach, it seems very difficult for the lender covertly to induce nonperformance to reap the benefits of the clause. Nevertheless, at initial glance, the cases appear to be contrary to economic theory since the clause is not enforced if the stipulated sum exceeds the amount to be paid plus damages. Upon closer inspection, however, these cases may perhaps be explained on a ground independent of the law of stipulated damages, namely that enforcing the clause may offend the policies underlying the usury laws. . . .

Clauses where there may be opportunity and incentive to induce nonperformance

. . . [C]lauses for delay in construction . . . [and] clauses forfeiting upon breach money paid at the formation of the contract . . . [are illustrative.] Construction contracts frequently stipulate damages for each day of delay in performance. Since delay can result for many reasons at least partially in the control of the party contracting for the construction, the opportunity to increase the probability of nonperformance is present. Our analysis implies that courts will carefully scrutinize the clause under the reasonableness test, and the cases once again are consistent. Although delay clauses are usually reasonable, particularly when stipulating damages that are often very difficult to calculate, courts have not hesitated to refuse enforcement to clauses that are unreasonable.

Contracts occasionally require one party to prepay (or post) a stipulated sum to be forfeited upon breach. Where there is opportunity and incentive to induce nonperformance, these clauses will only be enforced

159

if they are reasonable. For example, if a contractor executes a bond obligating it to pay the owner a stipulated sum unless it performs the construction, the owner has an incentive to induce nonperformance if the bond exceeds the likely actual damages. Courts will enforce such bonds only to the extent that they are reasonable.

Another example of a prepaid sum is a lease wherein the lessee prepays a deposit to be forfeited if he breaches. Given the close interaction that often exists between lessor and lessee, the lessor may be able covertly to induce nonperformance. Economic theory implies that courts should, therefore, scrutinize such clauses carefully for their reasonableness, and, here again, the cases and commentators state that the normal rules of stipulated damages apply.

* * *

Conclusion

Although the policy underlying the distinction has baffled the legal community, for hundreds of years courts have categorized stipulated damage clauses as either liquidated damages or penalties. Finding the previous explanations of this distinction to be unsatisfactory, we have asked whether economic efficiency could justify nonenforcement of stipulated clauses in certain situations, and, if so, whether that justification could explain the results, if not the reasoning, of the reported decisions. The answer to both questions supports an economic distinction between liquidated damages and penalties. Through a broad, poorly articulated reasonableness test, the courts appear to have attained efficient results.

* * *

Further thoughts on penalty clauses

VICTOR P. GOLDBERG

A penalty is just one element of the consideration for a contract. The party received something of value because it was willing to take the risk of having the penalty imposed upon it. Courts do not, in general, inquire into the adequacy of the consideration for a contract; yet if it is possible to characterize an element of a contract as a penalty, the court will scrutinize the adequacy of that element of the consideration more carefully.

The judicial hostility to penalties goes too far. Society would, I am quite certain, be better off if it adopted a more accommodating approach to liquidated damages and resisted the temptation to eliminate the right to terminate a relationship at will (if the initial contract allows for such terminations). There has been considerable effort to protect both employees and franchisees from such terminations, and courts have become more sympathetic to these efforts in recent years. Some of the hostility is undoubtedly due to a lack of appreciation of the mutual benefits to parties of arranging their affairs so that one could impose costs on the other. Nonetheless, I suspect that more than ignorance is involved.

It seems clear that the acceptability of certain penalties is culturally dependent. Society will simply not enforce certain penalties because that society perceives them to be wrong. You cannot contractually agree that in the event of breach you will become the other party's slave. At least you can't in twentieth-century America. It seems reasonable to take these social attitudes as given "tastes." That is not to say that economic analysis will be useless in generating propositions about these attitudes. It is probably true that "morality" is income elastic. That is, as the income of a society increases, it would trade off consumption of

161

goods for higher standards of concern for others.* One could conceivably relate the costs and benefits of, say, maintaining debtor's prisons to objective economic measures – perhaps the level and shape of the income distribution – and predict when a society might find the net benefits of imposing the penalty low or negative. It is at least plausible that the moral argument is more likely to succeed when the net benefits of the institution are low.

I suspect that there is a powerful social value that favors forgiving someone even if that individual knowingly accepted the certain imposition of a great penalty. Despite the fact that he sold his soul to the Devil in return for temporary rewards, there is great sympathy for Joe Hardy (*Damn Yankees* and *The Year the Yankees Lost the Pennant*), Jabez Stone (*The Devil and Daniel Webster*), and Doctor Faust. This sympathy can manifest itself in very different ways. At one extreme, courts can themselves feel this sympathy, and the law would tend to bail out those who would suffer great penalties, even if their vulnerability was due to their own careless behavior.† At the other extreme, courts can recognize that juries would exhibit this sympathy and attempt to structure the law so that juries could not act upon it. As a matter of law, certain defenses would be ruled out. Courts have, I think, tended to do a bit of both. Historically, I suspect that they have followed the former pattern regarding penalty clauses and (at least until recently) the latter regarding termination of "at-will" contracts.

There is, obviously, a wide middle range. Courts could concentrate on the "fault" of the party being penalized. The penalty would more likely be imposed if that party had behaved unreasonably. At least in part, that "fault" can have an economic interpretation. If the party had failed to perform because it had deliberately chosen to allocate its resources for this job to another, more profitable, contract, or if it had performed incompetently, the penalty would be upheld, but not, perhaps, if the failure to perform were due to an unforeseen complication. This economic interpretation of fault ought to look familiar; it is yet another variant on the *Boomer* story. Some of the line drawing distinguishing enforceable liquidated damages clauses from unenforceable penalty clauses quite likely reflects this economic notion of fault.

* Mack the Knife made the point somewhat more forcefully in the *Three Penny Opera*: "First feed the face, and then talk right and wrong; for even honest folk may act like sinners, unless they've had their customary dinners."

† A.W.B. Simpson (1979, p. 541) reports an English case decided over four centuries ago which gives no sympathy at all to the debtor who failed to deliver: "[I]f he has no Goods, he shall live of the charity of others, and if others will give him nothing, let him die in the Name of God, if he will, and impute the Cause of it to his own Fault, for his Presumption and ill Behaviour brought him to that Imprisonment."

Further thoughts on penalty clauses

Clarkson et al. (1978) focus on the other party, the one who is to collect the penalty. Their argument can be restated in a similar form. If one party to a contract can gain by enforcing a penalty, it has an incentive to bring about the situation in which the penalty would be assessed. If it cannot influence the occurrence of the situation, then this possible motive is irrelevant and the penalty should be enforced. If, however, both motive and means exist, it is possible that enforcement would result in an inefficient outcome.

It does not, however, follow that nonenforcement would be a wise policy. There remains the questions of how much the courts ought to police ex post opportunism, given that (a) the potential victim could have limited its vulnerability at an earlier stage, and (b) such an inquiry can undercut a powerful motive of the parties when they adopted a liquidated damages (or terminable-at-will) clause in the first place: avoidance of the costs of litigating.

163

Questions and notes on power and penalty clauses

1. Posner and Kronman (1979, p. 225) criticize Clarkson et al. (1978) by noting that the danger of the promisee's trying to provoke a breach should be reflected in the initial negotiations over the price and other terms of the contract. The parties could determine whether such external supervision was necessary. Hence, a refusal to enforce a clause on this ground presumes that the parties were incapable of weighing the merits of supervision on their own. A response to this is that since parties would want courts to fine-tune penalty clauses by selective enforcement, it is reasonable to incorporate such enforcement as an implied term. Do you think that parties would generally accept such a term? Should they be allowed to disclaim the implied term?

2. Ronko is a newspaper columnist whose contract provides him with a salary of $200,000 per year for five years. If he quits before the contract expires he is required to pay a penalty of $50,000 per year for each year he has worked. If he were to quit after the third year, therefore, he would owe his ex-employer $150,000. Should such a penalty be enforced? Compare this to the contract of Banks, a columnist at another paper. Banks's contract provides him with a salary of $150,000 per year plus $50,000 per year deferred income, which is paid only if he works all five years. Banks quits at the end of the third year and sues for his deferred compensation. Should he recover?

3. Merchants frequently buy security services to protect themselves against risks of theft and fire. Some might simply install burglar and fire alarms. Others might choose more elaborate systems known as central station alarm systems. In these, sensors at the merchant's establishment transmit signals to the alarm company's central office. Upon receipt of such a signal, the alarm company is to dispatch a

representative promptly to the premises to investigate and also contact the local police department. Insurance companies recognize the superiority of such systems and generally give discounts to merchants who install such systems.

The alarm contracts typically include a clause that states that the alarm company is not an insurer and that its liability for any loss suffered by the merchant is limited to $50 (or a similar nominal figure) no matter what the cause of the loss is.

Marvin Merchant (MM) enters into such an arrangement with the Honest Alarm Company (HAC). Subsequently, a burglary takes place and HAC fails to dispatch an investigator. MM's loss is $30,000. It sues HAC arguing that the failure was a breach of the contract. It argues that the $50 damage limitation is a penalty clause, not a liquidated damages clause. It also argues that, since all providers of such services have similar liability limitations, there is no real choice and the clause is unconscionable.

Should the liability limitation be upheld? Is there a problem of adverse selection? a problem of moral hazard? The merchant usually purchases the alarm services in conjunction with his buying property and casualty insurance. Does this fact weaken or strengthen MM's case? (See *Lobianco v. Property Protection, Inc.*)

4. It is not uncommon for a party to agree that its right to do something in the future will depend upon its receiving permission from the other party to a contract. Here are a few examples:

   (a) A franchisee has the right to sell its franchise, but the franchisor has the right to approve the new franchisee.

   (b) A tenant has the right to sublet, subject to the landlord's approval of the sublessee.

   (c) A shopping center owner has the right to build additional structures in the center, subject to a tenant's right to approve any new construction that reduces the amount of land allocated to parking below a specified amount.

   (d) An employee accepts a restrictive covenant that states that he will not work for any other chemical company in the United States for two years after leaving the firm. This is equivalent to saying that he could work for such a company only if the initial employer granted permission.

   4.1. Should there be an implied duty to act in good faith, so that one could not withhold permission without good cause? Should this duty be unwaivable, so that a clause that said "the landlord reserves the right to refuse to accept a subtenant on any grounds whatsoever" would be unenforceable?

165

4.2. Courts might refuse to grant specific performance for such clauses but might still be willing to award damages. If the contracts included a liquidated damages clause for breach of this specific covenant, should the courts enforce the clause?

4.3. Why might rational parties accept a clause that enables them to sublet (or engage in the other actions noted above) only if they can obtain the permission of the other party, if that permission might be withheld on any grounds at all?

PART VII

Standard forms and warranties

One of the benefits of editing a collection is that one can clarify, reinterpret, or recant one's own earlier writings. I shall take advantage of that opportunity here with regard to Selection [7.1]. The basic point is still correct. Rational buyer ignorance and adverse selection create the possibility that standard form contract terms will be inefficient; it is possible that judicial supervision or legislative intervention would improve the situation. Moreover, my argument was sufficiently qualified so that a sympathetic reader could conclude that I was only stating a possible case for overriding the terms included in the standard forms. Nonetheless, the tone suggests (and that coincides with my beliefs when the paper was written) that courts and legislatures should take a rather aggressive stance with regard to the secondary terms of standard form contracts. I am much less sanguine about the possible utility of such intervention today.

The roots of this change in opinion are both a decreased faith in the ability of courts and legislatures to do the job well and an increased faith in the ability of private parties to cope with, if not fully resolve, the problems associated with standard form contracts. Courts and legislatures have learned how to justify intervention. But they have not seemed to learn how to intervene. They have not come to appreciate the subtleties in designing efficient contract terms. It is not enough to say that a disclaimer of consequential damages was not understood or consented to by the buyer. One must also understand the possible rationale for such a disclaimer.

The possibility that markets might resolve some of the problems tolerably well is indicated by George Priest's [7.2] empirical study of warranty provisions. He argues that warranties will attempt to assign the task of controlling future costs to the party in the best position to contain them – a recurring theme in this book. The empirical evidence indicates that there is considerable variation in warranty terms across product lines and that the variation is reasonably consistent with an efficiency explanation.

Note that adverse selection is featured in both papers, but that it plays different roles. In my paper, consumers are ignorant of the content of a particular producer's hidden terms and there is a tendency for bad terms to drive out good. In Priest's paper, the producer who offers a warranty is concerned with the possibility that charging a price for this insurance would discourage the good risks from buying the product; he explains the incidence of various warranty exclusions (for example, consequential damages) as, in part at least, a way of coping with this adverse selection problem.

Institutional change and the quasi-invisible hand

VICTOR P. GOLDBERG (1974)

[Consider] the problem of the standard form contract. The . . . [standard economic] model treats the problem by assuming it away. If people voluntarily enter into contracts it is because it is in their best interest to do so. If the terms of one producer are unsatisfactory, the customer will shop around for others; if information on contract terms were costlessly available (and could be analyzed costlessly) he would continue shopping until he received precisely the desired combination of price, quantity, and other contract terms. This, implicitly, is how economists have handled the problem. Additional sophistication occasionally creeps in by the recognition of costs of attaining, processing, and evaluating information; the consumer then would engage in such information processing to the point at which the expected marginal benefits of the additional information are equated to the marginal costs of its acquisition.

Suppose, however, that rather than view the standard form contract as a voluntary agreement, we view it instead as private legislation; the legislature in effect delegates the lawmaking process to private parties. . . . We will first stipulate that we are interested here only in the "hidden" terms of the contract – those beside the basic price and quantity terms.* While such terms could be tailor-made for each contract, there are substantial economies to be gained by spreading the costs of producing

---

* The terms are sometimes literally hidden: warranty agreements for packaged consumer products are often placed *inside* the box; insurance policies are usually not sent to the buyer until *after* the insurance is purchased; yet the warranties and policies are considered to be contracts.

Reprinted from Victor P. Goldberg, "Institutional Change and the Quasi-Invisible Hand," Journal of Law and Economics 17 (1974): 461–92, with the permission of The University of Chicago Press.

(and analyzing the impact of) these terms over a large number of contracts. The firm, which regularly enters into the same type of transactions, will be able to achieve these economies (either by itself or by purchasing the service from specialists – lawyers); the consumer, generally, will not. The standard form contract therefore will be legislation produced in an arena which rewards the resources held by one party – the firm. The result, in Llewellyn's [1931, p. 734] words "has seemed even in such highly competitive spheres as installment sales, residence leases, investments, and commercial banking to be . . . [the] accumulation of seller-protective instead of customer-protective clauses."

We might expect competition in the market to constrain the firm's power in this arena. After all, the firm makes its price in this arena too, and if the industry is reasonably competitive we would expect that this competition would shield the price taker from the firm's power. Why will not competition among producers protect the contract term taker as well? The answer is twofold. On the one hand the cost of acquiring and processing information on contract terms is much greater than for price; unless the firm intentionally makes the particular term an important selling point – as is sometimes the case with the length or inclusiveness of the warranty – few, if any, customers will perceive the existence of variations in terms. Any movement toward contractual equilibrium due to the aggressive bargain-seeking of a few customers will be slow indeed due to both (1) the fewness of customers who will find it worthwhile to pay the costs of acquiring information and (2) the ease with which a producer can "contract term discriminate" – renegotiate the terms for the few aggressive customers while keeping the high information barrier for other customers virtually intact. The second answer is that the "aggressive bargain-seeking customer" is usually just a minor figure in the equilibrating process. More important, in general, is the role of new entry (or exit) of producers. If the firms in an industry are making profits because they have written standardized contract terms that are very favorable to them, they will attract new entrants into the industry. The entry will continue until excess profits are bid away. The benefits to the firms of the standardized terms will be capitalized into the firms' value. Thus, while competition between producers will in the long run yield zero profits, the firm will be able to attain a capital gain (or prevent a capital loss) by choosing the appropriate standard contract terms.

This does not necessarily mean, however, that the industry as a whole will be better off or that the industry's gains will come at the expense of the consumer. It might well be that the equilibrium terms arrived at are optimal for both producers and consumers, but there is no reason to presume this to be true. Consider, for example, the following scenario. Assume a competitive insurance industry with minimal government intervention. Firms in the industry compete by lowering their price and then compensate for this by decreasing the coverage (in as hidden a way as possible), with other firms being forced to cut also in order to remain competitive. A sort of "Gresham's Law" of bad policies driving out good would ensue. Both the quality of insurance contracts and the total sales of the industry are likely to fall.

This is not the end of the story. Both producers and consumers will have incentives to search for methods for improving upon this result. Ignoring solutions relying on an active government (to which we turn below) a number of solutions might arise. Brand names and advertising might be used as indicators of product quality in general (including the terms of the contract); consumers might take price as an indicator of quality; or private producers of information might appear. While such private market solutions will, to some extent, ameliorate the Gresham's Law problem considered in the previous paragraph, there is no reason to believe that the market will negate the standard form contract problem.

If the government's role is restricted to passive enforcement of private contracts, then there will be many standard form contract terms produced which are, in effect, legislation produced by a single party. The consumer need not necessarily suffer as a result, but his protection by market forces will in many instances be weak. Indeed, if we could argue that standard forms inevitably led to the enrichment of producers at the expense of consumers, the . . . [problem] would be considerably simplified. But this is not the case. In some instances all parties will benefit from the standard forms while in others all parties will be hurt. In many instances some consumers will benefit while others will be harmed. (For example, harsh terms will, in equilibrium, yield lower prices; those who would prefer the harsh term–low price combination will benefit at the expense of those who would have preferred an easier term–higher price combination.) Thus, the social engineer faces problems in identifying situations in which parties are likely to be helped by intervention and a further set of problems in balancing the anticipated benefits to some groups against the losses of others.

How should the courts react to the standard form contract? If they were to adopt the economist's faulty idealization of the contracting process, courts would accept the terms of the contract without question and hold the parties to them. Courts have essentially stuck to this approach although . . . they have often resorted to very liberal interpretations of the contract to reach what they regard as a fair result. A

171

number of commentators have argued that only by divorcing themselves from the fiction that the standard form contract is no different from the idealized contract between equals will courts be able to come to grips with the problem. Slawson [1971], for example, argues that the court must decide what the consumer could reasonably have been expected to consider as part of the transaction. This alone the court should accept as the contract to which the consumer has manifested agreement. The other terms must then be judged against some reasonable standards; essentially, all goods sold with a standard form have an "implied warranty of fitness for intended purpose." Even if an express warranty is included in the standard form it will not be treated as part of the contract if the court finds it inconsistent with the implied warranty.

This is not the place for a detailed analysis of Slawson's proposal. Clearly, courts will differ substantially in determining what part of a standard form contract has been agreed to and what part must pass the reasonableness test; they will further disagree as to what ought to determine reasonableness. The point, though, is that it is possible for judges to abandon the mythology of freedom of contract and to put limits on the ability of the firm(s) to produce legislation in the form of standard contracts.

While the courts might in the future be induced to take a more pro-consumer stance in litigation, this will likely prove of only marginal assistance to most consumers. Lawsuits are expensive, risky affairs with the expenses frequently in excess of the expected gains to the single individual, were he to win. Realizing this, firms would have little incentive to remove unenforceable terms from their contracts. (Many contracts carry unenforceable waivers of liability; a consumer when shown he had "agreed" to this provision would likely give up rather than bring the matter to a lawyer.) So, while some relief for the consumer might be possible in the judicial arena, it is doubtful that this in itself would be of much value.

One possible response to the standard form contract problem would be to provide consumers with an agent who would aid in the production of standardized terms. The government can fill the role of agent; assume initially an ideal government attempting to fill this role faithfully. The legislature could suggest terms that the parties might include in their contracts if they so agree, set terms that will hold unless the contract explicity replaces them, prohibit the inclusion of certain terms, or set terms which cannot be altered by the parties. Alternatively the legislature might choose to delegate the task to a regulatory agency (or other nonlegislative body). This arrangement permits an ongoing review of contract terms; the agency can adjust terms in light of past experience and can bargain with the producers concerning possible innovations.

Not all consumers will benefit equally from the agent's efforts. Indeed, in most instances some consumers are likely to be worse off, receiving protection from a clause that affected them little or not at all in exchange for a higher price. Given that the agent's costs must be spread over a large number of consumers with different preferences, it is inevitable that the agent must regularly engage in making interpersonal comparisons in producing contract terms. To be sure, the same is true without government intervention where the firm (or the market) in effect plays the role of agent in producing and modifying standard form contract terms.

It should come as no surprise that the agent will be at least in part a "double agent." Producers will seek a voice in determining who plays the role of agent and will ultimately try to influence the nature of the terms produced, the penalties for noncompliance, and the extent of public enforcement. The results will be substantially less favorable to consumers than those of an "ideal government." . . .

* * *

CHAPTER 7.2

A theory of the consumer
product warranty

GEORGE L. PRIEST (1981)

This article proposes a new theory of the standardized warranty and of
the determinants of the content of the warranties of individual products.
... A warranty is viewed as a contract that optimizes the productive
services of goods by allocating responsibility between a manufacturer
and consumer for investments to prolong the useful life of a product
and to insure against product losses. According to the theory, the terms
of warranty contracts are determined solely by the relative costs to the
parties of these investments. An insurance function of warranty coverage, of course, is well known. The novelty of the theory is its emphasis
on the variety of allocative investments that consumers may make to
extend productive capacity and its consideration of the difficulties of
drafting warranty contracts to encourage such investments. . . .

* * *

The basic theory defined

Let us . . . [try] to predict the contents of warranties where the costs of
extending product life and of insuring product losses are the sole determinants of their contents. Imagine that consumers are perfectly informed about the likelihood of a product defect and about the losses
that will be suffered should a product become defective. Imagine also
that consumers somehow make their preferences regarding warranty
terms known to manufacturers and that manufacturers are responsive
to those preferences. Imagine that warranty contracts are standardized

From George L. Priest, "A Theory of the Consumer Product Warranty." Reprinted by
permission of The Yale Law Journal Company and Fred B. Rothman and Company from
The Yale Law Journal, Vol. 90, pp. 1297–352. With the permission of the author.

only to reduce negotiation costs and thus that the standardized form itself does not affect the substantive obligations of consumers relative to manufacturers. Finally, imagine that all products are manufactured under conditions of perfect competition, so that each characteristic of a product – including warranty terms – serves to optimize the welfare of some dominant class of consumers. What would be the terms of product warranties?

In the common view, a warranty serves as both an insurance policy and a repair contract. As an insurance policy, a warranty provides that if, within a certain period, the product or some part of the product becomes defective, the manufacturer will compensate the buyer for the loss by repair, replacement, or refund of the purchase price. As a repair contract, a warranty fixes an obligation upon the manufacturer for some period of time to provide, without charge, services necessary to repair a defect in order to prolong the useful capacity of the product.

* * *

As a repair contract, a warranty reflects the respective costs to the consumer and the manufacturer of repair services. Repair by the consumer and manufacturer are substitutes, and the consumer can be expected to purchase repair services as part of the warranty wherever the manufacturer's price is less than the consumer's cost of providing the repair himself. Obviously, a consumer can (and frequently does) provide many repair services more cheaply than a manufacturer. It is plausible, for example, that where shelves fall in a refrigerator, repair by the consumer is cheaper. Of course, since the consumer and manufacturer are always free after the purchase of the good to negotiate for the provision of services of this kind, the warranty itself is valuable only if it reduces transaction costs for future agreements. Thus, a warranty may be expected to allocate responsibility to the manufacturer for those types of repairs that most frequently are difficult or burdensome for consumers to provide themselves.

Although the above example, as well as most uses of the word "repair," refers to investments designed to return a product to a condition it enjoyed at some previous period of time, it is worthwhile to consider "repair service" to a product more broadly as any investment designed to optimize the performance of the product over time. Viewed in this light, for example, restraining young children from swinging on a refrigerator door represents an investment in a form of "repair" that may well be less costly than hiring a serviceman at a later date to install new hinges. Similarly, a manufacturer may anticipate future repair services by technological investments in the design of the product that make its operation less susceptible to interruption – designing brackets to hold

175

refrigerator shelves more securely, for example – or by investments to control a consistent quality of production.

With respect to repair investments of this nature, however, a warranty serves a role beyond that of reducing transaction costs. The warranty promise establishes and enforces the obligation of the manufacturer to make investments in the design of the good or in quality control. Such an agreement between the parties subsequent to the sale could not achieve the same result as easily, so that there are advantages to "tying" the warranty to the sale of the product. The warranty in this regard operates as a performance bond of the manufacturer. The value of the bond is equal to the costs to the manufacturer of defective product claims. As long as the manufacturer makes appropriate investments, the bond will not be forfeited. The decision to allocate repair investments of this nature between the manufacturer and consumer, however, is identical to the decision of who should bear typical repair costs. As before, we would expect the parties to allocate between themselves, according to relative costs, all investments in "repair," whether in the form of direct reconditioning services, of product design, or of a consumer's care for or maintenance of the product so as to extend its useful life.

It is evident that the various activities described as repair are substitutes for insurance. Repair, like insurance, is a means of reducing the magnitude of a loss from an unexpected event such as a defect. It is important now, however, to depart from the common view of the warranty and to distinguish more clearly between repair as a redistribution of wealth over time, like insurance, and repair as an allocative investment which alters the productive capacity of the good. The first example of repair – the reinstallation of the refrigerator shelves by the consumer – is a form of self-insurance for the loss. The owner bears the full cost of time and energy necessary to replace the shelves after the event occurs, which, in this case, appears to be cheaper than buying market insurance requiring the manufacturer to replace the shelves. But neither repair by the consumer nor by the manufacturer directly alters the probability of the loss occurring and, thus, is like insurance. The second example – restraining the child from swinging on the refrigerator door – is an allocative investment by a consumer that extends the useful life of the product by reducing the probability of a future loss. Certainly, the burdens of a parent increase as the discipline of children becomes more strict or specific. But, again, it may well be cheaper for a consumer to restrain his child than either to buy market insurance for repair of the door or to pay the manufacturer to design a refrigerator with hinges as sturdy as playground equipment.

Thus, in this terminology, a consumer's decision to accommodate himself to a scratch in the surface of an appliance is an example of self-insurance of the defect. The consumer's earlier efforts to reduce the likelihood of the scratch, for example, by increasing the level of his care or by isolating the appliance, is an allocative investment by the consumer. The manufacturer's promise in a warranty to repair the scratch after it occurs is market insurance. And the manufacturer's production decision to make the surface more resistant to abrasion is an example of an allocative investment by the manufacturer.

* * *

A warranty in this view is the instrument that expresses consumer preferences for allocative or insurance investments. It is a contract that divides responsibility for allocative investments and insurance between the consumer and the manufacturer. The content of the contract is determined by the respective costs to the two parties of allocative investments or insurance. According to this approach, a manufacturer makes investments to prolong product life up to the point at which the marginal cost of such investments equals the marginal benefit. A manufacturer, then, offers market insurance for those losses or items of service for which market insurance is less costly than insurance or allocative investments by the consumer himself.

To the extent that a manufacturer disclaims liability or excludes or limits warranty coverage, however, it shifts to the consumer the obligation to make allocative investments to preserve the product or to self-insure for its loss. A disclaimer or an exclusion of coverage is the functional equivalent of provisions, common in other contracts, that explicitly require one of the parties to take certain actions to prevent breach or to insure for losses from uncertain events. The theory predicts that disclaimers of liability and exclusions of coverage will be observed in consumer product warranties for those specific allocative or insurance investments that the consumer can provide more cheaply than the manufacturer. In this view, disclaimers and exclusions can be said to be demanded by consumers because of the relative cheapness of consumer allocative investments or of self-insurance.

* * *

Defining standardized contracts: Reducing differences in risks

The task of defining optimal warranty provisions resembles the task of defining optimal rate classes in insurance contracts. In all insurance contexts, it is advantageous for an insurer to segregate applicants according to the level of risks added to the insurance pool. If the risk of loss of an individual can be predicted, then the insurance premium can be tailored to reflect the likelihood of future payouts. In particular, insurance coverage can be offered at a lower premium to an individual for whom the risk of loss is relatively low.

For most types of insurance, of course, it is prohibitively costly either to predict exactly the risk that an individual brings to a pool or to charge individual premiums. As a consequence, an insurer is forced to lump individuals into separate classes or, sometimes into a single class. The premium charged each member of the class must reflect the average level of risk of the class. Thus, the premium undercharges relatively high-risk individuals and overcharges relatively low-risk individuals. At the margin, some low-risk individuals are likely to find that the cost of market insurance exceeds the benefit and will shift to allocative investments that reduce the likelihood of the loss or to self-insurance. In the context of consumer products, these individuals will shift their purchases to products sold without, or with less, warranty coverage. The more precisely the insurer is able to construct classes comprising individuals with relatively similar levels of risk, however, the smaller the discrepancy will be between the premium and the value of insurance to the lower-risk members of the pool. Thus, the lower-risk members become less inclined to substitute self-insurance for market insurance. As a general proposition, therefore, discrimination that reduces differences in risk between members of a given insurance class optimizes the sale of insurance.

It is common for life, medical, accident, and home insurers to obtain information about applicants prior to making contracts in order to place applicants in appropriate insurance classes. Insurers routinely solicit information about age, sex, property location and value, as well as medical records and driving histories in order to construct rate classes. Some insurers make it possible for individuals with characteristics that tend to be correlated with low levels of risk, such as abstemious smoking and drinking habits, to identify themselves in order to qualify for lower premiums. Analogues to these methods of discrimination, however, are not immediately apparent in the context of consumer product insurance. Typically, insurance policies for consumer product losses are tied to the sale of the product itself, so that the insurance pool invariably consists of all consumers who have purchased the product.

Consumers may differ in two general ways with respect to risk under a product warranty. First, the amount of use of a product during the period of warranty coverage may vary considerably between consumers. Compare, for example, the expected service costs to a washing machine manufacturer from a family with many children and from a family with only a single child. The costs of service to the large family will almost certainly be greater. If the manufacturer could define warranty coverage in terms of number of washloads, however, as an automobile manufacturer defines coverage in terms of mileage, then the expected costs from the two families to the manufacturer might be similar. But for washing machines, as well as for most other consumer appliances, the least costly measure of use appears to be duration of ownership. As a consequence, no matter what the period of coverage, the amount of use of the machine by the two families is likely to differ greatly. The insurance premium must be set to cover all expected costs of service. Thus, smaller families at the margin may find warranty protection to be worth less than its cost.

Second, the risk of loss may differ between consumers with respect to what I will call the "intensity" of product use. Compare now for the large and small families, the expected service costs to a television manufacturer. The amount of use of the television – that is, the number of viewing hours might be identical for the two families. Nonetheless, the probability of a warranty claim is likely to be higher for the larger family, because of the greater number of individuals operating the set, because of the greater frequency of channel changes, and because of the greater risk in a large family that the set will be jostled, that the antenna will be struck, or that the machine will otherwise be treated roughly.

* * *

. . . [O]ne method of segregating consumers is to offer warranty contracts with different terms at different premiums in conjunction with the sale of a given product. Recently, the domestic automobile manufacturers have introduced insurance policies for separate fees extending coverage for periods beyond the basic twelve-month warranty. The optional service contract of many appliances is similar. These contracts segregate consumers according to the amount of insurance coverage they wish to buy. The warranty provides a term of basic coverage demanded by the lowest risk members of the pool. Those consumers for whom the risk is greater, however, can purchase more extensive coverage. Because relatively high-risk consumers are more likely to select such contracts, their premiums are likely to be proportionally higher for a given duration of coverage than the premiums of the basic warranty included in the sale price.

A more subtle method of differentiating consumers is the offer by many retailers of warranty coverage that is separate from and, typically, more extensive than the coverage offered by the product manufacturers themselves.

This additional coverage need not be explicit. It may take the form only of a more liberal or courteous return or exchange policy. It is not uncommon, however, for retailers to announce and, thus, to make contractual a guarantee of consumer "satisfaction" that far exceeds the typical manufacturer warranty. This practice enables consumers to segregate themselves according to the level of protection each desires. Those consumers who value their time highly and who avoid allocative investments in care and maintenance or insurance investments in self-repair of products, may seek out retailers with liberal policies, although the products can be purchased at lower retail prices elsewhere. Dealers who offer more extensive warranty coverage are undoubtedly fully compensated for doing so, but their customers are less likely to be those for whom the costs of allocative investments or self-insurance are relatively low.

Finally, a manufacturer may segregate consumers by means of explicit contractual provisions in the warranty. A manufacturer, for example, may exclude warranty coverage for a particular use of a product or specific class of consumers for which the volume or intensity of use is relatively high. The common provision that excludes coverage of commercial use is an obvious example. This provision narrows the class of those insured to domestic users of the product and may be incorporated to enforce a manufacturer's segregation of domestic and commercial purchasers by model design.

Some elements of product loss, however, may be excluded from coverage in the warranties of all product models. A common example is the exclusion of liability for consequential damages. The unavailability of any coverage of some loss, nonetheless, may be related to the reduction of differences in risk between members of the insurance pool. Where consumers differ substantially in the incidence of magnitude of a loss, such as consequential damages, there may be no single premium attractive to a sufficient number to justify offering coverage. Put another way, the increase in the premium required for coverage of such losses may be greater than the benefit of coverage to large numbers of consumers. If so, the sale of product insurance may be optimized by excluding coverage altogether.

* * *

The segregation of consumers by explicit contractual provisions, however, is effective only to the extent that the manufacturer can identify prior to sale those consumers, product uses, or elements of loss for which differences in risk across the set of potential consumers are great. All those not identified and segregated must be lumped into a common pool, high-risk and low-risk alike. The terms of the standard warranty, then, establish the minimum level of coverage that is demanded uniformly by each member of the large class of purchasers; that is, a base level that can be supplemented in the variety of ways suggested above by those consumers desiring more extensive protection. The standard level of coverage comprises the minimum performance bond necessary to encourage appropriate investments by manufacturers in the design or mechanical qualities of the product and the minimum insurance coverage demanded by the lowest-risk members of the consumer pool.

* * *

An empirical examination of the theories

... [Priest then reviews] the provisions of warranties issued in 1974 of sixty-two consumer products comprising sixteen different product groups.

The sample warranties were taken from a wide range of consumer products, including household appliances such as refrigerators, ranges, washers, dryers, and televisions, relatively inexpensive products such as cookware, and more significant durables such as automobiles, recreational vehicles, and onsite mobile homes.

* * *

Limitations of coverage to the original purchaser

Many warranties cancel coverage if the original purchaser sells or otherwise transfers ownership of the product prior to the expiration of the period of basic or extended coverage....

... To the extent that the intensity of the first purchaser's use cannot be detected by second-hand purchasers, those first purchasers who expect to transfer products to others may invest relatively less in care and maintenance or may subject products to a relatively greater volume or intensity of use prior to resale. If so, second-hand items are more likely to require servicing. As a consequence, purchasers who expect to retain products will prefer warranties that limit coverage to the original purchaser in order to remove second-hand items from the warranty pool. This explanation implies that the appearance of the limitation will not be universal but will be correlated, first, with the duration of basic or extended coverage – because the longer the term, the greater the opportunity for the owner to use the good intensively prior to resale – and, second, with the product's susceptibility to reduction in service life from intensive use.

An extension of this theory explains why markets for second-hand goods exist at all for some products and not for others. It is well known that the size of second-hand markets differs dramatically for different goods. The extent of the second-hand market in any product will be determined by the relationship between the difficulty of estimating the remaining productive life of the good and the product's susceptibility to deterioration from intensive use by earlier owners. . . . The investment explanation suggests that the inclusion of the original purchase limitation should be inversely correlated (roughly) with the size of the second-hand market. The more susceptible a product is to intensive use, the smaller the second-hand market for the product will be, and the more likely it will be that warranty coverage is limited to the original purchaser.

. . . [The data] appear to support the implication that an inverse relationship exists between the original purchaser limitation and the size of the used-goods market. The limited number of warranties of each product in the sample, however, makes the result only suggestive.

* * *

The disclaimer of the implied warranty of merchantability and the exclusion of consequential damages

The Uniform Commercial Code implies a warranty of merchantability in all sales contracts. The warranty requires that the item be of sufficient quality to "pass without objection in the trade" and that it be "fit for . . . ordinary purposes." The Code allows a disclaimer of the warranty of merchantability provided that certain technical requirements are met. At the time the warranties in the sample were issued, however, such a disclaimer was prohibited by statute in several states and was rendered ineffective by judicial decision in many others. If the warranty of merchantability or any other general warranty is breached, the Code awards the buyer the costs of repairing or replacing the product as well as consequential damages. Consequential damages represent losses that result from the inability of the buyer to make use of the product for a purpose that could be anticipated by the seller. In modern times, consequential damages of the greatest magnitude occur where product failure causes personal injury, and may include hospitalization costs, disability income, and the value of pain and suffering.

The disclaimer of the warranty of merchantability has always appeared suspect. It seems peculiar for a manufacturer to deny openly that its product can "pass without objection" or is ordinarily fit. . . .

. . . The effect of the legal implication of the warranty of merchantability is to delegate to a jury the judgment of what are the "ordinary" purposes to which a product may be put. A jury may appreciate the class of consumers and uses for which the product is designed. But if the jury errs, its verdict will charge a manufacturer for the failure of a product to satisfy a use not preferred by the dominant class of consumers, making both the class of consumers and the manufacturer worse off. Manufacturers whose products have a wide range of potential uses are exposed to greater risk from this delegation and will be more likely to disclaim the implied warranty of merchantability. On the other hand, manufacturers will exclude consequential damages where the expected differences among consumers in consequential losses are high.

. . . The disclaimers and exclusions are far from universal. Of sixty-two warranties, only twenty-four disclaim merchantability and only twenty-three exclude consequential damages. Furthermore, none of the manufacturers within six of the sixteen product groups disclaims merchantability and none within seven of the sixteen groups excludes consequential damages. . . .

. . . [I]t is warranties of the vehicular products that most frequently disclaim the warranty of merchantability and exclude consequential damages. The warranty of merchantability is disclaimed in sixteen of twenty-three vehicular product warranties, as compared with only six of thirty-four appliance warranties and two of four mobile home warranties. Similarly, consequential damages are excluded in seventeen of twenty-three vehicular product warranties, but in only five of thirty-four appliance warranties and in one of four mobile home warranties. With respect to the disclaimer, the range of potential uses may be greater for vehicular products than for appliances such as ranges, washers, and televisions. Moreover, the vehicular product warranties are those which most frequently incorporate exclusions of specific uses, such as racing, towing, or hauling heavy loads.

Similarly, differences among consumers in the potential magnitude of consequential damages may be greater for vehicular than for other products.

Many vehicular warranties enumerate several elements of loss stemming from the incapacity of the vehicle – loss of time, meals, lodging, the cost of a rental car – that are specifically excluded from coverage. The magnitude of these losses, of course, varies with the driving patterns of each consumer. A more significant element of consequential loss is damage to property where a defect leads to a traffic accident. The exclusion of recovery for this loss, however, is likely to reflect only the relative superiority of consumer self-insurance – by means of an accident or collision policy more carefully designed to the individual's needs. These explanations of the data, however, are only suppositions. They cannot be confirmed or refuted from the warranty sample.

* * *

Questions and notes on warranties

1. Farmers often buy their seeds from seed companies. Sometimes the seeds are defective (they carry disease, they include weeds, they are an inferior variety, and so on) and the net result is a disappointingly small crop. The farmer's loss would be disproportionate to the price of seeds, since if the seeds are bad his expenses on other inputs (labor, land, irrigation, and so forth) are all for nought. Seed companies usually include limitations on liability in their contracts (or on their packages and in their catalogues). Typically, liability is limited to the purchase price of the seeds.

   Such disclaimers do not fare well in the courts. Some courts have found the disclaimers unconscionable for a variety of reasons: (a) all the competitors' using a similar clause, (b) the farmers have relatively little bargaining power, (c) farmers are uncounseled laymen, (d) the fact that the defect is usually within the control of the seed company, which is in a better position to prevent the defect, and (e) the fact that the farmer could lose his entire livelihood while the seed company would lose only a relatively few dollars. (See, for example, *Martin v. Joseph Harris Co., Inc.*)

   Is the disclaimer unconscionable? Try to draft a clause between a seed company and a large corporate farm so that there are no problems with relative bargaining power or buyer ignorance. Would that clause assign liability differently?

2. A construction company used a spread sheet program on its personal computer to prepare its bid. However, when calculating costs it inserted its figure on general expenses in such a way that the figure appeared on the screen but it was not added to the total costs. As a result, the firm underestimated its costs by $250,000 and therefore it suffered a substantial loss when it performed the contract. The con-

struction company sued the software company that distributed the spread sheet program for the $250,000. The only warranty issued with the program was that the company would replace a defective disk. Should the software company be liable for the damages suffered by the user? If users were able to bargain over this issue, what sort of warranty would they agree to? (For discussion of such a case, see Gilman and Bulkeley [1986]).

3. One rationale for permitting a seller to exclude liability for consequential damages is that the purchaser is in the best position to control those losses. Making the purchaser strictly liable for those damages gives it the proper incentive to control losses. It could be argued that the incentives would be the same if the seller were held liable and the buyer was required to mitigate its damages. Why would sellers opt for the former?

PART VIII

Duress, preexisting duty, and good faith modification

Because conditions will change after parties enter into a contract, there are tremendous advantages to maintaining flexibility to adjust the arrangement in the light of changed circumstances. There will also, however, be opportunities for one party to take advantage of the other's isolation from market alternatives and insist that an existing contract be modified in its favor. Contract law faces the difficult task of facilitating the former while attempting to restrict the latter. The common law utilized the preexisting duty concept to police attempts to modify contracts while the Code has utilized the notion of good faith modification.

The four selections in Part VIII are all concerned with this problem. It should be clear to the reader that the problem is another variation on the *Boomer* problem. The party requesting the modification is in the same position as the party that might get the injunction. The more it appears that this party is simply taking advantage of the other's vulnerability, the more likely it is that the court will intervene (providing only damages in the case of the cement company and invoking some variant of the preexisting duty doctrine in the contract case). On the other hand, the more the opposite party was responsible for its own plight, the less willing a court will be to bail it out. One can perhaps read *Hackley et al. v. Headley* (discussed by Dalzell [8.1]) as holding that if a party is vulnerable to a request to modify because it is on the verge of bankruptcy, this condition is entirely of its own making; its "fault" makes it extremely unlikely that the opposite party's behavior would be found unlawful. The party had the "last clear chance" to avoid the damage to the victim, but it had no obligation to do so.

Duress by economic pressure, I

JOHN DALZELL (1942)

It seems . . . reasonable to say that a contract or payment secured by duress is defective not because of some difference in the nature of the consent, but because of the impropriety of the alternative presented; that is, of the pressure used. However, not every improper pressure is duress, since our legal system provides remedies that are reasonably effective in protecting the innocent against improper pressures under ordinary circumstances, and it is better to require the use of such remedies where practicable than to resort to an indiscriminate overhauling of transactions in court. The theory underlying this article is that, to constitute duress, the following elements are both essential and sufficient: (1) The transaction must be induced by a wrongful threat, (2) for which the law offers no adequate remedy, that is, no remedy which (by practical laymen's standards, not those of the common-law nor even of equity) is really sufficient to compensate for the wrong suffered if the threat should be carried out. . . .

* * *

Private individuals are . . . aware of the effectiveness in some situations of a threat to break a contract. In some contractual dealings, the two parties cannot always keep abreast of each other in performance as the work progresses. Inequalities of investment in preparation and performance, or other inequalities between the parties, create situations where one can exert considerable pressure on the other by a threat of disregard of contract obligations. A threat to break a contract is always a threat to commit a wrong (except in situations where there is a legal excuse, which are of course excluded from this discussion), and the common law allows damages for that wrong. Our courts have usually but not invariably refused to see any relievable duress in contracts or payments made under such a threat.

Consider first a simple threat to refuse payment of money due under a contract. A release or a new contract induced by such a threat is none the less entitled to some protection as a transaction between competent parties; we do not want our courts to overturn such transactions wholesale. Something is to be said in favor of the policy of repose, protecting the security of agreements between man and man in an organized society. It is better to have parties settle their business matters finally between themselves without resort to judicial tribunals, in normal circumstances. And, even though a transaction is induced by threat to refuse to pay money due, which is a threat of a wrong, if the commonly available remedy for that wrong, an action for breach of contract, is sufficient to meet the needs of the person threatened, the transaction should not be set aside. This reasoning will apparently support many decisions where the courts refused to find relievable duress in such a threat, there being no reference to any facts showing the inadequacy, by reason of delay or otherwise, of an action for damages as a remedy.

But the same conclusion has been generally applied to situations where there was good reason to doubt the sufficiency of the protection afforded by the normal legal remedy. In the fields where the doctrine of economic duress is already established, duress of goods and duress by utilities, . . . the cases seem to turn on a wrongful threat and inadequate remedy; in the present group of cases, and most of those discussed hereafter, this analysis has not yet been generally accepted, or else a different test of remedial adequacy is usually applied.

Here is a debtor representing a partnership who, after computing their liability from their own records for work already completed, in one sentence, admits owing $4,260 and offers a $4,000 note in full settlement, adding that the creditor can take the note or sue, just as he likes. But the creditor is faced with pressing financial obligations, which have been awaiting this payment – so pressing that any considerable delay in meeting them will mean ruin for the creditor. He, accordingly, takes the $4,000 note and gives a receipt in full; later he attacks the settlement on the ground of duress. The Michigan Supreme Court, in one of the important decisions in this field, *Hackley et al. v. Headley*, reversed the trial court and rejected the claim of duress, saying:

In what did the alleged duress consist in the present case? Merely in this: that the debtors refused to pay on demand a debt already due, though the plaintiff was in great need of the money and might be financially ruined in case he failed to obtain it. It is not pretended that Hackley & McGordon had done anything to bring Headley to the condition which made this money so important to him at this very time, or that they were in any manner responsible for his pecuniary embarrassment except as they failed to pay this demand. The duress, then, is to be found exclusively in their failure to meet promptly their pecuniary obligation. But this, according to the plaintiff's claim, would have constituted no duress whatever if he had not happened to be in pecuniary straits; and the validity of negotiations, according to this claim, must be determined, not by the defendants' conduct, but by the plaintiff's necessities. The same contract which would be valid if made with a man easy in his circumstances, becomes invalid when the contracting party is pressed with the necessity of immediately meeting his bank paper. But this would be a most dangerous, as well as a most unequal doctrine; and if accepted, no one could well know when he would be safe in dealing on the ordinary terms of negotiation with a party who professed to be in great need.*

Inadequacy of the remedy available for a threatened wrong had little weight in that decision. The last-quoted statements seem based on the doctrine that a subjective test for duress is impracticable; this theory has been widely discarded since the above decision. The other argument by the court against duress was that the debtor did not cause the embarrassing circumstances which made his threat effective. Where the debtor consciously took advantage of those circumstances, however, the fact that he did not create them should be treated as of little importance. It is so in cases of duress. When the employer whose funds have been embezzled secures repayment from the guilty employee's mother by reminding her of the danger of criminal prosecution of the son, there is relievable duress; but the employer's threat is effective because of the crime committed by the son, not because of any circumstances for which the employer is responsible. The debtor in the Michigan case knew of the creditor's financial embarrassment and threatened a wrong, a breach of contract, knowing that threat would be practically irresistible because of the circumstances.

* * *

These decisions admit that a wrong is threatened, yet deny the victim an efficient protection against that wrong, and thus have the effect of denying him all remedy. These cases are typical of the weight of authority, but there are some decisions which have treated a refusal to pay money due under a contract as relievable duress. Where a seaman's wages, payable at the end of a voyage, were withheld until he gave a release on a disputed claim, comparatively early American decisions

---

* *Hackley v. Headley*, at 569. In subsequent litigation the release involved in this case was held invalid for lack of consideration; *Headley v. Hackley*.

treated the release as of no effect. [See *Whitney v. Eager* and *Thomas v. McDaniel*.] Another employee was given the same relief against a settlement agreed to, at the end of a term of employment in Panama, as the only means of collecting out of sums due him from the employer, enough to pay passage money back home; in this case the court looked on the threat used, since it in effect was a threat to keep the employee in a distant country, as analogous to duress by imprisonment. [See *Rourke v. Story*.]

* * *

Our system of free competition or Anglo-Saxon individualism also encourages the seller to refuse delivery on his contract in order to force payment of higher prices, where the buyer is unable to supply his needs elsewhere. The payment or contract secured by these means is not the result of duress, according to practically all our decisions.

In the days when ice was a product of nature rather than of electricity, and a summer's supply depended almost entirely on the amount cut out of lakes and stored during the preceding winter, a firm of brewers had contracted for a year's supply of ice at $1.75 a ton, or $2 if scarcity developed. The brewers had chances during the spring to buy ice elsewhere, and talked to the ice company here involved about making such arrangements, but were assured that the contract would be carried out. In May, however, when it was too late to get ice elsewhere, the seller refused further deliveries at the contract price, because of failure of the winter's ice crop. Five dollars a ton was the price originally demanded by the seller, but this was finally reduced to three dollars and fifty cents. The only ice available was that of this seller, and it was shown that lack of ice for two days, or possibly even one day, would have ruined all the good beer in the making. Of course the brewers gave in, paid three dollars and fifty cents a ton for eight months, and then when sued on a note given to the seller, sought relief on the ground of duress. The decision resulting, *Goebel v. Linn*, is another leading authority from Michigan; the court said, of the defendant brewers' claim of duress:

It is to be observed of these circumstances that if we confine our attention to the very time when the arrangement for an increased price was made the defendants make out a very plausible case. They had then a very considerable stock of beer on hand, and the case they make is one in which they must have ice at any cost, or they must fail in business. If the ice company had the ability to perform their contract, but took advantage of the circumstances to extort a higher price from the necessities of the defendants, its conduct was reprehensible, and it would perhaps have been in the interest of good morals if the defendants had temporarily submitted to the loss and brought suit against the ice company on their contract. No one disputes that at their option they might

191

have taken that course, and that the ice company would have been responsible for all damages legally attributable to the breach of its contract. [At 492]

After pointing to eight months of acquiescence by the brewers as some evidence that the new arrangement was voluntary, the decision concludes:

But if our attention were to be restricted to the very day when notice was given that ice would no longer be supplied at the contract price, we could not agree that the case was one of duress. It is not shown to be a case even of a hard bargain; and the price charged was probably not too much under the circumstances. But for the pre-existing contract the one now questioned would probably have been fair enough, and if made with any other party would not have been complained of. The duress is therefore to be found in the refusal to keep the previous engagements. How far this falls short of legal duress, was so recently considered by us in *Hackley v. Headley*, that further discussion now would serve no valuable purpose.*

The rule which this concluding language expresses, and for which the decision is generally cited, that a threat to refuse delivery of goods according to contract necessarily falls far short of legal duress, indicates a total blindness to business realities, and sometimes works a serious injustice. The ice dealer's threat was a gun pointed at the heart of the brewer's business, and should be treated as such. The court says that if the victim, "in the interest of good morals," had refused to pay the higher price, "all damages legally attributable" to the wrong would have been recoverable. This assurance is not very satisfactory to one who learns that there may be a vast difference between the damages recoverable as "legally attributable" to the wrong, and the damages *actually resulting* for the wrong. Moreover, the remedy of damages is about as satisfactory after the business is dead, as it would be after the pistol had been discharged and the man was dead.

There are other arguments in the decision, almost certainly mere make-weights to support the conclusion already settled upon to follow the rule in *Hackley v. Headley*. The court talks of the fairness of the substituted agreement, or rather of the lack of evidence that it was unfair considering market prices at the time the new agreement was made. In German law, duress problems are decided by looking at the reasonableness of the transaction compelled by the duress, and even by altering

---

* At 494. It may not be surprising that there are two other "ice" cases among the authorities on economic duress, both cases where the seller refused delivery unless paid more than the price he had agreed upon. In *Secor v. Ardsley Ice Co.*, the buyer was allowed recovery of the excess paid, with no discussion of the problem of duress. In the other, *Mandel v. National Ice & Coal Co.*, it was shown that the buyer could have gotten ice elsewhere at the same price the seller demanded, and the claim of duress was rejected.

the terms when necessary to make the agreement reasonable; but Anglo-American law is devoted to the theory that the courts should avoid wherever possible all consideration of the reasonableness of the terms of the contract. Although reasonableness of the terms of the contract may be indirect evidence of the absence of coercion, in measuring the reasonableness of the terms for this purpose, something other than current market prices of the product should be considered; from the viewpoint of the buyer who has a valid contract entitling him to the goods at less than market prices, the payment of market prices is not reasonable. And if society is interested in enforcing contracts, this is also the social viewpoint, "in the interest of good morals," as the Michigan decision admitted. It was also suggested that possibly the brewers agreed to the increase in price as the only means of assuring a supply of ice for themselves, because without it the ice dealer's business would collapse and he would be unable to perform any of his contracts. If there had been evidence that this was the situation, it should have been considered; but the court's suggestion was admittedly a hypothesis in its most naked form, without a shred of evidence to cover it. The idea is intriguing in its troublesome possibilities,* but should not play any part under the evidence in this case.† The fact that the brewers had sufficient bargaining leverage to reduce the ice dealer's price from the originally demanded $5.00 a ton to $3.50 a ton, is substantial evidence that the brewers had some influence over the ice dealer; but the threat of the latter against the business life of the brewer was the controlling factor in the situation, and was as a matter of plain business fact, simply irresistible.

---

* What if a situation is such that, unless the terms agreed upon are changed, both businesses must collapse? Or suppose it can be shown that the continuation of one enterprise depends on the contract being performed as written, while the other business will surely break up unless a change is made? What will be the effect of subsequent developments, so that when the case is tried, the crisis is past, both enterprises are prosperous, and each is well able to carry its liability for past wrongs?

† In fact the evidence in the case went far to make the court's suggestion ridiculous. In the spring, after the ice supply for the year was in the ice house, the ice dealer assured the brewer the contract would be carried out; after he has laid in his season's supply, an ice dealer is not likely to become insolvent because the market value of ice goes up.

* * *

Gratuitous promises in economics and law

RICHARD A. POSNER (1977)

Often it is possible for a party to make a binding promise, unsupported by any fresh consideration, to modify a term of an existing contract. For example, the payor in a construction contract might agree to pay a higher price to a builder who had encountered unexpected soil conditions. The motives for such promises are various: to gain a reputation for "fair dealing" (really risk sharing), to avoid driving the promisee into bankruptcy (which might prevent his completing performance or raise the cost of his doing so), or even to be altruistic (the contingency giving rise to modification may have dramatically altered the relative wealth position of the parties). In any event, the stakes are often substantial in such cases, while the increment in utility to the promisor may also be substantial because of the length of time over which optimal performance may extend.

Consider the example of the house purchaser who promises the builder a higher than contract price because the builder has encountered some unexpected difficulty which may make it impossible* to complete the contract at the agreed price. If the purchaser merely declares his intention of paying the builder a higher price, but is free to renege, the builder may decide not to complete performance but instead to take his chances in bankruptcy court. Yet the promisor dare not pay him the extra price in advance in exchange for the builder's promise to continue, for if the contractor is financially shaky for other reasons, the prepayment may end up in the hands of a trustee in bankruptcy, with the

---

* Yet not fall within the bounds of the contract doctrine that allows discharge on grounds of "impossibility." . . .

Reprinted from Richard A. Posner, "Gratuitous Promises in Economics and Law," *Journal of Legal Studies* 6 (1977): 411–26, with the permission of the author and The University of Chicago Press.

purchaser relegated to the status of an unsecured creditor. This is a clear case where the enforcement of a promise not supported by fresh consideration enhances the welfare of the promisor.

The facts of a real case upholding enforceability of such a promise, *Goebel v. Linn* are rather similar to those of the last example. The defendants were brewers who had a contract with the plaintiff in the case, an ice company, to supply them with ice at a price not to exceed $2 a ton. An unusually mild winter ruined the local ice "crop" and the ice company informed the defendants that it would not continue to supply them with ice at the contract price. The defendants had a large stock of beer on hand that would spoil without refrigeration, and therefore agreed to pay the ice company $3.50 to continue the supply of ice under the contract. The defendants later repudiated the agreement and the ice company sued. In upholding the plaintiff's claim, the court observed that the defendants

... chose for reasons which they must have deemed sufficient at the time to submit to the company's demand and pay the increased price rather than rely upon their strict rights under the existing contract.... Suppose, for example, the defendants had satisfied themselves that the ice company under the very extraordinary circumstances of the entire failure of the local crop of ice must be ruined if their existing contracts were to be insisted upon, and must be utterly unable to respond in damages; it is plain that then, whether they chose to rely upon their contract or not, it could have been of little or no value to them. Unexpected and extraordinary circumstances had rendered the contract worthless; and they must either make a new arrangement, or, in insisting on holding the ice company to the existing contract, they would ruin the ice company and thereby at the same time ruin themselves. [At 492–3]

The result in this case has been criticized on the ground that it exposes promisees to extortion. In economic terms, the making of a contract may confer on the seller a monopoly vis-à-vis the buyer which the seller can exploit by threatening to terminate the contract unless the buyer agrees to pay a higher price than originally agreed upon. The court in *Goebel* was aware of this danger but found that the ice company's claim was not extortionate in this sense. This raises the question, however, whether extortion can be given a meaningful definition in the modification setting. To answer this question, it is helpful to distinguish three situations in which modification might be sought:

1. Nothing has changed since the contract was made, but the promisor, realizing that the remedies for breach of contract would not fully compensate the promisee, gives the promisee the unhappy

195

choice of either paying the promisor more to complete the contract or pursuing his legal remedies.

2. Something has changed since the contract signing: The promisee has given up alternative sources of supply or otherwise increased his dependence on the promisor. If modification is permitted, the promisor can extract a monopoly rent from the promisee.
3. Something has changed since the contract signing: an unexpected event which, as in *Goebel v. Linn*, prevents the (willing) promisor from completing the promised performance without a modification of the contract.

The third case is the clearest for allowing modification. The inability of a willing promisor to complete performance removes the factor of strategic behavior that is present in cases one and two. No exploitation of a monopoly position or of the inadequacy of contractual remedies is involved in allowing modification in the third case. The first case might also seem one where modification should be allowed, on the basis of Holmes's "bad man" theory of contract law, which has close affinities with the economic approach. The legal obligation of a promisor is to perform or pay damages. If the promisee wants more – wants in effect specific performance – he must pay extra for it. That is all that seems to be involved in the first case, but if we pause to ask why the promisee in the first case would ever agree to pay extra, we shall see that the first case is in reality a version of the second, the monopoly case. If the promisee in the first case has equally good alternative sources of supply, or at least no worse than he had when he made the original contract, he will have no incentive to pay a premium above the contract price for the promisor to perform as agreed; he will allow the promisor to breach and turn elsewhere. He will pay the premium only if his dependence on the promisor has increased since the signing of the contract, i.e., only if the contract gave the promisor a monopoly position vis-à-vis the promisee.

Alaska Packers' Ass'n v. Domenico was such a case. The plaintiffs (technically "libelants") hired out as sailors and fishermen to the defendant (appellant), but soon after beginning work stopped and threatened to quit unless their wages were raised above the agreed amount. Defendant's agent agreed to pay the higher wage demanded but defendant later reneged. The court refused to enforce the modified contract, noting that

... the libelants agreed in writing, for a certain stated compensation, to render their services to the appellant in remote waters where the season for conducting fishing operations is extremely short, and in which enterprise the appellant had

196

a large amount of money invested; and, after having entered upon the discharge of their contract, and at a time when it was impossible for the appellant to secure other men in their places, the libelants, without any valid cause, absolutely refused to continue the services they were under contract to perform unless the appellant would consent to pay them more money. [At 102]

This seems a clear case where the motive for the modification was simply to exploit a monopoly position conferred on the promisors by the circumstances of the contract. It might seem that the promisee would have been in even worse shape if the men had quit as they threatened to do. However, since their only motive for threatening to quit was to extract a higher wage, there was probably little danger of their actually quitting. The danger would have been truly negligible had they known that they could not extract an enforceable commitment to pay them a higher wage.

The court in *Alaska Packers'* criticized the earlier result in *Goebel v. Linn*, yet the cases are readily distinguishable, with the help of economic analysis. In *Goebel* without a modification the promisor might well have terminated the contract, so the modification conferred a real benefit on the promisee. But in *Alaska Packers'* the likelihood of termination was much less since the threat to terminate was not a response to external conditions genuinely impairing the promisor's ability to honor the contract but merely a strategic ploy designed to exploit a monopoly position. A firm rule of nonenforceability in such cases solves the monopoly problem and thereby facilitates the making of contractual arrangements in which the promisee will be dependent on the good faith of the promisor.

One can relate this distinction back to the basic theme of this paper by noting that one effect of enforcing the kind of modification attempted in the *Alaska Packers'* case would be to reduce the benefits of contracting to people in the same situation as the plaintiffs in that case. Seamen thereafter could not expect to be promised a high wage in exchange for agreeing to work for a stated period at that wage, since the employer would know that the seamen were not obliged to honor their promise but could at any time "hold him up" for a higher wage. In a different form, this is the same problem as that of the man who derives little value from promising a future gift because the promise is not binding on him.

An intermediate case between the involuntary threat to terminate (*Goebel v. Linn*) and the monopolistic (*Alaska Packers' Ass'n v. Domenico*) is that of a promisor who threatens to terminate only because a third party has offered him a higher price for his goods. Because the higher price is a genuine opportunity cost of continued compliance with

197

the contract, the promisor should be allowed to terminate subject only to his obligation to make good the promisee's loss from the breach, and hence he should be allowed to negotiate with the promisee over a modification that will compensate the promisor for the lost opportunity. This was the result in *Schwartzreich v. Bauman-Basch, Inc.**

* * *

* Indeed, from an economic standpoint a foregone benefit is no different from a direct cost; both are opportunity costs.

CHAPTER 8.3

The mitigation principle: toward a general theory of contractual obligation (2)

CHARLES J. GOETZ AND ROBERT E. SCOTT (1983)

Contract rules policing contractual modification are another response to the heightened risk of extortion in specialized environments. For example, the common-law preexisting duty rule can be usefully contrasted with the more permissive regulation of contractual modification under the Uniform Commercial Code. The preexisting duty rule denies enforcement of a renegotiation or contractual modification where an obligor agrees merely to do that which he is already contractually obligated to do. The rule is primarily designed to reduce the incidence of extortionate modification in construction, employment, and other specialized contractual relationships. . . .

The preexisting duty rule, however, often fails accurately to mirror the underlying bad faith behavior. First, the rule discourages cost-reducing negotiations in addition to threats. Moreover, the obligor satisfies the rule by assuming *any* additional obligations whether or not the "additional" duties are themselves part of the strategic maneuver. The Code [U.C.C. 2-209(1)] abandoned this ill-fitting rule of thumb and instead applies a general good faith standard. . . . Because this standard is substantially more difficult to enforce, however, the Code may not deter extortionate renegotiation as effectively as did the common law. Nonetheless, if parties generally execute contracts for the sale of goods in the context of a well-developed market for substitutes, the costs saved through legitimate renegotiations will exceed the increased enforcement costs of policing bad faith modification.

Courts also express concern with bad faith extortion through the rules

Reprinted from Charles J. Goetz and Robert E. Scott, "The Mitigation Principle: Toward a General Theory of Contractual Obligation," *Virginia Law Review* 69 (1983): 967–1025, with the permission of Virginia Law Review Association and Fred B. Rothman & Company.

restraining economic duress. Such cases arise when the obligor has *performed* the modified contract, but the "injured party" seeks restitution of the value of his performance because economic duress forced his agreement to the modified terms. . . . The market for substitutes is the key variable in economic duress cases. For example, "a mere threat by one party to breach the contract by not delivering the required items, though wrongful, does not in itself constitute economic duress. *It must also appear that the threatened party could not obtain the goods from another source of supply.*" [*Austin Instrument, Inc. v. Loral Corp.*, at 130–1. (emphasis added)] Because a market for substitutes will effectively control a defendant's behavior with no need for legal rules, a prima facie claim of economic duress thus requires a plaintiff to show a specialized environment.

It is difficult to police such bad faith behavior, however, because the distinction between legitimate requests for renegotiation and bad faith threats lies entirely in the honesty of a party's assertion that a readjustment contingency made *performance* less attractive than quasi-performance (breach with damages). When a professional athlete requests renegotiation because he now prefers lying in the sun (and paying appropriate compensation) to playing football or basketball, the issue turns on whether that claim is true or represents a bluff designed to obtain additional compensation. Because such a claim is almost impervious to accurate proof, the law must choose between no *legal* regulation and crudely devised rules of thumb.

* * *

CHAPTER 8.4

The law of contract modifications: the uncertain quest for a benchmark of enforceability

VAROUJ A. AIVAZIAN,
MICHAEL J. TREBILCOCK,
AND MICHAEL PENNY (1984)

... Static efficiency considerations will generally require that contract modifications be enforced on the grounds that the immediate contracting parties perceive mutual gains from recontracting that cannot, at the time modification is proposed, be realized as fully by any alternative strategy. On the other hand, dynamic efficiency considerations focus on the long-run incentives for contracting parties at large imparted by a set of legal rules. In the modification context, these dynamic efficiency considerations adopt an ex ante perspective, rather than the ex post perspective implicit in the static efficiency considerations. Adopting the former perspective, rules that impose no constraints on recontracting may increase the overall costs of contracting by creating incentives for opportunistic behavior in cases where "holdup" possibilities arise during contract performance. As well, even where a genuine change has occurred in the economic environment of the contract between the time of formation and the time of modification such that, in the absence of modification, one party faces an increase in the costs of performance relative to expectations at the time of contract performance, allowing recontracting may facilitate the reallocation of initially efficiently assigned risks. This leads to moral hazard problems that may attenuate incentives for efficient risk minimization or risk insurance strategies by the party who subsequently seeks the modification. Thus, what is in the best interests of two particular contracting parties ex post contract formation when a modification is proposed and what is in the interests ex ante of contracting parties generally in terms of legally ordained incentives and

From Varouj A. Aivazian, Michael J. Trebilcock, and Michael Penny, "The Law of Contract Modifications: The Uncertain Quest for a Benchmark of Enforceability," *Osgood Hall Law Journal* 22 (1984): 173–212. © 1984 by the Osgood Hall Law Journal. With the permission of the publisher and the authors.

constraints that minimize the overall costs of contracting may lead to divergent policy perspectives. Our framework of analysis emphasizes the dynamic or long-run incentive effects created by legal rules in the modification context and seeks to identify those rules that will reduce the long-run costs of contracting.

* * *

We shall follow Posner [Selection [8.2]] and initially distinguish two alternative sets of cases in which contract modifications might be sought. In one set of cases there are no changes in the underlying economic conditions governing the initial contract except that the promisee has acquired some monopoly power ex post and exploits this power by forcing higher returns than provided for in the initial contract. Posner argues for the nonenforcement of contract modifications in such cases. The second set of cases is characterized by changes in the underlying economic conditions, or the emergence of new information about the underlying economic conditions governing the contract which prevent or inhibit the promisee from completing the promised performance without a modification of the contract. Posner argues that modification is justified in such cases because without that ability mutually advantageous exchanges may be precluded.

First, in relation to both sets of cases, it must be emphasized that the potential for opportunism in the course of contractual performance is likely to be constrained in various ways. The party demanding a modification on threat of breach will need to take account of: the impact of this on future dealings with the other party if repeat transactions are envisaged; the reputation effects on other potential trading partners in the market; ease of substitution by the party from whom the modification is demanded; initial contractual terms that may make the latter party unreceptive to a modification (for example, liquidated damage or penalty clauses, if enforceable, performance bonds, or backend loading in payment schedules); the possibility of the latter party obtaining specific relief in the form of an injunction or specific performance; exposure to a damages claim in the event that modification is refused and breach occurs. However, despite these constraints, there will be situations where there may be gains from engaging in opportunism – repeat transactions are not envisaged, market networks may imperfectly disseminate information about contractual performance, substitution may be difficult or costly, initial contractual provisions may not fully penalize or constrain opportunism and may be costly to negotiate in great detail, specific relief may be unavailable, and damages for breach may not fully compensate the nonbreaching party for the costs associated with procuring a substitute and other consequential damages induced by the breach, . . . [and] limited liability or bankruptcy may preclude effective enforcement of a damages judgment.

* * *

. . . [I]n cases where contract modifications occur purely and simply as a result of changes in the strategic circumstances of the contracting parties, the enforcement or nonenforcement of modified contracts in a zero transaction costs environment with complete information about future contingencies and rational expectations will have no bearing on resource allocation or economic welfare. In an environment with positive transaction costs or incomplete information, a law which disallows contract modifications will economize on transaction costs and maximize the gains from contractual agreements. Hence, efficiency considerations dictate that contract modifications in this context be nonenforceable.

The second set of cases in which contract modifications may be sought (supervening changes in the economic environment of the contract) are those in which modifications can represent mutually advantageous positive-sum games. The Coase theorem implies that with zero transaction costs, Pareto efficient allocations – an allocation of resources is Pareto efficient if it is impossible to reallocate resources to make one or more individuals better off without making at least one other individual worse off – corresponding to such mutually advantageous (recontracting) exchanges will always emerge, provided that contract modifications are allowed by law. If recontracting between the parties in a particular ex post state of nature is mutually advantageous, then it will occur, leading to an optimal restructuring of contractual terms. These considerations suggest that contract modifications are necessary for the attainment of Pareto efficiency and should be allowed by law in this second set of cases. However, as we will see, such a conclusion is premature since there are additional considerations that bear on the problem.

* * *

. . . Suppose a promisee (supplier) of a product can avoid bankruptcy only if the promisor (buyer) agrees to a higher price than stipulated in the initial contract. If there are alternative suppliers of the product with identical or lower cost functions to the promisee, the nonenforceability of contract modifications will not affect resource allocation provided the transaction costs of turning to an alternative supplier are negligible. If these transaction costs are nonnegligible and if a suit for damages for breach will not fully compensate the nonbreaching party for the costs associated with procuring a substitute, then nonenforceability of contract modifications may adversely affect resource allocation. If alternative suppliers of the product have higher costs than the promisee, then contract modifications may be Pareto efficient. Of course, in this circumstance the modified price demanded by the promisee cannot exceed what his higher-cost competitors would charge, otherwise the promisor would turn to them. Thus, the smaller the promisee's effective monopoly power (reflected in the degree of availability of substitutes for his product and the effectiveness of a legal action for breach), the lower the scope for Pareto efficient contract modifications.

* * *

... Posner's treatment of this second class of case, while perhaps superficially attractive, ignores a counterpart problem to that of strategic behavior in the first class of cases, namely the problem of moral hazard; to allow risk reallocation through modification away from the superior risk bearer attenuates incentives to take efficient risk reduction or risk insurance precautions.

In developing our analysis of the category two modification cases, we are, perhaps ironically, adapting in large part the framework of analysis developed by Posner and Rosenfield [Selection [9.1]] in the context of the doctrine of frustration/impossibility. In effect, we view enforceable modifications as a substitute for the doctrine of frustration: Contracting parties, facing the occurrence of some intervening event that substantially affects the cost of performance may, under some circumstances, rearrange their contractual rights and obligations either through invocation of the assistance of the courts pursuant to the doctrine of frustration or through private recontracting. In other cases, while the underlying factual circumstances of the contract may not have changed, new information about those circumstances may have been uncovered. The parties may have contracted on the basis of incomplete or inaccurate information about the underlying factual environment of the contract. This situation is the domain of the doctrine of mistake. The economic considerations bearing on permissible rearrangements by virtue of contract modifications, the doctrine of frustration, or the doctrine of mistake would seem to be similar.

* * *

Posner endorses the result of *Goebel v. Linn* on the basis of his distinction between modifications entered into where there has been a change in underlying circumstances and those where there has not. However, our emphasis on efficient risk allocation suggests a more cautious approach to evaluating the correctness of this decision. If mild winters were one of the occupational hazards of running an ice business during the era in question, the ice company would seem clearly to be the superior risk bearer, both in terms of risk reduction (for example, making different inventory or standby subcontractual arrangements) and in terms of risk insurance (that is, being better able to appraise the impact of climatic variations on the supply of ice and adjusting the initial contractual fixed price accordingly). Only where the winter in question was quite out of the ordinary so that the gains from recontracting were likely to outweigh the long-run costs of moral hazard problems associated with permitting recontracting in these circumstances, could one support the decision. Otherwise, permitting recontracting is inefficient.

Another leading American decision which seems suspect for similar reasons is *Pirrone v. Monarch Wine Co. of Georgia*. Pirrone, a modest-quantity winemaker had agreed to sell to Monarch, America's largest purchaser of peach brandy, 150,000 gallons in 1968 and again in 1969. As it had overbought brandy and because the market price fell to two-thirds of the contract price, Monarch breached its shipping schedule. In 1969, with Pirrone complaining of financial difficulties, its facilities loaded with brandy, its production of more profitable wine curtailed, and its ability to ship controlled by Monarch, which was required to initiate a shipping permit, the parties agreed to a modification that provided for shipments to Monarch of the residue of the 1968 year but terminated Pirrone's rights in respect of the 1969 sale. The Court of Appeal for the Fifth Circuit refused an action by Pirrone for loss of profits on the 1969 sale, holding the termination agreement to be binding and dismissing a claim of duress.

Clearly this seems to be a case where the risk in question was more efficiently borne by Monarch – the risk of a fall in the American market price for peach brandy (of which they were America's largest purchaser) was a risk that they could much better evaluate than Pirrone and at least partially diversify against. Moreover, the fluctuation in price seems not to have been entirely out of the ordinary and might reasonably be assumed to have been impounded in the terms of the original contract. The modification, in effect, reallocated this initially efficiently assigned risk to Pirrone, the less efficient risk bearer. This is a clear case where the enforcement of a modification generates significant moral hazard type incentives.

* * *

Our analysis assumes that in the pure strategic modification cases the static efficiency gains to the immediate contracting parties from modification relative to breach are outweighed by the long-run or dynamic efficiency losses from encouraging opportunistic behavior. Moreover, in most pure strategic modification cases a rule rendering modifications unenforceable will ensure contractual performance rather than breach – the economically optimal state of affairs. In the changed circumstances cases, the trade-off between static and dynamic efficiency is not so straightforward. Precluding modification in all such cases runs the real risk of breach (and attendant costs), given our assumption here of changes in underlying cost conditions (or perceptions thereof). However, to allow modification in all such cases, while permitting the parties to realize the static efficiency gains from recontracting relative to breach, creates long-run or dynamic efficiency losses as a result of the attenuation of incentives to efficient risk reduction or insurance, as well as generating transaction costs on recontracting. Only in cases where the efficient allocation of risks is indeterminate, both subjectively and objectively, or where the risk in question is extremely remote so that the expected costs of bearing it do not induce significant efficient precautionary responses, is it likely that the static efficiency gains from recontracting will outweigh the dynamic efficiency losses from permitting the reallocation of risks through modifications exacted and acceded to in large part because of limitations in the remedial system available to parties on breach. It should be added that efficient constraints on contractual modifications in all cases must apply not only to modifications per se but also to transactional substitutes (for example, rescission of the original contract and formation of a new contract, compromises, of suits, and so on), so that these constraints are not reduced to largely formal significance.

In central respects, the problems entailed in formulating optimal modification rules are a function of legal limitations on remedies available for breach that prevent a nonbreaching party from obtaining relief that puts him in the same position as if the contract had been performed. For the purposes of this paper, we have accepted these limitations as given, but without a reevaluation of these limitations at least in some contexts (for example, the availability of specific performance, the recovery of consequential damages, the enforceability of penalty clauses), we are often left in a realm of second-best solutions to the question of the enforceability of contractual modifications.

As our analysis has attempted to show, neither a legal regime that enforces all contract modifications nor one that invalidates all modifications is efficient, apart from the savings in adjudication costs associated with a clear legal policy favoring one polarity over the other. The rather more complex and less definite regime suggested by our analysis, while generating higher adjudication costs than the polar choices, appears to weigh all the relevant economic variables. Because these involve difficult, or at least different, trade-offs from one class of case to the next, it is unrealistic to assume that a simple set of legal rules governing contract modifications is ever likely to evolve. The tangled history of the evolution of legal doctrine seems to reflect this reality. However, clear identification of the relevant variables seems a useful, albeit modest step towards reducing the conceptual confusion that has characterized this area of law.

Questions and notes on duress

1. *Goebel v. Linn* is discussed in three of the selections. Which do you find most persuasive?
   1.1 Suppose that Goebel accepted the modified contract until the end of the season. Instead of defaulting on the note, Goebel then sued the ice company for damages for breach of contract and argued that the second contract was simply the "cover" contract. Should it be able to recover the difference between the original contract price ($2.00) and the modified contract price ($3.50)? See *Endiss v. Belle Isle Ice Co.*
   1.2 The fact that the size of the ice crop would depend upon the weather is obvious and one would expect that ice contracts would reflect this. The twenty-five cent premium in the event of a small ice crop in Goebel's contract is one way to deal with this contingency. A second device would be to include a prorationing arrangement. Such a clause was used by at least one other seller of ice in that era. See *Kemp v. The Knickerbocker Ice Co.*
   1.3 Suppose that Goebel's contract did call for prorationing and that some buyers used their quotas to resell to those who were desperate for ice at prices in the $10- to $15-per-ton range. (In *Kemp* some ice was reported being sold at $16 per ton despite a contract price of $2.50.) Should the ice company, Belle Isle, be allowed to terminate sales to the resellers? Should the fact that a lot of buyers are reselling at a premium influence the decision as to whether the contract modifications extracted by Belle Isle should be allowed to stand?
2. A grower of carrots has a contract to deliver his entire output to a large soup company. There is a tremendous shortage of this type of carrot and the market price rises to three times the contract price.

208

The grower threatens to breach unless the soup company agrees to a modification. The company does so because it believes that if it does not get these carrots it would have to close down some of its production lines for the entire canning season and that it would not be able to recover these damages if it refused to negotiate and later sued the grower for breach. After the season is over, the canner sues for the difference between the prices in the original and modified contracts. It argues that there was no consideration for the second promise and that the modified contract was signed under conditions of duress. How should its claim be resolved?

3. Suppose that in *Hadley v. Baxendale*, after the shaft had been turned over to Baxendale, he had informed Hadley that the shaft would be delivered late because the train had been rerouted to pick up some profitable cargo. Hadley then offered additional payment to prevent the delayed delivery; subsequently, he asked for a refund, arguing that the second promise was extracted under duress. Would it make sense to argue that Hadley should have had an extra shaft on hand to protect him from the carrier's negligence (hence no consequential damages) but that his failure to have a second shaft available is irrelevant when determining whether the new bargain was extracted under conditions of duress?

PART IX

Impossibility, related doctrines, and price adjustment

If conditions change after parties enter into a contract, one of them might want to be excused from performance or at least have its obligations revised. Under certain circumstances courts have excused performance invoking the doctrines of impossibility, frustration, impracticability, or mutual mistake. Courts will sometimes keep the contract alive, but rewrite it. It is not uncommon for German courts to revise the price term in a long-term contract; see Dawson (1983). While that is rarely done in American courts, it is not unheard of.

Richard Posner and Andrew Rosenfield [9.1] attempt to provide an economic explanation of the impossibility doctrine. They emphasize the importance of putting liability on the party that is the superior risk bearer. In part, this means the party that is in the best position to avoid costs. But they also place great emphasis on the risk aversion of the parties and the relative costs of insuring against risk. I am, it should be recalled, generally hostile to explanations centering on attitudes toward risk. In the following selection, I present an alternative explanation that does not require explicit assumptions as to the risk preferences of the parties. The explanation hinges on an understanding of why contracts will often include *force majeure* clauses, which state that in the event of certain "acts of God" – fire, breakage of machinery, strikes, and so forth – performance will be excused.

Contracting parties can anticipate the need for change by including in their initial agreement some mechanisms for adjusting the contract price – for example, a price index. In Selection [9.3] I discuss the reasons why parties might want to include price adjustment mechanisms and some of the techniques that are available. I then turn to a discussion of the only American case in which a court has overtly revised the price term of a contract, *Alcoa v. Essex Group, Inc.*

211

Impossibility and related doctrines in contract law: an economic analysis

RICHARD A. POSNER AND
ANDREW M. ROSENFIELD (1977)

... The typical case in which impossibility or some related doctrine is invoked is one where, by reason of an unforeseen or at least unprovided-for event, performance by one of the parties of his obligations under the contract has become so much more costly than he foresaw at the time the contract was made as to be uneconomical (that is, the costs of performance would be greater than the benefits). The performance promised may have been delivery of a particular cargo by a specified delivery date – but the ship is trapped in the Suez Canal because of a war between Israel and Egypt. Or it may have been a piano recital by Gina Bachauer – and she dies between the signing of the contract and the date of the recital. The law could in each case treat the failure to perform as a breach of contract, thereby in effect assigning to the promisor the risk that war, or death, would prevent performance (or render it uneconomical). Alternatively, invoking impossibility or some related notion, the law could treat the failure to perform as excusable and discharge the contract, thereby in effect assigning the risk to the promisee.

From the standpoint of economics – and disregarding, but only momentarily, administrative costs – discharge should be allowed where the promisee is the superior risk bearer; if the promisor is the superior risk bearer, nonperformance should be treated as a breach of contract. "Superior risk bearer" is to be understood here as the party that is the more efficient bearer of the particular risk in question, in the particular circumstances of the transaction. Of course, if the parties have expressly

From Richard A. Posner and Andrew M. Rosenfield, "Impossibility and Related Doctrines in Contract Law: An Economic Analysis," *Journal of Legal Studies* 6 (1977): 83–118. With the permission of the authors and the University of Chicago Press.

assigned the risk to one of them, there is no occasion to inquire which is the superior risk bearer. The inquiry is merely an aid to interpretation.

A party can be a superior risk bearer for one of two reasons. First, he may be in a better position to prevent the risk from materializing. This resembles the economic criterion for assigning liability in tort cases. It is an important criterion in many contract settings, too, but not in this one. Discharge would be inefficient in any case where the promisor could prevent the risk from materializing at a lower cost than the expected cost of the risky event. In such a case efficiency would require that the promisor bear the loss resulting from the occurrence of the event, and hence that occurrence should be treated as precipitating a breach of contract.

But the converse is not necessarily true. It does not necessarily follow from the fact that the promisor could not at any reasonable cost have prevented the risk from materializing that he should be discharged from his contractual obligations. Prevention is only one way of dealing with risk; the other is insurance. The promisor may be the superior insurer. If so, his inability to prevent the risk from materializing should not operate to discharge him from the contract, any more than an insurance company's inability to prevent a fire on the premises of the insured should excuse it from its liability to make good the damage caused by the fire.

To understand how it is that one party to a contract may be the superior (more efficient) risk bearer even though he cannot prevent the risk from materializing, it is necessary to understand the fundamental concept of risk aversion. Compare a 100 percent chance of having to pay $10 with a one percent chance of having to pay $1,000. The expected cost is the same in both cases, yet not everyone would be indifferent as between the two alternatives. Many people would be willing to pay a substantial sum to avoid the uncertain alternative – for example, $15 to avoid having to take a one percent chance of having to pay $1,000. Such people are risk averse. The prevalence of insurance is powerful evidence that risk aversion is extremely common, for insurance is simply trading an uncertain for a certain cost. Because of the administrative expenses of insurance, the certain cost (that is, the insurance premium) is always higher, often much higher, than the uncertain cost that it avoids – the expected cost of the fire, of the automobile accident, or whatever. Only a risk-averse individual would pay more to avoid bearing risk than the expected cost of the risk.

The fact that people are willing to pay to avoid risk shows that risk is a cost. Accordingly, insurance is a method (alternative to prevention) of reducing the costs associated with the risk that performance of a contract may be more costly than anticipated. It is a particularly important method of cost avoidance in the impossibility context because the risks with which that doctrine is concerned are generally not preventable by the party charged with nonperformance. As mentioned, if they were, that would normally afford a compelling reason for treating nonperformance as a breach of contract. (Stated otherwise, a "moral hazard" problem would be created if the promisor were insured against a hazard that he could have prevented at reasonable cost.)

The factors relevant to determining which party to the contract is the cheaper insurer are (1) risk-appraisal costs and (2) transaction costs. The former comprise the costs of determining (a) the probability that the risk will materialize and (b) the magnitude of the loss if it does materialize. The amount of risk is the product of the probability of loss and the magnitude of the loss if it occurs. Both elements – probability and magnitude – must be known in order for the insurer to know how much to ask from the other party to the contract as compensation for bearing the risk in question.

The relevant transaction costs are the costs involved in eliminating or minimizing the risk through pooling it with other uncertain events, that is, diversifying away the risk. This can be done either through self-insurance or through the purchase of an insurance policy (market insurance). To illustrate, a corporation's shareholders might eliminate the risk associated with some contract the corporation had made by holding a portfolio of securities in which their shares in the corporation were combined with shares in many other corporations whose earnings would not be (adversely) affected if this particular corporation were to default on the contract. This would be an example of self-insurance. Alternatively, the corporation might purchase business-loss or some other form of insurance that would protect it (and, more important, its shareholders) from the consequences of a default on the contract; this would be an example of market insurance. Where good opportunities for diversification exist, self-insurance will often be cheaper than market insurance.

The foregoing discussion indicates the factors that courts and legislatures might consider in devising efficient rules for the discharge of contracts. An easy case for discharge would be one where (1) the promisor asking to be discharged could not reasonably have prevented the event rendering his performance uneconomical, and (2) the promisee could have insured against the occurrence of the event at lower cost than the promisor because the promisee (a) was in a better position to estimate both (i) the probability of the event's occurrence and (ii) the magnitude of the loss if it did occur, and (b) could have self-insured, whereas the promisor would have had to buy more costly market in-surance. As we shall see, not all cases are this easy.

. . . Two hypothetical cases will illustrate the nature of the economic analysis of a discharge case.

(1) A, a manufacturer of printing machinery, contracts with B, a commercial printer, to sell and install a printing machine on B's prem-ises. As B is aware, the machine will be custom-designed for B's needs and once the machine has been completed its value to any other printer will be very small. After the machine is completed, but before instal-lation, a fire destroys B's premises and puts B out of business, precluding B from accepting delivery of the machine. The machine has no salvage value and A accordingly sues for the full price. B defends on the grounds that the fire, which the fire marshal has found occurred without negli-gence on B's part – indeed (the same point, in an economic sense), which could not have been prevented by B at any reasonable cost – should operate to discharge B from its obligations under the contract.

The risk that has materialized, rendering completion of the contract uneconomical, is that a fire on B's premises would prevent B from taking delivery of the machine at a time when the machine was so far completed (to B's specifications) that it would have no value in an alternative use. The fact that the fire occurred in premises under B's control suggests that B had the superior ability to *prevent* the fire from occurring. This consideration is entitled to some weight even though the fire marshal found that B could not, in fact, have prevented the fire (economically); the fire marshal might be wrong. Certainly as between the parties B had the superior ability to prevent the fire. But in light of the fire marshal's finding, ability to prevent cannot weigh too heavily in the decision of the case.

Turning to the relative ability to the parties to *insure* against the machine's loss of value as a result of the fire, we note first that while B was in a better position to determine the probability that a fire would occur, A was in a better position to determine the magnitude of the relevant loss (the loss of the resources that went into making the ma-chine) if the fire did occur. That loss depended not only on the salvage value of the machine if the fire occurred after its completion but also on its salvage value at various anterior stages. A knows better than B the stages of production of the machine and the salvage value at each stage.

Assuming the actuarial value of the risk has been computed, there remains the question which of the parties could have obtained insurance protection at lower cost. Depending on the volume of A's production and on A's prior experience with contingencies such as occurred in the contract with B, A may be able to eliminate the risk of such contingencies simply by charging a higher price – in effect, an insurance premium – to all of its customers; A may in short be able to self-insure. B is less likely to be able to do so: The magnitude of its potential liability to A in the event of a default may greatly exceed any amount it could hope to pass on to its customers in the form of higher prices. As for market insurance, it seems unlikely that B could obtain for a reasonable price a fire insurance policy that protected it not only against the damage to its premises (and possibly to its business) caused by a fire but also against its contractual liability to A which, as mentioned, depends on the stage in the production of the machine at which the fire occurs, a matter within the private knowledge of A.

We are inclined to view A as the superior risk bearer in these circumstances and thus to discharge B. . . .

(2) For our second hypothetical case, let C be a large diversified business concern engaged in both coal mining and the manufacture and sale of large coal-burning furnaces. C executes contracts for the sale of furnaces to D, E, F, etc. in which it also agrees to supply coal to them for a given period of time at a specified price. The price, however, is to vary with and in proportion to changes in the consumer price index.

A few years later the price of coal unexpectedly quadruples and C repudiates the coal-supply agreements arguing that if forced to meet its commitments to supply coal at the price specified in its contracts it will be bankrupted. Each purchaser sues C seeking as damages the difference between the price of obtaining coal over the life of C's commitment and the contract price. C argues that the rise in the price of coal was unforeseeable and ought to operate to discharge it from its obligations.

On these facts the case might be decided against C simply on the ground that the contract explicitly assigned to it all price risks (except those resulting from changes in the value of money). If, however, C were able to convince a court that the risk had not been specifically assigned in the instrument (either on the theory that C was really contracting for the sale of a furnace and the coal provisions of the contract were incidental, or that the source or magnitude of the price change that occurred was not within the parties' contemplation), it would then be necessary to determine whether C or the purchasers were the superior risk bearer(s).

With regard to the parties' relative abilities to forecast the consequences for contract performance of a steep change in the price of coal, two factors seem critical: the amount of coal that C has contracted to deliver forward at a fixed price, and the degree of C's exposure to coal price changes. C's exposure depends on the amount of coal sold forward that is not covered either by C's existing coal stocks or by its forward purchase contracts, multiplied by the spread in price between the average forward sale price and the average forward purchase price. Thus the magnitude of the potential loss from the price increase is simply C's net short position, and C is in a better position than any of its (typical) customers to estimate this magnitude since only C has precise knowledge of its own net asset position and contractual commitments.

The likelihood (as distinct from magnitude) of loss in this case *appears* to depend crucially on the probability of a large movement in the price of coal, a movement which C may have no greater ability to predict than its purchasers. But the appearance is deceptive. The critical variable is again the extent of C's exposure. If C had a perfectly neutral hedge position in coal, no movement in the price of coal could affect it. The closer C is to a neutral hedge position, the less impact a given movement in price will have on its balance sheet. Hence the ability to forecast the relevant probability here depends ultimately on knowing C's net coal position, and C knows it best.

Moreover, C can readily insure against the contingency involved in this case. Its owners can self-insure against the financial risks to C of having to make good on its coal-supply commitments at the price specified in the contract either by holding a diversified portfolio of common stocks or by purchasing shares just in the firms that are on the buying side of C's contracts. To be sure, the shareholders of C's customers may be able to insure themselves in the same fashion at no greater cost. But an additional factor is that, as suggested above, C can self-insure by purchasing covering contracts to perfect a neutral hedge. Since there are transactional economies of scale in making forward contracts, C could execute the hedge at lower cost than each of its purchasers.

* * *

. . . In the discussion of our two hypothetical cases, we applied the standard of efficient discharge developed earlier directly to the facts of the case. This is not necessarily the optimum approach. A broad standard makes it difficult to predict the outcome of particular cases. If the purpose of contract law (so far as relevant here) is to supply standard contract terms in order to economize on negotiation, it will be poorly served by a legal standard so vague and general that contracting parties will encounter great difficulty in trying to ascertain the judicially implied terms of their contract; if the allocation of risks in the contract is unclear, neither party will know which risks he should take steps to prevent or insure against because he will be held liable if they materialize.

217

Our second hypothetical case is a particularly good illustration of the dangers of a broad standard. The contract seemed on its face to allocate the risk of coal price changes (save those due to inflation) to C; if the allocation is instead to depend on how a court decides years later who the superior risk bearer was, the apparent definitiveness of the contract terms evaporates. One way of avoiding this result in the coal hypothetical is to deem the case outside the scope of the discharge defense by noting the absence of any showing that performance under the contract was uneconomical. We assume the coal company's position is not that it could not comply with the contract at an economically reasonable price (it could buy on the open market all of the coal that it needed to fulfill its contractual obligations), but that compliance would bankrupt it. This is tantamount to arguing that a breach of contract should be excused when the breaching party for some reason lacks the resources to make good on the other party's damages.

Another approach one can take in the coal case to rule out discharge is to reason that when a contract explicitly assigns the risk of price changes to one party, discharge should not be allowed simply because the price change is greater than anticipated, regardless of which party is the superior bearer of the unanticipated portion of the change. The theory here would be that since the parties must negotiate with regard to price anyway, they can, at the same time and at little additional negotiating cost, place a limit on the promisor's price exposure. If they do not do so, the court will not do it for them.

* * *

... [A] common issue in the impossibility area is the effect of wars or other unexpected events on transportation contracts. To illustrate the relative abilities of the parties to bear risk in cases of this sort, consider the effect on shipping contracts of the closing of the Suez Canal by the Egyptian government in 1956. The closing required ships passing between Atlantic ports and ports in the Middle East to sail around Africa, a longer and more expensive voyage, and gave rise to voluminous litigation. The general result was the enforcement of the shipping contracts. For example, in *Transatlantic Financing Corp. v. United States* a shipowner argued that its contract with the United States to transport wheat from the U.S. to Iran was discharged by the closing of the Suez Canal. The issue was framed by Judge Wright as follows:

First, a contingency – something unexpected – must have occurred. Second, the risk of the unexpected occurrence must not have been allocated either by agreement or by custom. Finally, occurrence of the contingency must have rendered performance commercially impracticable. [At 315]

218

The court found that the closing of the canal was unexpected and that the risk of its occurrence had not been expressly allocated between the parties. It then addressed the ultimate question: Was the closing grounds for discharge?

To answer the question, Judge Wright sought to determine which party – the owner of the ship or the government – was the superior risk bearer. His answer addressed itself to the precise elements of our economic framework:

Transatlantic was no less able than the United States to purchase insurance to cover the contingency's occurrence. If anything, it is more reasonable to expect owner-operators of vessels to insure against the hazards of war. They are in the best position to calculate the cost of performance by alternative routes (and therefore to estimate the amount of insurance required), and are undoubtedly sensitive to international troubles which uniquely affect the demand for and cost of their services. [At 319]

This passage makes the decision on whether to discharge the contract turn on an examination of the key economic parameters that we have identified. The shipowner is the superior risk bearer because he is better able to estimate the magnitude of the loss (a function of delay, and of the value and nature of the cargo, which are also known to the shipowner) and the probability of the unexpected event. Furthermore, shipowners who own several ships and are engaged in shipping along several routes can spread the risks of delay on any particular route without purchasing market insurance or forcing their shareholders to diversify their common-stock portfolios. And the shipping company could, if it desired, purchase in a single transaction market insurance covering multiple voyages. Of course, the shipper in the particular case – the United States Government – was well-diversified too, but decision should (and here did) turn on the characteristics of shippers as a class, if an unduly particularistic analysis is to be avoided.

It might appear that the owner of the shipment would have a better idea than the shipowner of the consequences of delayed arrival. But consequential damages of this type are not relevant to the discharge question, because the rule of *Hadley v. Baxendale* places liability for such damages (in the absence of express agreement to the contrary) on the shipper rather than on the carrier – and properly so from the standpoint of economics. The question of discharge thus arises only with respect to that portion of the damages that the carrier can estimate without knowing the details of the shipper's business.

* * *

... The next group of cases we consider concerns contracts to supply agricultural products, and illustrates how the courts can arrive at an economically efficient result yet disguise it as an apparently meaningless semantic distinction. The cases have similar facts. A supplier contracts to deliver a particular quantity of and quality of an agricultural product; an unexpected event such as a flood or an exceptionally severe drought prevents delivery; the buyer seeks damages. The courts generally discharge the contract where the supplier is a grower, but enforce it where the supplier is a wholesaler or large dealer. The result is both consistent and efficient; it places the risk of extreme weather conditions on the superior risk bearer. The purchaser from the grower can reduce the risk of adverse weather by diversifying his purchases geographically; there is empirical evidence to suggest that in some climatic regions geographical separation of only a few miles can dramatically reduce the risk of a large loss. When the seller is a wholesaler or large dealer there is no reason to allow discharge since he can diversify his purchases and thereby eliminate the risk of adverse weather.

Here as elsewhere the courts have not explicitly characterized the problem as one of identifying the superior risk bearer. They usually state that discharge will be allowed when the contract contemplates a single crop to be grown on a specific tract of land. Similarly, a comment to the relevant section of the Uniform Commercial Code allows discharge if and only if the contract refers to crops grown on land designated explicitly in the agreement. [UCC 2-615 (Comment 9)] This factor is irrelevant save as a reasonable instrumental variable that distinguishes cases in which the seller is a grower from those where he is a wholesaler. However, consistently with our analysis, one observes a tendency in both the pre-Code and later cases to mitigate the mechanical operation of this rule by either expansive construction of the contract or equitable reformation of its terms.

* * *

220

CHAPTER 9.2

Impossibility and related excuses

VICTOR P. GOLDBERG (1988)

The importance of the impossibility defense is circumscribed by the ability of the parties to contract around the law. If the law were too liberal in excusing performance, the parties could narrow the range of acceptable excuses by explicit contractual language. Conversely, if the law were too niggardly, the parties could enumerate additional circumstances that would justify discharge of the contractual obligations. If the law were badly out of line in either direction, the problems could be vitiated by proper drafting of *force majeure* clauses. Such clauses, which are very common, will suspend or discharge a promisor's obligations for "acts of God."

Indeed, it should not really matter whether we frame the problem of excuse in terms of implementing the parties' decision ("Does the fire constitute an act of God that excuses performance as per the initial agreement?") or of identifying the conditions that would justify excusing performance ("Does the fire make performance impossible?"). Even if a contract had no *force majeure* clause, a court might infer that the parties would have included one had they thought of it. That is, instead of recognizing an impossibility defense, the court could achieve the same result by interpretation of a *force majeure* clause, express or implied.

Regardless of how the doctrine is labeled, courts, when considering a plea to excuse performance, should be constrained by the fundamental question: What would the parties have chosen? I will argue that, as a general rule, parties would not agree to excuse performance because of changed market conditions (neither supply nor demand shocks). The

Reprinted from Victor P. Goldberg, "Impossibility and Related Excuses," *Journal of Institutional and Theoretical Economics* 144 (1988): 100–16, with the permission of the publisher.

fact that market prices have doubled or tripled would be irrelevant.* Parties are more likely to excuse performance if the supervening events adversely effect the costs of performing this particular contract for reasons that are essentially unrelated to overall market conditions.

* * *

Many contracts include a *force majeure* clause which would discharge a seller's obligation if, for example, his factory were to burn down. If he did not want to deliver for other reasons, perhaps because he could get a better price elsewhere, he would not be excused. Why would reasonable businessmen agree to excuse performance for the first reason but not the second? It is useful to note first that not all contracts would discharge the seller's obligation even in the first situation. If the subject matter of the contract were fungible, the contract would be less likely to provide for discharge. For example, suppose that Smith agrees to pay $1,000 for an item. His wallet, with $1,000 in it, is consumed in flames. It is unlikely that the parties would want to excuse his performance on this ground since there is no reason to presume that this $1,000 was connected in any way with performance of this contract. The loss of his wallet makes Smith poorer, but does not otherwise impair his ability to perform the contract. He simply substitutes other dollars for those destroyed in the fire. If, instead of cash, Smith had lost a ton of a fungible commodity or his factory for producing the fungible commodity had burnt down, the same story holds. He does not need to produce the commodity; he can meet his contractual obligation by buying it on the open market.

Let us consider then, a contract for delivery of something other than a fungible commodity from the seller, Smith, to the buyer, Brown. If the seller does not perform and remains liable for damages, then the court must assess damages and ascertain the reasonableness of buyer's cover. These tasks present some of the same problems that arise with monitoring specific performance. Because the good is not fungible, the buyer has some leeway in choosing the goods with which to cover. If Brown bears the costs, he will have an incentive to choose the most efficient substitute. If, however, Smith must bear the costs, Brown's incentive to economize is weaker. For example, suppose that Brown was purchasing a computer system. His choice of alternatives to the original system that Smith had promised include one firm with somewhat

---

* This is not to say that parties would never adjust the contract price. Price concessions in the face of changed market conditions are commonplace. But the grantor of the concession often expects a quid pro quo, either express (e.g., an increase in the term of the contract) or implied (e.g., enhanced good will). The grantor, that is, maintains the right to make (or not make) price concessions.

better hardware and somewhat inferior software and after-sale services. A second alternative has the opposite features and is considerably more expensive. If Brown had to pay out of his own pocket, he would choose the superior hardware at the lower price. If, however, the costs were to be borne by Smith, the buyer would choose the latter.

This is a routine moral hazard problem. The greater the moral hazard, the greater the *joint* costs of the parties. Even though nondischarge would result in greater costs for Smith and increased benefits for Brown, the net result is that both are worse off. The costs of the substituted performance are greater than the value of that performance to Brown – that is the essence of the moral hazard problem. Since in the long run the sellers must cover their costs, the costs of moral hazard will be reflected in the price of the goods. In this indirect way do the buyers share in the costs.

If not excusing the seller would result in these increased costs, why would the parties ever fail to excuse? The reason is that the benefits from holding the seller to the agreement will generally outweigh the costs, but these benefits are likely to be much lower in the event of the occurrence of a condition covered by a *force majeure* clause. If the plant for building a particular machine burns down or a farmer's entire carrot crop is destroyed, the overall market conditions do not change, although the costs of the individual producer do. If the occurrence of the particular event is uncorrelated with market conditions, then the expected value of the change in price between the date of contract formation and the date of the occurrence is zero. If the seller were excused, the buyer would gain when the market price fell and lose when it rose; leaving consequential damages aside, those two effects should roughly wash out.* That is, the buyer's *expected* damages from this source at the contract formation stage are low. The *actual* damages could turn out to be very high, however.[†]

The critical point is this. If the occurrence of a *force majeure* condition is not correlated with market conditions, the expected change in the market price is zero, and, therefore, the benefits anticipated at the contract formation stage from holding the promisor liable are likely to

---

* If the buyer could have recovered consequential damages that would arise because a substitute performance could not be completed until after the original performance was due, then discharge could be expensive for the buyer. The analysis is cleaner where it is clear that consequential damages would not be granted. When damages from delay are anticipated, a *force majeure* clause would be likely to suspend the seller's obligation, rather than terminate it.

† One cost of excusing performance is that the existence of a *force majeure* condition is a question of fact which could be costly to litigate. The greater the contract versus market differential, the greater the incentive to allege the existence of such a condition.

be low. However, if the seller refuses to perform because events subsequent to the formation of the contract have shown that the contract price is too low, the buyer does suffer. If the seller could perform, but would prefer not to, we can reasonably infer that the reason is that the contract price is too low; the seller could do better selling elsewhere. The changed conditions affect the market for the good or service involved. There is a widespread drought, the Suez Canal closes, etc. Discharging the contract in this instance carries a greater cost. If a seller could be excused simply because the contract price was below the market price, the substantial benefits from entering into a contract in a timely manner are sacrificed. While this sacrifice might be acceptable in some cases, it is clear that the costs of excusing a seller's performance when the contract price is too low are greater than excusing its performance in the event of a fire or other act of God.

Thus, it is at least plausible that contracting parties would find it efficient to excuse a seller in the event of a fire or similar seller-specific occurrence, but not on other grounds. It should be emphasized that discharge does not allow the seller to get off scot-free. If a fire destroys the seller's factory and its contract is discharged, it still bears all the costs of the destruction. The buyer bears the risk of a subsequent price change and any consequential damages. It should also be noted that the "impossibility" label is misleading. It might be impossible for the seller to perform what had been promised, but it is not impossible for him to pay the expectation damages. All he'd have to do is write a check. The justification for discharge is that the expected value of the check at the contract formation stage is likely to be low compared to the costs associated with holding the seller liable.

CHAPTER 9.3

Price adjustment in long-term contracts

VICTOR P. GOLDBERG (1985)

The economics of price adjustment

A. The benefits of price adjustment

Business firms have ample incentives to include some form of price adjustment mechanism in their contracts even if both parties are risk neutral. Firms do not generally enter into multiyear contracts because of their concern for the future course of prices. Rather, they enter into the agreements to achieve the benefits of cooperation. Having entered into such an agreement, the parties have to make some decision regarding the course of prices during the life of the agreement. That is, price adjustment will probably be ancillary to the main purposes of the agreement.

Price adjustment can be difficult and costly. Why then bother? Why not simply establish a price or a schedule of prices for the duration of the agreement? I will suggest four reasons that might lead business firms to consider using some form of price adjustment. First, if the contract concerns a complex product that will be continuously redefined during the life of the contract, a price adjustment mechanism can price the "amendments" to the original agreement. Examples include cost-plus pricing of sophisticated defense hardware and complex construction projects. Second, to properly coordinate their behavior, the parties want correct price signals. If the price of an input were below the market price (and if the buyer could not resell at a price greater than the contract price) the buyer would have an incentive to use "too much" of the input.

From Victor P. Goldberg, "Price Adjustment in Long-Term Contracts," *Wisconsin Law Review* 1985 (1985) 527–43. © 1985 by the University of Wisconsin. With the permission of the Wisconsin Law Review.

Since this should be anticipated at the formation stage, the costs of poor coordination are borne by both parties. This is a pure "moral hazard" problem akin to an insured person consuming too much health care because the postinsurance price is too low.

Two other reasons are, analytically at least, more interesting: reduction of precontract search and postagreement jockeying. In both these explanations, the success of price adjustment depends upon its ability to reduce the variance of outcomes. The reduced variance is not, however, valued directly. Rather, it enables the parties to curtail mutually harmful behavior, thereby increasing the value of the agreement to both parties.

A contract establishes gains to be divided between the parties; a fixed-price contract determines the distribution of these gains. The parties could attempt to increase their share of the gains before signing the contract by improving their information on the future course of costs and prices. The more they each spend on this search, the smaller the pie. *Ceteris paribus*, the larger the variance of the outcomes, the more resources would be devoted to this effort. The parties, therefore, have an incentive to incorporate into the initial agreement a device that would discourage this wasteful searching. Price adjustment mechanisms can do precisely that by reducing the value of the special information. This argument applies even for standardized commodities sold in thick markets.

If after the firms enter into a long-term agreement the contract price fails to track changing market conditions, the loser will be reluctant to continue performance. It could breach and suffer the legal and reputational consequences, but other, less severe, alternatives to willing compliance exist. A buyer could, for example, insist upon strict compliance with quality standards. The aggrieved party could read the contract literally – "working to the rules" as in labor disputes or in centrally planned economies. This is a variation on the pure moral hazard story. The incorrect price induces the aggrieved party to expend resources in attempting to renegotiate the terms of the agreement. The costs can arise directly from the effort to renegotiate or indirectly in strategic bargaining. That is, the loser might threaten to engage in acts which impose costs upon the other party but do not constitute a legal breach. These costs are a result of the failure to coordinate behavior in the face of changed circumstances. These costs would be unimportant if the parties had easy access to market alternatives; *ceteris paribus*, the more isolated from alternatives the contracting parties are, the more significant are the potential losses from poor coordination. Again, to the extent that the parties can anticipate these problems at the formation stage, the value of the exchange is reduced. If the probability of wasteful behavior increases as the divergence between contract price and the opportunity cost of the aggrieved party widens, price-adjustment rules which narrow the gap become increasingly attractive.

B. The mechanics of price adjustment

The easiest way to adjust the price is to index. But what should the parties be indexing? The overall price level? Input costs? Market price? Ideally the parties would index the market price. The payoff from indexing, after all, is from the reduction in the divergence between contract price and the market price. However, practical exigencies usually lead parties to index other prices as proxies. Indeed, in a long-term contract there often is no unique external market price. The implications of this fact will become clearer in the discussion of *Alcoa v. Essex*, below.

Cost changes will be a reasonably good proxy for changes in the market price if demand doesn't fluctuate too much or if industry supply is very elastic. However, changes in input prices are not necessarily the same as changes in input costs. If the relative prices of inputs change, the firm has an incentive to alter factor proportions to take advantage of the new price relationships. Also, if factor productivity changes, the connection between input prices and costs deteriorates. Nevertheless, indexing to input prices is common.

While indexing would be the easiest price adjustment mechanism to implement, it has the obvious disadvantage of tracking changing conditions imperfectly. The poorer the correlation between the index and what it is supposed to be tracking, the less attractive it will be. Another relatively simple mechanical rule is permitting one party to solicit outside offers with the other party having the right of first refusal. This allows better tracking of that party's opportunity cost, but it discourages making relation-specific investments. That is, the direct costs of price adjustment would be low, but the indirect costs of discouraging entering into a long-term relationship in the first place might be quite high. Cost-plus pricing tracks cost changes more closely but is more subject to manipulation; it also gives the seller poorer incentives to control costs and requires that the parties devote more resources to monitoring performance.

Negotiation is, of course, always an option. Even if the contract explicitly utilizes one of the methods mentioned in the previous paragraph or unambiguously states that the contract is a fixed-price agreement, one party could propose that the price be renegotiated. The

227

contract price, the clarity of the legal rule, and the costs of invoking the legal rule provide the background against which the renegotiation might take place.

Renegotiation allows use of accurate, current information in revising the contract; but reopening the contract could result in cost-generating strategic behavior, especially if one of the parties is vulnerable to the threat of nonrenewal. Renegotiation is not a zero-sum affair with one side's gains offset by the other's loss. In exchange for an increased price, for example, a seller could offer a contract extension and the prospect of not working to the letter of the contract. (A threat, after all, is just a promise with the sign reversed.)

The contract could explicitly establish the conditions under which renegotiation is to take place. It could require renegotiation at fixed intervals or have it triggered by specific events (for example, a rise in a price index of more than 20 percent). Gross inequity clauses call for renegotiation if the contract price is too far out of line, but typically do not spell out the criteria for determining when a gross inequity exists. The parties could agree to renegotiate in good faith and determine what would happen if the negotiations break down. The failure to negotiate a new price could result in continued performance at the current price, termination, mediation or arbitration, and so forth.

There are, in sum, a lot of mechanisms available for adjusting price within a long-term contract. All are imperfect. Their relative costs and benefits will determine which, if any, the parties should choose.

Alcoa v. Essex

A. The facts

In 1967, Alcoa and Essex entered into a twenty-year agreement in which Alcoa agreed to convert Essex's alumina into molten aluminum at Alcoa's Warrick, Indiana, plant. Essex purchased its alumina from an Alcoa subsidiary under a second long-term contract. The trial judge insisted that the two contracts were separate and that by design Alcoa's left hand did not know what the right hand was doing. After conversion the molten aluminum would be loaded into crucibles owned by Essex and taken by truck to Essex's fabricating plant built specifically to receive it. The contract was for fifty million pounds per year and included options for three additional blocks of twenty-five million pounds each. (By 1973, the parties had deleted

228

the last two blocks.) Hence, the contract quantity at the time the litigation arose was seventy-five million pounds per year.

The initial contract price was fifteen cents per pound, composed of a "demand charge" of five cents per pound, and a "production charge." The latter included a fixed component of four cents per pound (which was the "profit" on the plant constructed to fulfill this contract) and three cents each for nonlabor (primarily fuel) and labor costs. The former was indexed by the Industrial Component of the Wholesale Price Index and the latter by Alcoa's average hourly labor cost at the Warrick plant. The contract included a ceiling price of 65 percent of the price of a specified type of aluminum as reported in a trade journal; however, it did not specify a minimum price.

The demand charge was to be paid regardless of whether Essex took any aluminum. In effect Essex "rented" a portion of Alcoa's Warrick plant at a fixed rate of $7.09 million per year ($4.09 million for the demand charge and $3 million for the fixed charge) and paid a service fee of six cents per pound that was indexed.

Problems arose following the large increase in fuel prices in 1973. In the ensuing years the market price of aluminum and the cost of producing it in Warrick increased far more rapidly than did the contract price. By 1979, Essex received aluminum from Alcoa under the contract at thirty-six cents per pound and resold some of it in the open market at seventy-three cents. Nonlabor production costs rose from 5.8 cents to 22.7 cents in 1973–8, while the wholesale price index less than doubled. Alcoa attempted to renegotiate the price as early as 1975. In 1978, the dispute went to trial.

The trial court ruled in Alcoa's favor. Indexing nonlabor production costs to the Wholesale Price Index was deemed a "mutual mistake" because it tracked those costs so badly. The court also accepted Alcoa's alternative theories of impracticability and frustration. The court reformed the contract, since rescission would result in a windfall for Alcoa and deprive Essex of the benefits of its long-term supply contract. The court rewrote the price term of the contract to include a minimum price assuring Alcoa a one cent per pound "profit."

The disputed contract represented only a small part of the business of Alcoa and Essex. Alcoa's sales and total assets in 1979 were each almost $5 billion. Essex by the time of the trial had been acquired by United Technologies, another multibillion dollar firm. Despite its losses on this contract, Alcoa's overall profits in 1979 were around $500 million; its rate of return on equity in 1978 exceeded 14 percent for the first time in twenty-two years. This is not, clearly, a case in which a bad contract jeopardized the survival of a firm, as in *Westinghouse*. Rather, it is more instructive to view this contract as a poor performer in the firm's much larger portfolio of contracts, a portfolio which was performing very well overall.

B. The $75 million misunderstanding

The court placed considerable emphasis on the fact that projected losses from 1977 to 1978 were in the range of $75 million. This is one of those funny numbers that means nothing but could end up as a fundamental part of the *Alcoa* doctrine, were one to emerge. Alcoa was excused because they stood to lose $75 million; we won't excuse X because it cannot prove that it will lose such a large amount. (As I will note below, the *Alcoa* judge distinguished another case on precisely this ground.) It is, therefore, useful to look at how the court determined the magnitude of the loss.

The "profits" are the revenue minus the actual production costs minus the demand charge (the 5 + cents per pound). The court assumed something (the decision doesn't make it quite clear what) about future costs and prices for the remaining life of the contract and then added them up. There are three obvious problems with this. First, the future profits are undiscounted. A dollar lost in 1984 is just as important as a dollar lost in 1979. Second, the estimates are based on guesses about the future course of prices; there's nothing wrong with guesses, but time has a way of transforming guesses into facts. But these are quibbles. The most important point is that the estimate, even if done right, is irrelevant.

What does Alcoa lose if it must fulfill the contract? It loses the chance to sell the aluminum to someone else. That is the true measure of the loss, and in this case it is considerably greater than the figure cited by the judge. In the year the suit was brought the loss was over thirty cents per pound, over $20 million. The original cost of construction of the plant is a red herring equivalent to "par value" for a stock, a vestige of the past with no economic content.

The error is important. In an earlier case, the court refused to allow Gulf Oil to escape its obligation to deliver jet fuel under a five-year contract despite the fact that the price index utilized had inadequately tracked the course of oil prices. The court held that the cost data presented were insufficient to ascertain how much it cost Gulf to produce a gallon of jet fuel, and, therefore, Gulf had failed to prove that it had suffered losses on the contract. The *Alcoa* judge applied the "negative accounting profit" test in distinguishing this decision from *Alcoa*.

When faced with a claim of changed circumstances, courts or arbitrators should not look to accounting cost data to determine the merits of the claim. The relevant question is whether the difference between the contract price and the aggrieved party's next best option is large enough to warrant relief. An accounting cost or profit standard is an invitation to produce lots of information with a low expected value.

C. Alcoa's mistake

In retrospect, of course, Alcoa made a big mistake. However, the mistake singled out by the court to justify reformation of the contract was not the most important one. The failure of the price index to accurately measure the change in fuel prices accounted for only about ten to twelve cents of the difference between the contract price and the market price for aluminum in 1979 (that difference being over thirty cents). The main problem was caused by the fact that the contract did not track changing demand conditions, and the demand for aluminum was soaring in the late 1970s.

Moreover, the contract was not designed to adjust to large changes in the overall price level. Sixty percent of the initial contract price (the demand charge plus the fixed "profit") was unadjusted for the life of the contract. A very simple example gives an indication of the type of problem this could cause. Suppose that the price level rises about 7 percent per year (doubling roughly every ten years); assume that the factors of production remain equally productive and that they continue to be used in the same proportions. The indexed production costs would then rise from six cents per pound to twenty-four cents per pound in the twentieth year. However, the remaining costs are unindexed, so the final contract price would rise only to $(24 + 9 =)$ thirty-three cents. To keep the real price of aluminum constant the contract price would have had to increase to sixty cents.

The relevant question is not whether Alcoa made what turned out to be a bad decision. They did. But was it a bad decision at the time they made it? The answer to that is less certain. When I began this project it seemed clear that Alcoa could have, and should have, done better. At a minimum, I thought, they should have indexed the remaining 60 percent of the costs. However, a more careful look leads me to believe that it is a much closer question.

This long-term contract is in many respects similar to a lease or sale of part of Alcoa's Warrick production capacity to Essex. A fixed rental for long-term leases is not uncommon. Moreover, if one firm sells a durable asset to another, it is the rule, rather than the exception, that the price is not to be readjusted after the sale has taken place. It can be argued, then, by analogy, that this component of the long-term contract that looks so much like a lease should also be at a fixed price.

If the contract price of a long-lived asset were to be readjusted to better track the market price, the parties would expend less resources today in pursuit of special information. If this benefit were great, we would expect the parties to incorporate price adjustment arrangements in their sales and leases of assets. However, the benefits will often be very small. Information regarding the future price level, for example, is already incorporated in the term structure of interest rates. It is not necessarily *accurate* information, ex post; however, the key question is whether it is *improvable* information, ex ante. Incorporating a general price index, therefore, need not result in reduced information costs.

The lease/sale analogy, however, has difficulties. A pure lease or sale is similar to a contract for a standardized commodity because further coordination between the two parties is unnecessary; the only issue is whether price adjustment reduces the initial price search. However, the more the outcomes depend upon future coordination by the parties, the less likely they will use a fixed price contract. For example, shopping center leases in which the lessor engages in activities which generate business for the tenants will base at least part of the compensation on a percentage of the gross (which automatically provides for some price adjustment). If Alcoa were leasing the plant to Essex and allowing Essex to operate it, the fixed price arrangement would be routine. The fact that operation of the plant was in Alcoa's hands reduced the likelihood that a fixed price would be successful. The increased divergence between the contract price and Alcoa's best alternative would induce Alcoa to engage in strategic behavior, thereby reducing the value of the contract to both parties.

However, it is unlikely that indexing capital costs would result in a more accurate contract price. I would speculate that the pre-1973 experience would confirm that indexing this cost component to the general price level, construction costs, or any other conceivable cost-based measure would have resulted in a poorer fit between the market and contract price.

Instead of using a cost-based price adjustment, the parties could have attempted to track market conditions by, for example, indexing to a particular aluminum price. Using output prices to index is not without problems. First, other goods with published prices that are sufficiently close to the output that we are attempting to index might not exist. Second, the observable external prices are typically list prices, not transaction prices. If these diverge, the index suffers. It is plausible that the two would diverge in a concentrated industry like aluminum since list prices typically change more slowly in such industries. Further, if the contract price were linked to the list price of a type of Alcoa's aluminum, then Alcoa would have an incentive, however modest, to set the list price in excess of the transaction price.

Even if list prices were accurate measures of transaction prices, a more fundamental difficulty remains. The parties do not necessarily confront the same external price. That is, the relevant price to each party is its opportunity cost – the net price it could get from the next best trading partner. In a market for a standardized commodity, the list price and these two opportunity costs would be roughly the same. However, in a long-term contract in which the parties deliberately isolate themselves from the external market, these three prices are more likely to diverge. Generally, the more isolated the contracting parties are from market alternatives, the poorer the relationship between these three prices is likely to be. Thus, while the parties might desire to index their agreement to a published market price, the very nature of a long-term contract makes it likely that the index price would not perform its function adequately. It is, therefore, not at all obvious that indexing the contract to changes in the published price of a particular type of output would be in the interest of the two parties.

In the instant case, Alcoa's opportunity cost is the net price it could receive by using the Warrick capacity to produce ingot for export to other customers. Essex's opportunity cost is the price of delivered aluminum ingot. There is no a priori reason to believe that these will be close to each other. However, for an index to work it is not necessary that the prices be close, only that they move together over time. Whether these two opportunity costs (and the market price for aluminum ingot) do move together over time is an empirical question which I intend to explore in a later paper.

Essex chose to incorporate the output price information in the form of a maximum price. Alcoa, however, was not willing to pay (by agreeing to a lower initial contract price) for a price minimum. The failure to do so might well have been a mistake ex ante, but it is at least plausible that a ceiling indexed to published prices would be more valuable to Essex than a similarly indexed floor would have been to Alcoa. Alcoa's superior knowledge of the aluminum industry might make Essex suspicious of the manner in which costs were indexed. A bias in favor of Alcoa, because of Alcoa's superior knowledge, would make a bound on the index relatively more valuable to Essex.

Conceivably, therefore, Alcoa's failure to index plant costs or include a minimum price was not an error ex ante. Looking at the new contract

233

may provide some insight on this issue. We know that the parties rejected the judicially imposed minimum price based on ex ante accounting costs. But we do not know whether that was a reason for rejection and we do not know what replaced it. I would speculate that the new contract includes a minimum and that the minimum depends upon output prices. If so, that would suggest that Alcoa had erred initially.

Resolution of price adjustment disputes

Suppose that contracting parties assign the task of resolving price adjustment disputes to an outsider (a court or an arbitrator). The outsider can be asked to resolve two very different questions: (a) have conditions changed sufficiently to justify relief; and (b) what form should relief take – what will the new price (or price formula) be? Since the parties bear the costs of producing the evidence, they must reckon the expected costs of producing evidence on production costs, accounting profits, market prices, opportunity costs, and so forth, and weigh these against the expected benefits (in terms of reducing the costs arising from the divergence of contract price from market price). These evidentiary costs provide the backdrop for subsequent renegotiation. Thus, for example, if a standard required that one party spend a lot to produce evidence to forestall price revision, its opposite party could use those potential costs as a bargaining chip in renegotiation.

For determining whether relief is justified, I think it is reasonably clear that accounting cost data of the sort relied upon by the *Alcoa* judge are largely beside the point. The relevant question is whether the difference between the contract price and the aggrieved party's next best option is large enough to warrant relief. The requisite price differential would vary across contracts. There is no "magic number": If price goes up by at least X percent or losses total at least $\$Y$, adjust the price. A large divergence between the market and contract price for a standardized commodity, for example, would have little adverse effect on the expected value of a contract; it would, therefore, be unlikely that the parties would benefit from revision. Conversely, if a modest price divergence would generate considerable joint costs, revision could be effective. The problem is complicated by the fact that making relief easy to obtain generates additional joint costs as well. Rational parties might easily find that the potential benefits from price revision come at too high a cost.

This is especially true if there is no obvious standard for determining a new contract price. My initial presumption was that if a reasonable measure of the output price were available, the parties would want the arbitrator to use this to guide his decision. Further consideration has led me to conclude that this might not be very helpful. A simple example illustrates the problem. Suppose that when the contract was written Alcoa would have received ten cents a pound for its aluminum on the open market, Essex would have paid twenty cents per pound, and the contract price was fifteen cents. When the case is litigated, Alcoa could sell at fifty cents and Essex buy at seventy, and the contract price is thirty-five cents. What should the contract price be? Even if this information were costlessly produced and absolutely accurate, are the parties better off putting the decision in the hands of an arbitrator? What decision rule would they want him to apply? When the opportunity costs of the buyer and seller diverge, it is not at all clear what should guide the arbitrator in setting a new price. Thus, the possible divergence not only impairs the value of a published price as an index, but makes it more difficult for the parties to rely upon outsiders (arbitrators and judges) to revise price.

* * *

Questions and notes on impossibility and price adjustment

1. It seems a rather curious use of language to view strikes as acts of God. Why are they usually included as an excuse in a *force majeure* clause?

2. Posner and Rosenfield argue that the Suez Canal cases were rightly decided. Why do they argue that the carrier's obligation should not be excused? Do you find their explanation persuasive?

   2.1 Suppose that the port at which a carrier is supposed to deliver its cargo is blockaded. As a result, the carrier discharges the goods at another port. Completion of the contract (that is, delivery of the goods to the original destination) would require that someone incur additional expenditures. Who should bear the additional costs, the carrier or the shipper? How would Posner and Rosenfield decide that matter?

   2.2 In fact, contracts for ocean shipping of grain routinely include a War Risks clause that holds that in the event of a blockade (and related risks), the carrier who delivers to a safe port would be paid the amount specified in the original contract, and, upon such delivery, the contract would be discharged. The shipper would be responsible for any additional costs that might be incurred by bringing the goods to their original destination. Why might this be the case?

   2.3 This allocation of risks can be reconciled with the allocation in the Suez cases. How? HINTS: What is the likely effect of a blockade of a particular destination on the market price of ocean shipping services? What is the likely effect on that price of the closing of the Suez Canal? In the two cases, what is the likelihood that the shipper would want the goods to be delivered to the original destination if the costs of completion had to be borne by the shipper?

236

3. Posner and Rosenfield suggest that the explicit identification of the crops with a particular plot of land is a proxy for the distinction between a farmer and a wholesaler, the latter being better able to diversify risks. Is this persuasive? The farmer still bears the entire risk of the destruction of his crop. The only question is assignment of the additional risk of a price rise. If the farmer had assumed this risk in the initial contract, why should the risk be shifted when his crop is destroyed?

   3.1 One could argue that the destruction reduces the farmer's wealth and therefore he would want more protection from risk – the poorer they are, the more risk averse. Does this seem plausible? This explanation would suggest that rich farmers or corporate farmers use different contracts than poorer farmers, other things equal. Do you think that this would be true?

   3.2 Can you develop an alternative explanation for excusing contracts that specify that the crop be grown on a particular plot of land and not others? HINT: Consider the contracting parties' desire to specify quality and the moral hazard problem inherent in arranging a cover transaction.

4. *Force majeure* clauses are often symmetrical, in that either party could be excused if a fire or similar event prevented its performance. Would that be consistent with an explanation based on relative attitudes toward risk?

5. A retailer, Rogers, leases a store for five years at a fixed monthly rental rate from the landlord, Lewis. Rogers does not intend to make any significant improvements on the leased property; he is just renting the space. One possible contingency for which they might want to plan is the possibility that a government agency might take the property for a public use (for example, construction of a highway). There is a Constitutional requirement that the government compensate the owner for such a taking. Since the leasehold interest is recognized as a separate property interest, the government must compensate both the landlord and the tenant. The tenant's interest is the difference between the contractually specified rental payments and the rent that would have to be paid given current market conditions. So, for example, if at the time of condemnation the lease had five years to run, the agreed-upon rent was $5,000 per year, and the current market rent was $10,000, the tenant would be entitled to receive the discounted value of the difference ($5,000 per year).

   Designating the tenant's interest a property interest only defines a default position. If the lease is silent on the matter, then the tenant will receive the compensation. The parties are free, however, to draft around the law and specify contractually how the award should be distributed. In fact, they typically do include "condemnation clauses" in their leases and these clauses typically give the entire award to the landlord. Why might they choose this arrangement? See Goldberg, Merrill, and Unumb (1988).

6. In anticipation of the coronation of Edward VII, rooms along the anticipated route of the procession were rented at a substantial premium for the day of the event. A sudden illness of the soon-to-be monarch, however, resulted in postponement of the proceedings and a spate of litigation. In *Krell v. Henry* and *Chandler v. Webster* the courts held that the frustrated viewers were excused from performance; however, money that had been paid prior to the announcement of the illness would not be refunded, and money that was due prior to the announcement must still be paid by the renter. Dawson and Harvey (1969, p. 636) characterize the result in this way: "The parties were left suspended at the particular point where they had planned to be when the unforeseen event occurred, despite the conclusion . . . that their contractual plan had been so shattered that the contract could not be enforced." This, they claim, is absurd. Is it? Suppose that the parties had anticipated that such an illness was possible. How do you think careful planners would have allocated the risks of postponement. HINT: Think of the owners of flats along the route as selling options. If payment is not made by a particular date, the option lapses.

7. The Snow Mountain Ski Lodge rents out its rooms during the peak season at $200 per day. A mild, dry winter leaves them with no snow on the ground in February. People who had booked the rooms back in October realize that without snow these rooms aren't even worth $20 a day. They cancel their reservations and demand the return of their deposit claiming that the unexpected weather frustrated the basic purpose of their contract. Should their obligation be discharged? Should their down payments be refunded? Posner and Rosenfield (in a portion of their article not reproduced here) note that this situation is similar to the coronation cases. They argue that the contract should not be discharged because the ski lodge is less able to diversify its risks than the customers. "Skiers as a class are superior self-insurers against poor ski conditions compared to ski lodges; the skier can find adequate conditions somewhere but the lodge cannot diversify away the risk of poor conditions (save by merger with lodges in other ski areas)" (1977, p. 110). Is that

238

persuasive? How do you think this issue would be resolved if the parties dealt with it explicitly in the contract?

8. Smith agrees to manufacture customized machinery to be sold to Brown for $100,000. Brown's factory burns down when the contract is purely executory. That is, Smith has done nothing and Brown has paid nothing. Should performance be excused?

   8.1. Now, suppose that Brown's fire occurred four months after the contract had been entered into. Smith has incurred an expenditure of about $25,000 and Brown has made payment to Smith of $15,000. Brown sues for restitution of its $15,000 payment and Smith countersues for payment of its expenditures in reliance. How should these claims be disposed of? See *Fibrosa Spolka Akcyjna v. Fairbairn L.C.B., Ltd.* If you were designing a contract, how would you draft the agreement to take contingencies of this sort into account. HINT: What purpose is served by having Brown make payments prior to completion of the contract?

9. The Posner–Rosenfield coal hypothetical is based on Westinghouse's breach of its uranium supply contracts in the 1970s. Westinghouse's refusal to honor its contractual commitments precipitated a huge lawsuit that was settled before a decision was rendered. For a description of some aspects of the *Westinghouse* litigation, see Joskow (1977). Westinghouse had promised to sell a considerable amount of uranium that it did not own. That is what Posner and Rosenfield mean when they say that the seller was in a net short position. Westinghouse would not have been net short had it owned sufficient uranium to meet its contractual obligations or had some contractual commitment to purchase the uranium at a fixed price. Is it likely that Westinghouse would have tried to breach if it had owned a sufficient amount of uranium?

   9.1 In *Alcoa* the failure of the contract formula to track costs adequately is analogous to the seller having a net short position in the Posner–Rosenfield hypothetical. That did not play any role in my analysis of the case in Selection [9.3]. Nor did the analysis depend upon the fact that the Essex contract was only one contract in Alcoa's portfolio of contracts, a portfolio that increased in value during the period. Should courts accept evidence on these points when considering a request to provide relief or excuse performance?

10. Suppose that the coal company in the hypothetical realized that buying the coal on the open market in order to meet its contractual

obligations would have been futile since the obligations would eventually place the firm in bankruptcy. It informed the buyers that if they did not renegotiate the price, it would simply walk away from the contract. The buyers agreed to a higher price and accepted coal at that higher price for a period of time. However, the buyers then claimed that the price adjustment was extracted under duress and that they should not be liable for the higher price. Should the modification be enforced? Compare this problem with *Goebel v. Linn* (discussed in Part VIII).

10.1 Suppose that after the price of coal quadrupled it became clear that the buyers had no use for the coal. They would simply resell it to others. Should the contracts be discharged because the basic purpose of the contracts had been frustrated?

10.2 Most long-term (i.e., thirty- to fifty-year) coal supply contracts include a gross inequity clause that enables either party to request a modification of the contract price in the event of changed circumstances. See Joskow (1985). Why would parties enter into such long-term supply contracts and why would they include the gross inequity clause?

References

Cases

Alaska Packers' Ass'n. v. Domenico, 117 Fed. 99 (9th Cir. 1902)

Alcoa v. Essex Group, Inc., 499 F. Supp. 53 (W.D. Pa. 1980)

Anglia Television Ltd. v. Reed, 3 All. E.R. 690 (C.A. 1971)

Austin Instrument, Inc. v. Loral Corp., 29 N.Y. 2d 124, 272 N.E.2d 533, 324 N.Y.S.2d 22 (1971)

Boomer v. Atlantic Cement Co., 26 N.Y. 2d 219, 257 N.E.2d 870, 309 N.Y.S.2d 312 (NY 1970)

British Columbia Sawmill Co. v. Nettleship, L.R. 3 C.P. 499 (1868)

Campbell v. Wentz, 172 F.2d 80 (1948)

C. Czarnikow Ltd. v. Koufos (Heron II), 1 A.C. 350 (1969)

Chandler v. Webster, 1 K.B. 493 (1904)

Chatlos Systems Inc. v. National Cash Register Corp., 670 F.2d 1304 (1982)

Chicago Coliseum Club v. Dempsey, 265 Ill. App. 542 (1932)

Compania Naviera Asiatic v. The Burmah Oil Co., Findings of Fact and Conclusions of Law in No. 74–2025 (S.D.N.Y. Apr. 27, 1977) (Frankel, J.)

Endiss v. Belle Isle Ice Co., 49 Mich. 279, 13 N.W. 590 (1882)

Fibrosa Spolka Akcyjna v. Fairbairn L.C.B. Ltd., (1943 A.C. 32

Frederick Raff Co. v. Murphy, 110 Conn. 234, 147 A. 709, 712 (1929)

Goebel v. Linn, 47 Mich. 489, 11 N.W. 284 (1882)

Hackley & McGordon v. Headley, 45 Mich. 569, 8 N.W. 511 (1881)

Hadley v. Baxendale, 9 Ex. 341, 156 Eng. Rep. 145 (1854)

Hawkins v. McGee, 84 N.H. 114, 146 A. 641 (1929)

Headley v. Hackley, 50 Mich. 43, 14 N.W. 693 (1883)

Hoffman v. Red Owl Stores, Inc., 133 N.W. 2d 267, 26 Wis. 2d 683 (1965)

In re Westinghouse Electric Corp. Uranium Contracts Litigation, No. 235 (E. D. Va. October 27, 1978) (bench opinion).

J'Aire Corp. v. Gregory, 24 Cal. 3d 799, 598 P. 2d 60, 157 Cal. Rptr. 407 (1979)

Kemble v. Farren, 6 Bing. 141, 130 Eng. Rep. 1234 (C.P. 1829)

Kemp v. The Knickerbocker Ice Co., 51 How. Pr. 316 (N.Y. 1876)

References

Krell v. Henry, 2 K.B. 740 (1903)

L. Albert & Son v. Armstrong Rubber Co., 178 F.2d 182 (1949)

Lobianco v. Property Protection, Inc., 437 A.2d 417 (Pa. Super. Ct. 1981)

Mandel v. National Ice & Coal Co., 180 N.Y. Supp. 429 (1st Dept. 1920)

Martin v. Joseph Harris Co., Inc., 767 F.2d 296 (1985)

Neri v. Retail Marine Corp., 30 N.Y. 2d 393, 334 N.Y.S.2d 165, 285 N.E. 2d 311 (1972)

Oloffson v. Coomer, 11 Ill. App. 3d 918, 296 N.E. 2d 871 (1973)

Parsons v. Uttley, 1 Q.B. 791 (1978)

Pirrone v. Monarch Wine Co. of Georgia, 497 F.2d 25 (5th Cir. 1974)

Rourke v. Story, 4 E.D. Smith 54 (N.Y. 1855)

Schwartzreich v. Bauman-Basch, Inc., 231 N.Y. 196, 131 N.E. 887 (1921)

Secor v. Ardsley Ice Co., 133 App. Div. 136, 117 N.Y. Supp. 414 (2d Dept. 1909), aff'd mem. 201 N.Y. 603, 95 N.E. 1139 (1911)

Security Stove & Manufacturing Co. v. American Railway Express Co., 227 Mo. App. 175, 51 S.W. 2d 572 (1932)

Sullivan v. O'Connor, 363 Mass. 579, 296 N.E. 2d 183 (1973)

Teradyne Inc. v. Teledyne Industries, Inc., 676 F. 2d 865 (1st Cir. 1982)

Thomas v. McDaniel, 14 Johns. 185 (N.Y. 1817)

Transatlantic Financing Corp. v. United States, 363 F.2d 312 (D.C. Cir. 1966)

Ultramares Corp. v. Touche 255 N.Y. 170, 174 N.E. 441 (1931)

Victoria Laundry (Windsor) v. Newman Industries, 2 K.B. 528 (1949)

Walters v. Marathon Oil Co., 642 F.2d 1098 (1981)

Whitney v. Eager, 29 Fed. Cas. No. 17584, at 1073 (E.D. Pa. 1841)

Articles

Aivazian, Varouj A., Michael J. Trebilcock, and Michael Penny. "The Law of Contract Modifications: The Uncertain Quest for a Benchmark of Enforceability." *Osgood Hall Law Journal* 22 (1984): 173–212.

Akerlof, George A. "The Market for 'Lemons': Quality Uncertainty and the Market Mechanism." *Quarterly Journal of Economics* 84 (1970): 488–500.

Arrow, Kenneth J. "Uncertainty and the Welfare Economics of Medical Care." *American Economic Review* 53 (1963): 941–73.

——. "The Economics of Moral Hazard: Further Comment." *American Economic Review* 58 (1968): 537–8.

Birmingham, Robert. "Notes on the Reliance Interest." *Washington Law Review* 60 (1985): 217–66.

Bishop, William. "The Contract–Tort Boundary and the Economics of Insurance." *Journal of Legal Studies* 12 (1983): 241–66.

——. "The Choice of Remedy for Breach of Contract." *Journal of Legal Studies* 14 (1985): 299–320.

Buchanan, James M. *The Inconsistencies of the National Health Service.* Occasional Paper No. 7. London: Institute of Economic Affairs 1964.

Calabresi, Guido, and A. Douglas Melamed. "Property Rules, Liability Rules, and Inalienability: One View of the Cathedral." *Harvard Law Review* 85 (1972): 1089–128.

Clarkson, Kenneth W., Roger LeRoy Miller, and Timothy J. Muris. "Liquidated Damages v. Penalties: Sense or Nonsense?" *Wisconsin Law Review* 1978 (1978): 351–90.

Coase, Ronald A. "The Nature of the Firm." *Economica* 4 (1937): 386–405.

———, "The Problem of Social Cost." *Journal of Law & Economics* 3 (1960): 1–44.

Cooter, Robert. "Unity in Tort, Contract, and Property: The Model of Precaution." *California Law Review* 73 (1985): 1–51.

Dalzell, John. "Duress by Economic Pressure, I." *North Carolina Law Review* 20 (1942): 237–77.

Danzig, Richard. "Hadley v. Baxendale: A Study in the Industrialization of the Law." *Journal of Legal Studies* 4 (1975): 249–84.

Darling, Sir Malcolm. *Punjabi Peasant in Prosperity and Debt,* 3d ed. Oxford: Oxford University Press (1932).

Dawson, John P. "Judicial Revision of Frustrated Contracts: Germany." *Boston University Law Review* 63 (1983): 1039–98.

———, and William B. Harvey. *Cases on Contracts and Contract Remedies.* Mineola: Foundation Press, 1969.

Demsetz, Harold. "Wealth Distribution and the Ownership of Rights." *Journal of Legal Studies* 1 (1972): 223–32.

Dickerson, O. D. *Health Insurance.* Homewood, Ill.: Irwin, 1959.

———. *Health Insurance,* rev. ed. Homewood, Ill.: Irwin, 1963.

Feinman, Jay M. "Promissory Estoppel and Judicial Method." *Harvard Law Review* 97 (1984): 678–718.

Fuller, Lon, and William Perdue. "The Reliance Interest in Contract Damages." *Yale Law Journal* 46 (1936): 52–98.

Gilman, Hank, and William M. Bulkeley. "Can Software Firms Be Held Responsible When a Program Makes a Costly Error?" *Wall Street Journal,* August 4, 1986, p. 15.

Goetz, Charles J., and Robert E. Scott. "The Mitigation Principle: Toward a General Theory of Contractual Obligation." *Virginia Law Review* 69 (1983): 967–1025.

———. "Measuring Seller's Damages: The Lost-Profits Puzzle." *Stanford Law Review* 31 (1979): 323–73.

Goldberg, Victor P. "Institutional Change and the Quasi-Invisible Hand." *Journal of Law and Economics* 17 (1974): 461–92.

———. "Relational Exchange: Economics and Complex Contracts." *American Behavioral Scientist* 28 (1980): 337–52.

———. "An Economic Analysis of the Lost-Volume Retail Seller." *Southern California Law Review* 57 (1984a): 283–97.

———. "Production Functions, Transactions Costs and the New Institutionalism." In *Issues in Contemporary Microeconomics,* edited by George Feiwel, 395–402. New York: Macmillan, 1984b.

References

———. "A Relational Exchange Perspective on the Employment Relationship." In *Organization and Labor*, edited by Frank Stephens, 1984c.

———. "Price Adjustment in Long-Term Contracts." *Wisconsin Law Review* 1985 (1985): 527–43.

———. "Relational Exchange, Contract Law, and the *Boomer* Problem." *Journal of Institutional and Theoretical Economics* 141 (1985): 570–5.

———. "Impossibility and Related Excuses." *Journal of Institutional and Theoretical Economics* 144 (1988): 100–16.

———, Thomas W. Merrill, and Daniel Unumb. "Bargaining in the Shadow of Eminent Domain: Valuing and Apportioning Condemnation Awards Between Landlord and Tenant." *UCLA Law Review* 34 (1987): 1083–137.

Hicks, John F. "The Contractual Nature of Real Property Leases." *Baylor Law Review* 24 (1972): 443–544.

Joskow, Paul L. "Commercial Impossibility, the Uranium Market and the Westinghouse Case." *Journal of Legal Studies* 6 (1977): 119–76.

———. "Vertical Integration and Long-Term Contracts: The Case of Coal-Burning Electric Generating Plants." *Journal of Law Economics and Organization* 1 (1985): 33–80.

Kitch, Edmund W. "The Nature and Function of the Patent System." *Journal of Law & Economics* 20 (1977): 265–90.

Klein, Benjamin. "Transaction Costs Determinants of 'Unfair' Contractual Arrangements." *American Economic Review, Papers and Proceedings* 70 (1980): 356–62.

———, Robert G. Crawford, and Armen A. Alchian. "Vertical Integration, Appropriable Rents, and the Competitive Contracting Process." *Journal of Law and Economics* 21 (1978): 297–326.

Knight, Frank. *Risk, Uncertainty, and Profit*. Boston: Houghton Mifflin, 1921.

Kronman, Anthony T. "Specific Performance." *University of Chicago Law Review* 45 (1978): 351–82.

Llewellyn, Karl N. "What Price Contract? – An Essay in Perspective." *Yale Law Journal* 40 (1931): 704–51.

Macaulay, Stewart. "Non-contactual Relations in Business: A Preliminary Study." *American Sociological Review* 28 (1963): 55–61. [check pages]

Mentschikoff, Soia. Testimony in *New York Law Review Commission Hearings on the Uniform Commerical Code* 2 (1954): 1391.

Muris, Timothy J. "Cost of Completion or Diminution in Market Value: The Relevance of Subjective Value." *Journal of Legal Studies* (1983): 379–400.

Murray, John E. *Cases and Materials on Contracts*, 3d ed. Charlottesville, Va.: Michie, 1983.

Parsons, Theophilus. *A Treatise on the Law of Marine Insurance and General Average*, Volume 1. Boston: Little, Brown, 1868.

Pauly, Mark V. "The Economics of Moral Hazard: Comment." *American Economic Review* 58 (1968): 531–7.

Posner, Richard A. "Gratuitous Promises in Economics and Law." *Journal of Legal Studies* 6 (1977): 411–26.

———, and Andrew M. Rosenfield. "Impossibility and Related Doctrines in

Contract Law: An Economic Analysis." *Journal of Legal Studies* 6 (1977): 83–118.

———."Some Uses and Abuses of Economics in Law." *University of Chicago Law Review* 46 (1979): 249–84.

———, and Anthony T. Kronman. *The Economics of Contract Law*. Boston: Little, Brown, 1979.

———. *The Economic Analysis of Law*, 3d ed. Boston: Little, Brown, 1988.

Priest, George L. "The Theory of the Consumer Product Warranty." *Yale Law Journal* 90 (1981): 1297–352.

Schwartz, Alan. "The Case for Specific Performance." *Yale Law Journal* 89 (1979): 271–306.

Shavell, Steven. "The Design of Contracts and Remedies for Breach." *Quarterly Journal of Economics* 99 (1984): 121–48.

Simon, Herbert A. "A Formal Theory of the Employment Relationship." *Econometrica* 19 (1951): 293–305.

Simon, David, and Gerald A. Novack. "Limiting Buyer's Market Damages to Lost Profits: A Challenge to the Enforceability of Market Contracts." *Harvard Law Review* 92 (1979): 1395–438.

Simpson, A. W. B. "The Horwitz Thesis and the History of Contracts." *University of Chicago Law Review* 46 (1979): 533–601.

Slawson, David. "Standard Form Contracts and Democratic Control of Law Making Power." *Harvard Law Review* 84 (1971): 529–66.

Tullock, Gordon. "On Effective Organization of Trials." *Kyklos* 28 (1975): 745–62.

———. "Efficient Rent Seeking." In *Toward a Theory of the Rent-seeking Society*, edited by James M. Buchanan, Robert D. Tollison, and Gordon Tullock. College Station: Texas A&M University Press, 1980.

Ulen, Thomas S. "The Efficiency of Specific Performance: Toward a Unified Theory of Contract Remedies." *Michigan Law Review* 83 (1984): 341–403.

Williamson, Oliver E. *Markets and Hierarchies: Analysis and Antitrust Implications*. New York: Free Press, 1975.

Index of cases

Alaska Packer's Ass'n v. Domenico, 196, 197
Alcoa v. Essex Group, Inc., 211, 227, 230, 239
Anglia Television Ltd. v. Reed, 96
Austin Instrument, Inc. v. Loral Corp., 200

Boomer v. Atlantic Cement Co., xi, 50, 52, 69, 70, 71, 100, 126, 134, 162, 187
British Columbia Sawmill Co. v. Nettleship, 88

Campbell v. Wentz, 134
C. Czarnikow Ltd. v. Koufos (Heron II), 88, 90, 100, 101
Chandler v. Webster, 238
Chatlos Systems Inc. v. National Cash Register Corp., 135
Chicago Coliseum Club v. Dempsey, 96
Compania Naviera Asiatic v. The Burmah Oil Co., 84

Endiss v. Belle Isle Ice Co., 208

Fibrosa Spolka Akcyjna v. Fairbairn L.C.B. Ltd., 239
Frederick Raff Co. v. Murphy, 63

Goebel v. Linn, 191, 195–7, 204, 208, 240

Hackley v. Headley, 187, 189, 190, 192
Hadley v. Baxendale, 71, 86–90, 95, 96, 100–3, 209, 219

Hawkins v. McGee, 135
Headley v. Hackley, 190
Hoffman v. Red Owl Stores, Inc., 96, 97, 104

In re Westinghouse Electric Corp. Uranium Contracts Litigation, 230, 239

J'Aire Corp. v. Gregory, 73

Kemble v. Farren, 157
Kemp v. Knickerbocker Ice Co., 208
Krell v. Henry, 238

L. Albert & Son v. Armstrong Rubber Co., 94, 98, 101
Lobianco v. Property Protection, Inc., 165

Mandel v. National Ice & Coal Co., 192
Martin v. Joseph Harris, 185

Neri v. Retail Marine Corp., 106, 113, 116, 118

Oloffson v. Coomer, 85

Parsons v. Uttley, 90
Pirrone v. Monarch Wine Co. of Georgia, 205

Rourke v. Story, 191

Index of cases

Schwartzreich v. Bauman-Basch, Inc., 198
Secor v. Ardsley Ice Co., 192
Sullivan v. O'Connor, 135
*Security Stove & Manufacturing Co. v.
American Express Co.*, 92–4, 96, 101,
102

*Teradyne Inc. v. Teledyne Industries,
Inc.*, 115
Thomas v. McDaniel, 191

*Transatlantic Financing Corp. v. United
States*, 218

Ultramares Corp. v. Touche, ix

*Victoria Laundry (Windsor) v. Newman
Industries*, 88, 90

Walters v. Marathon Oil Co., 97, 104
Whitney v. Eager, 191

Author index

*Note: **italicized** numbers indicate an article included in this volume.*

Aivazian, Varouj A., *201–7*
Akerlof, George A., 2, *24–8*
Alchian, Armen A., 140
Arrow, Kenneth J., 2, 26, *33–4*

Birmingham, Robert, 75, 76, *92–8*, 101–4
Bishop, William, *86–91*, 99–101, 121, *122–5*
Buchanan, James M., 32

Calabresi, Guido, 107
Clarkson, Kenneth W., 138, *152–60*, 163, 164
Coase, Ronald A., 21
Cooter, Robert, 51, 52, *53–60*
Crawford, Robert G., 140

Dalzell, John, 187, *188–93*
Danzig, Richard, 99
Darling, Sir Malcolm, 28
Dawson, John P., 211, 238
Demsetz, Harold, 112, 114
Dickerson, O. D., 26, 31, 32

Feinman, Jay M., 97
Fuller, Lon, 75, *77–9*, 80, 81, 94, 95, 97, 103

Gilman, Hank, 186
Goetz, Charles J., 51, *61–8*, 73, 106, 109, *199–200*

Goldberg, Victor P., 1, *16–20, 21–3*, 52, *69–71*, 105, *106–13*, 121, *126–7*, 137, *147–51*, 167, 168, *169–73*, 211, *221–4*, *225–35*, 238

Harvey, William B., 238
Hicks, John F., 83

Joskow, Paul L., 239, 240

Kitch, Edmund W., 81, 82
Klein, Benjamin, 137, *139–46*, 140
Knight, Frank H., 2
Kronman, Anthony T., 121, 122

Llewellyn, Karl N., 170

Macaulay, Stewart, 1, *4–15*, 118
Melamed, A. Douglas, 107
Mentschikoff, Soia, 9
Merrill, Thomas W., 238
Miller, Roger LeRoy, 138, *152–60*, 163, 164
Muris, Timothy J., *128–32*, 135, 138, *152–60*, 163, 164
Murray, John E., 93, 96

Novack, Gerald A., 84

Parsons, Theophilus, *29–30*
Pauly, Mark V., 2, *31–2*, 33, 34
Penny, Michael, *201–7*

Author index

Perdue, William, 75, *77–9*, 80, 81, 94, 95, 97, 103
Posner, Richard A., x, 85, 138, 164, *194–8*, 202, 204, 211, *212–20*, 236–9
Priest, George L., 167, 168, *174–84*

Rosenfield, Andrew M., 85, 204, 211, *212–20*, 236–9

Schwartz, Alan, 121, 122
Scott, Robert E., 51, *61–8*, 73, 106, 109, *199–200*

Shavell, Steven, 121–5, 135
Simon, Herbert A., 19, 84
Simpson, A.W.B., 162
Slawson, David, 172

Trebilcock, Michael J., *201–7*
Tullock, Gordon, *3, 35–42*, 43, 44, 47, 82

Ulen, Thomas S., 121
Unumb, Daniel, 238

Williamson, Oliver E., 140

Subject index

Adverse selection, 2, 26, 86, 87, 90, 91, 165, 167, 168
Anticipatory repudiation, 83
"At will" termination, 139, 149, 161–3

Battle of the forms, 6, 7
Blunderbuss clause, 157
Brennan, Geoffrey, 42

Capacity utilization, 116, 117
Coase theorem, 112, 114, 203
Commons, John R., 78
Consequential damages
    exclusion of (or disclaimer against) 72, 167, 168, 180, 182, 183, 186
    foreseeability, 71, 100
    recoverability, 202, 206, 209, 219, 233
    reliance, relation to, 76, 101, 103
    specific performance, relation to, 126, 134
Cost of completion, 76, 121, 129–31, 135
Culpa in contrahendra, 104

Diminution of value, 121, 128–31
Discrete transaction, 1, 52, 134, 137
Duress, 56, 71, 126, 188–92, 200, 205, 209, 240

Economic waste, 126, 131, 132, 134
Efficient breach, 73, 124
Excuse (of performance)
    changed circumstances, in face of, 86, 100, 136, 211

conditions under which parties would agree to, 221–4
    duress, 126
    incentive effects of liberal, 51, 56, 57
Expectation damages, 56, 116, 224
    versus specific performance, 123, 125
Expectation interest, 75, 76
    protection of, 77–9
    reliance interest, compared to, 92–8

Fault, 52, 71, 72, 100, 127, 162, 187
Firm-specific
    capital, 18
    investment, 140, 142
    skills, 20, 147
Force majeure, 100, 211, 221–3, 236, 237
Forseeability
    doctrine, 59, 71, 76, 86, 99, 100, 103, 104
    tort versus contract, 90
Frustration, 86, 87, 204, 211, 229. *See also* Impossibility

Governance, of contractual relationships, 19, 147, 150
Gresham's law, 25, 28, 171
Gross inequity clause, 228, 240
Gross margin, 105, 107, 108, 109, 111

Holdup, 139–41, 145, 197, 201

Impossibility, 56, 57, 86, 136, 194, 204, 211, 212, 214, 218, 221, 224

Impracticability, commercial, 56, 211, 218, 229. *See also* Impossibility
Indexing. *See* Price index
Injunction, 69, 70, 71, 75, 126, 133, 159, 187, 202

Job-specific
  human capital, 149
  skills, 147

Least cost avoider, 51, 52, 71
Lemons, 2, 25–7
Liquidated damages, 130
  efficient reliance and, 58, 59
  lost-volume seller, and, 105, 113, 119
  penalties, and, 137, 152–66, 202
Lost profits, 59, 72, 76, 93, 97, 104, 155
  seller's, 108–10, 113, 115, 118, 119
Lost volume, 105, 106, 115. *See also* Lost profits, seller's

Marx, Karl, 78
Marxist concept of "nonproductive labor," 22
Mitigation, 52, 56, 60–3, 65–8, 71, 186
Modification, of contracts, 126, 187, 194–209, 240
Moral hazard, 2, 26, 31–4, 66, 165, 201, 204, 205, 214, 223, 226, 237

Neumann, John von, 37

Opportunism. *See* Opportunistic behavior
Opportunistic behavior, 17, 18, 19, 51, 61, 62, 66, 68, 107, 127, 140–6, 148, 163, 201, 202, 205
Opportunity cost, 22, 68, 81, 97, 150, 197, 198, 227, 233, 234, 235

Penalty clause, 113, 130, 138, 143, 155–65, 202, 206
Pre-existing duty, 187, 199
Price adjustment, 16, 50, 211, 225–7, 232, 234, 240
Price index, 19, 211, 216, 227–33, 235
Prisoner's dilemma, 31
Progress payments, 18, 119
Promissory estoppel, 97

Property, in the contract price, 75, 76, 78, 83, 91

Quasi-rents, 70, 140, 141

Relational, 1, 16, 17, 19, 52, 69, 144
Relation-specific
  assets, 137
  investment, 149, 227
Reliance, 18, 19, 89, 103, 122, 124, 135, 148, 149
  enforcing executory contract when there is no, 50, 75, 76–8, 80
  harm caused by promisor's breach and, 51, 53, 55–60
  relation to expectation interest and, 75–6, 92–8, 101–2
Rent seeking, 3, 35–42, 43, 44, 48–50, 51, 70, 71, 81, 126
Requirements contract, 8
Restatement of contracts, 75, 97, 157, 158
Restitution, 75, 135, 200, 239
Risk aversion, 1, 2, 211, 213, 237

Specific capital, 70, 141
Specific investment, 145
Specific performance, 65, 75, 107, 121–7, 133, 134, 135, 166, 196, 202, 206, 222
  cost of completion and, 129, 130
  uniqueness and, 121, 133, 134
Standard form contract, 167, 169–72
Stipulated damages. *See* Liquidated damages
Strategic behavior, 17, 61, 64, 66, 68, 135, 196, 199, 204, 226, 228, 232. *See also* Opportunistic behavior
Superior risk bearer, 204, 211–3, 216, 218–20

Transaction costs, 1, 21, 22, 23, 89, 124, 139, 142, 144, 146, 175, 176, 203, 206, 214
  zero, 21, 22, 89, 203

Unconscionability, 56, 139, 155, 165, 185

Warranty, 76, 87, 91, 167, 168, 169, 170, 172, 186
  disclaimer of implied warranty of merchantability, 182–3
  Priest's theory of content, 174–84